Cosmopolitans & Parochials

Cosmopolitans & Parochials

MODERN ORTHODOX JEWS IN AMERICA

Samuel C. Heilman and
Steven M. Cohen

THE UNIVERSITY OF CHICAGO PRESS
CHICAGO & LONDON

SAMUEL C. HEILMAN, professor of sociology at Queens College and the Graduate Center of the City University of New York, is the author of *A Walker in Jerusalem, The Gate Behind the Wall, The People of the Book,* and *Synagogue Life,* the latter two also published by the University of Chicago Press. STEVEN M. COHEN, professor of sociology at Queens College of the City University of New York, is the coauthor of numerous books and the author of *American Assimilation or Jewish Revival?, American Modernity & Jewish Identity,* and *Interethnic Marriage and Friendship.*

The University of Chicago Press, Chicago 60637
The University of Chicago Press, Ltd., London
© 1989 by Samuel C. Heilman and Steven M. Cohen
All rights reserved. Published 1989
Printed in the United States of America
98 97 96 95 94 93 92 91 90 89   5 4 3 2 1

Library of Congress Cataloging-in-Publication Data

Heilman, Samuel C.
    Cosmopolitans & parochials : modern Orthodox Jews
    in America / Samuel C. Heilman and Steven M.
Cohen.
        p. cm.
    Bibliography: p.
    Includes index.
    ISBN 0-226-32495-8 (alk. paper)
    ISBN 0-226-32496-6 (pbk.: alk. paper)
        1. Orthodox Judaism—United States. 2. Jews—
United States—Cultural assimilation. I. Cohen, Steven
Martin. II. Title. III. Title: Cosmopolitans and
parochials.
    BM205.H42 1989
    305.6'96073—dc20   89-34306
                                                    CIP

⊛The paper used in this publication meets
the minimum requirements of the American National
Standard for Information Sciences—Permanence of
Paper for Printed Library Materials, ANSI Z39.48-1984.

Contents

Preface   vii

1   Introduction   1

2   *Mitzva:* Ritual Practices and Orthodox Jews   39

3   The Religious Faith and Fervency of
       Orthodox Jews   83

4   *Kehilla:* Orthodox Insularity and
       Community Boundaries   113

5   The Ethos of Orthodoxy: Political,
       Social, and Sexual Attitudes   153

6   Whither Orthodoxy?   181

7   Conclusion   207

Notes   217

Bibliography   235

Index   245

Preface

Since the early 1970s, beginning with the publication of *Synagogue Life,* an ethnographic study of an Orthodox Jewish synagogue in the American urban Northeast, one of us (Samuel C. Heilman) has been engaged primarily in the qualitative study of Orthodox Jews; while the other (Steven M. Cohen) has been engaged primarily in quantitative, survey research studies of American Jews, of whom the Orthodox are a small fraction. This study on variations in American Jewish Orthodoxy represents a joining of our two research agendas and strengths. We hope it will support the conclusion Kohelet reached: "Two are better than one, because they have good reward for their labor, for if they fall the one will lift up the other" [Eccles. 4:9–10].

Orthodoxy has been increasingly on the mind of America, especially since it did not fulfill the expectations of many that it would disappear in the atmosphere of modern Western civilization. A number of social scientists have sought to explore the phenomenon, including such researchers as Charles Liebman who has written about the organization and ideology of Orthodoxy, and Egon Mayer who has focused on the Orthodox neighborhood of Borough Park in Brooklyn and who along with Chaim Waxman analyzed some of the data from the National Jewish Population Survey and other sources from which they gleaned information about the Orthodox in America. Heilman's work, although focusing on the Orthodox, was, as already pointed out, primarily ethnographic in nature. William Helmreich has examined the Yeshiva world. David Ellenson has looked at the historical roots of Orthodoxy and in particular at one of its major rabbinical pioneers.

Similar efforts focused on the history of Yeshiva University have been an important part of Jeffrey Gurock's contribution to the subject. And Reuven Bulka has collected a series of essays by contemporary thinkers on various dimensions of Orthodox Judaism. No one, however, has attempted to systematically survey and describe the character—or what we call the many faces—of Orthodox Jews in America.

In the quantitative study of contemporary American Jews, the Orthodox often have constituted, at best, a point of comparison for the study of the 90% or so of American Jewry who are not Orthodox. Studies of American Jewry typically do not embrace a large enough number of Orthodox to allow for internal examination of processes and variations.

To fill these needs, we combined our complementary skills and overlapping interests to produce this study of American Orthodoxy or, more modestly, of a sample of a significant segment of Orthodox American Jews. Several parties contributed in all sorts of ways to this monograph. Students in Heilman's course "Orthodox Jews in America" and Cohen's "The American Jewish Community," which we taught for several years at Queens College of the City University of New York, helped sharpen the focus of our interest and our curiosity.

We received financial support from the Memorial Foundation for Jewish Culture and from the City University of New York Research Foundation. Claire Semel and several student aides associated with the Queens College Jewish Studies Program provided valuable clerical and research assistance. The friends and colleagues who critically reviewed our draft chapters include Robert Chazan, Calvin Goldscheider, Charles Liebman, and Peter Medding.

We also wish to thank those persons who helped us to assemble our sample—Rabbi Shlomo Riskin and Ephraim Buchwald (both then affiliated with the Lincoln Center Synagogue), as well as those who chose to remain anonymous, the various Jewish magazine editors, organizational secretaries, and synagogue officers who provided us with lists of people whom we might survey. Of course, we thank those many who completed questionnaires and allowed us to interview them. We hope the information contained in the pages that follow will provide some compensation for their efforts.

There is hardly an author who does not feel a profound sense of gratitude to family—in our cases, wives and children—for their understanding and stimulation. We are no exception. To our wives, Ellin Heilman and Susan Wall, as well as our children, we extend our affectionate appreciation for their patience and support.

Samuel C. Heilman
Steven M. Cohen

June 1988/Sivan 5748

1 Introduction

> One of the central puzzlements of recent American
> Jewish history is the growing strength of Orthodox
> Judaism. . . . Orthodox Judaism cannot only make
> its peace with modernity, but actually thrive in the
> modern world.
>
> Leonard Fein

Throughout the early generations of American Jewry, the predominant assumption was that in one way or another Jews would enter fully into the mainstream of American cultural life. Some analysts and lay observers speculated that Jews would be swallowed up by the host society without a trace.[1] Others thought they would retain some sort of ethnic or religious identity in spite of becoming Americanized. But whatever their views of the ultimate outcome, few doubted that the overwhelming trend in American Jewry was away from the parochialism of the ghetto, the sectarianism of tradition, and all this implied.

In this assimilation perspective, Orthodoxy was perceived as being at best a residual category, a vestige of another era, and unsuited to the circumstances of contemporary culture.[2] People committed to the parochial truths of an eternal yesterday—with its predictable traditions, secure beliefs, and tribal ties—could not be expected to survive in an open world, a world that emphasized the promises of endlessly novel tomorrows, one that valued spontaneity and glorified the intellectual and social emancipation of the individual from the shackles of archaic dogmas and ancient tribal loyalties and rites.

Moreover, because during the last years of the previous century and the early years of this one Orthodox Jews failed to share fully in the cultural and therefore the economic wealth of the outside world, Orthodoxy became for the most part the preserve of the least affluent and most foreign Jews. With the passing of generations and with the inevitability of Americanization, as American Jews rose to a position of higher social status, it was commonly assumed the poor, foreign, aging Orthodox segment of

1

American Jewry would concomitantly shrink in size and in significance.

Indeed, in 1955, in the context of writing about Conservative Judaism, which he called "an American religious movement," Marshall Sklare described Orthodoxy in America as "a case study of institutional decay."[3] Even in 1977, two prominent sociologists prognosticating about Orthodoxy in America by the year 2000, suggested that "the number of Orthodox Jews is bound to decline in the coming decades."[4]

In brief, Orthodox Jews were expected gradually to vanish from the main stage of American Jewish life. They would at best become a memory, the observant grandparents of an assimilated American Jewry. "Orthodoxy was doomed to a lingering senility," as one prominent non-Orthodox rabbi suggested.[5] But, Orthodox Jews did not disappear.

In the late nineteen-eighties, over a hundred years after the onset of the large waves of Jewish immigration from Eastern Europe, nearly 150 years following the influx of German Jewry, and a generation after the arrival of holocaust survivors to these shores, Orthodoxy in America has not vanished. For all the tides of change that have crossed American Jewish life, these have failed to wash away those who call themselves Orthodox. As a group, they have for over a generation remained constant at about 10 percent of the American Jewish population of nearly six million.[6] In fact, after years of attrition during the nineteenth and early twentieth centuries, the years of mass Jewish immigration to America, the Orthodox population size may even be rebounding.[7] As Sklare was forced to admit in his "new, augmented edition" of *Conservative Judaism*, "Orthodoxy has refused to assume the role of invalid. Rather, it has transformed itself into a growing force in American Jewish life."[8] In "Orthodoxy Faces Modernity," Charles Liebman affirms that "this is the first generation in over 200 years (i.e., since its first formulation as the effort by traditional Judaism to confront modernity) in which Orthodoxy is not in decline."[9]

Orthodox institutions have grown in number and influence in the last few decades. Some mark the beginning of its new growth with the years during and immediately after the Second World War. We shall more fully outline the dimensions of Orthodox strength in America later in these pages.

Support for this appraisal comes from the fact that by 1940 American Orthodoxy was becoming congregationally large and growing.[10] Between 1933 and 1943, major new advanced yeshivot (academies of higher Jewish learning) had opened their doors in America. Furthermore, "1940 marks the beginning of phenomenal growth for the Jewish Day School movement. Two hundred and seventy-one yeshivot [i.e., at the primary and secondary level], 91 percent of all existing day schools, were established after this date."[11]

Many Orthodox Jews who were refugees and survivors of the Nazi firestorm in Europe arrived in America during this time. They became the lifeblood of many of these institutions.[12] While those who had immigrated earlier had come to an America that was weak in Orthodox institutions, a place that was considered by many a *trefe medina* (a defiled land), these later immigrants came to a place that already had some basic Orthodox institutions and organization. Even so, before the Nazi era many of these refugees had not been eager to risk their Jewish attachments by moving to America. Unlike earlier immigrants, those Orthodox Jews who had come to America in the late thirties and after the Second World War held on to their Jewish way of observance in Europe, the heartland of tradition, until at last there was nothing left to hold onto. Then and only then had they run for their lives. Even as refugees, however, few if any were interested in escaping tribal attachments and religious bonds. And when they came, they came convinced, indeed almost with a sense of mission, that they could continue to hold onto the tradition, to their Orthodox way of life. Anything else would have been for many a betrayal.[13] These highly committed Jews, who had remained attached to the intensive Jewish community of Europe till the last, now resolved to maintain their brand of Orthodox Judaism in America as much as possible. As survivors, they had already demonstrated a tenacity of spirit; that they were likewise tenacious in holding onto their Jewish way of life should therefore not be surprising.

In 1944, for example, these immigrants founded Torah Umesorah, a confederation of Orthodox day schools, and the growth of the day school movement, the primary pipeline for Orthodoxy, began. By 1975, "every city in the United States with a Jewish population of 7500 had at least one [Jewish] day school, as did four out of five of the cities with population of 5000 to 7500."[14] The overwhelming number of these (which included 425 days schools and 138 Jewish high schools) were under Orthodox auspices.[15]

And there are other signs of American Orthodoxy's vitality. The Union of Orthodox Jewish Congregations of America, founded in 1898 to perpetuate "loyalty to Jewish law and custom" and to protect "Orthodox Judaism whenever occasions arise in civic and social matters," by now has become a firmly established feature of American life; its certifications of *kashruth*, among its most prominent accomplishments, have grown from approximately 400 to over 10,000 in the last thirty years, an increase of 2,500%.[16] The number of congregations affiliated with the organization has increased from 700 to over 1,000 in the last thirty years.[17] And its youth division, the National Conference of Synagogue Youth, had by the early 1980s over 200 chapters in fifteen regions of the country.[18] The various Orthodox rabbinical organizations, including the Union of Orthodox Rabbis (Agudath HaRabbonim) and the Rabbinical Council of America, counted over 1,500 rabbis in their membership by the 1980s.[19] And the National Council of Young Israel, one of the major Orthodox synagogue movements, counts over 25,000 families among its members.[20] Where in the early years of the American Jewish community large numbers of children of Orthodox parents once abandoned Orthodoxy, fewer do so today, setting the stage for demographic growth.

But not only is the Orthodox "retention rate" growing; so is its visibility. In fact, the perception—if not the actuality—of growth and stability has coincided with a certain triumphalism on the part of Orthodox leaders, evident in their dealings with non-Orthodox Jews as well as with American society in general. In many instances, Orthodoxy "has reasserted its claim of being *the* authentic interpretation of Judaism."[21]

In short, the ubiquitousness of skull-capped men and women dressed in the "modest" style associated with traditional Jewish religious norms, everywhere from the board room to the college classroom, the large-scale entry of the Orthodox into the professions, the apparent vigor of the *baal t'shuva* movement in which the non-Orthodox adopt the ways of tradition, and the economic and numerical expansion of Orthodox institutions all suggest that Orthodoxy in America survives quite well indeed.

And what is the character of this survival? Who are today's American Orthodox Jews? How do they live their Orthodoxy? What are their practices, beliefs, affiliations, and worldviews? Have they chosen to turn their backs completely on contemporary American values, associations, and practices in favor of a contra-acculturative parochialism, or do they live in a tension between the demands of Orthodoxy and those of American life? Have they developed a way to "mediate between the claims of classical Judaism, the work of ages of faith, archaic, supernatural, and sacred, and the ineluctable demands of contemporaneity, secularity, unbelief and worldliness?"[22] And if so, what is that way? Finally, how do the answers to these questions reveal the distinctions among the Orthodox? To what extent are all Orthodox Jews alike in their responses to life in contemporary America? Are the young and the old identical? Are men and women identical? The pages that follow will try to answer these questions, in the process painting a portrait of the many faces of contemporary Orthodoxy.

These are faces with a variety of poses and profiles. One Orthodox face turns inward—away from the larger society—and appears significantly traditional, rejecting many of the essentials of contemporary secular American society and culture. Framed by apparent loyalty to the strictest tenets of faith and Jewish law *(halacha)*, it is punctilious in ritual observance, solidly attached to a network of parochial ties with other like Jews, and rather conservative in outlook.[23]

Another Orthodox face appears to turn outward—toward the larger society—seeming in many ways barely distinguishable from other American Jews. Here we find people who embrace much that is essential about conventional American life. While careful about certain ritual observances, devoted to basic articles of Jewish faith and socially linked to other Orthodox Jews, they are neither very remote from nor untouched by life in the contemporary world around them. In some cases, such Jews are little more than Orthodox in name.

In the center, situated between these two, we find an Orthodoxy that seems to be turning both inward and outward. Here we find people who are both traditionalist and modernist in orientation, parochial and cosmopolitan, orthodox and liberal, dogmatic and tolerant, deeply influenced by the cultural currents of the world around them while often acting to maintain their cultural separateness.

To be sure, all Orthodox Jews to some extent share these dualist traits; everyone—as sociologist Peter Berger once explained—is "in the situation of modernity." And that includes those who are most traditionalist. We only wish to impart the idea of an Orthodox gradient, with two groups tending toward the extremes and one revolving about the center. The division of Orthodox into traditionalist, modernist, and centrist camps is in some respects an arbitrary exercise akin to dividing Americans into conservative, liberal, and moderate political groupings. As we try to demonstrate in our ensuing analysis, however, these divisions do reflect significant and patterned distinctions among Orthodox Jews along several dimensions, and Orthodox Jews themselves are capable of classifying themselves in a reasonably precise fashion along these lines. These are not different faces that only the outsider sees (in fact, the true outsider may be ignorant of them); they are, however, recognized by the Orthodox themselves.

To speak of "faces" is suggestive, but such metaphorical characterizations are imprecise, the sorts of descriptions that while current in conversation and anecdotal evidence are insufficient for the social scientist or in fact for anyone who wishes to get beyond the level of broad and easy generalizations. What follows here, then, is for those who wish a more definitive portrait, a clearer vision of what Orthodoxy in America has become. It is as well one chapter in the larger story of the persisting presence of religion in modern society.

The Emergence of Orthodoxy

To portray contemporary Orthodoxy we must begin with at least a brief examination of the factors that led to its emergence and to the circumstances in which it finds itself today. Our purpose here is not to review the entire history of Orthodoxy; that has been done admirably—particularly in the case of American Orthodoxy—by a variety of others.[24] Nor is this the place to repeat the entire story of the modernization of Judaism, a story in which the emergence of Orthodoxy is but one chapter.[25] Rather, we wish simply to suggest the ideological panorama in which the face of Orthodoxy first appears.

That face emerges in the last third of the eighteenth century in Europe, particularly in Central and Western Europe, the precincts of Ashkenazic Jewry. Here the old order of life was beginning to change. Venerable truths and established customs were being deluged by new ideas and orders. Life was in flux. The age of reason of the seventeenth century evolved into the industrial revolution of the late eighteenth and early nineteenth centuries.

First, there were important changes in the actual conditions of life that left a mark on social existence. Industrialization bolstered the rise of the cities. In search of work and in the quest for a better life, people left home and moved to the rapidly growing cities. It was a movement not only of place but of world order. Ineluctably, the future became more important than the past. Change rather than stability was a hallmark of existence. As faith gave way to reason, it was a time when one could easily say that "the old gods are growing old or already dead."[26]

Political changes also accompanied the needs of industrialization for a free pool of labor. These changes included the disintegration of feudal society. This was a movement, in the words of Henry Sumner Maine, "from Status to Contract," from a society organized around people's tribal

7

and familial ties to one ordered by "the free agreement of individuals."[27] Edicts of tolerance, political upheavals, and revolutions spread like a wave eastward across the continent. Out of these came the new category of "citizen," an identity bonded only to the nation-state and not to any religious or parochial entity. All citizens were, at least in principle, supposed to be equal. In this atmosphere, parochial orientations gave way to cosmopolitanism. And the character of life inexorably changed.

In this new world governed by the marketplace and industry, what people could do and what their ideas were mattered far more than who they were or with which group they associated, or even which god—if any—they worshipped. Increasingly independent and emphasizing their own new achievements over those ancient ties, people simultaneously turned away from the mystical bonds of tradition and received truths, and moved toward goal-oriented rationality, the engine of industrialization.[28]

Ashkenazic Jews, who found themselves dispersed among those peoples who were undergoing these transformations, discovered that they too experienced these effects. Although for generations separated from the host cultures among whom they lived, Jews found that in some places more than others, but everywhere to some degree, the ramparts of tradition which enclosed them in ghettoes and a world ruled by the eternal yesterday of Judaism began to crumble.[29] In a sense, in spite of the fact that they held onto a despised faith in an overwhelmingly Christian civilization, the Jews, precisely because they were not bonded to place or part of the landed aristocracy or Christian nobility who had based its authority and power on ascription, had more to gain by these changes than many others. And they did. Jews (in some places at first only grudgingly and in principle rather than in fact, but ultimately in both) began to share in the new world order. This process was referred to both by historians and contemporaries of the time by a variety of terms: naturalization, civic betterment, amalgamation, assimilation, and (most commonly) emancipation.[30]

In the course of emancipation, the Jews were no longer to be treated as a corporate group, whose leaders spoke for and served as intermediaries between the governing powers of the host societies and individual Jews. Throughout Europe, as society moved from Status to Contract and individuals became freed from formal community controls and began to fend for themselves, so was this true as well for the Jews. While in traditional (preemancipation) Jewish society "the observance of the Jewish tradition could and would be enforced by the organs of the Jewish community," a kind of tribal, quasi-familial order, the *new* Jewish community which emerged *after* emancipation, the modern one, "was denied the right to impose its will concerning thought and action on the individual."[31] It was voluntary, far more contractual than based on ascription and status. The result was, as historian Jacob Katz concludes: "Everywhere the individual gained a certain amount of freedom in evolving or absorbing ideas and determining his conduct accordingly. Jews also gained this leeway in their relation to the community and the traditional values represented in it."[32] Where individuals were freed from formal community control and sanction, the Jewish community had to exercise its authority informally, through social norm, more, custom, or folkway.

Among the first to experience these changes were probably the merchants, itinerant travelers who, in the quest for material sufficiency, found themselves inexorably traversing not only the boundaries of the Jewish ghetto but also its view of the world. Then too there were the intellectuals, the enlightened, who saw themselves increasingly as part of a pluralistic, cosmopolitan elite of freethinkers, who also experienced the impact of emancipation in its earliest stages. Finally, the people in the cities, exposed to and brushing shoulders with Gentiles who were being swept by these changes, also were affected by these processes.[33]

But, as the Jews quickly discovered, there was a moral cost for emancipation. In order to enter into the mainstream of the host societies in which they found themselves, to be truly emancipated, to be good citizens, they had to change. Epitomizing the attitude of the hosts who were taking in the Jews, Voltaire, for example, wrote that he would sit and eat with "even a Jew, provided the Jew frees himself first of his hateful Jewish superstitions and prejudices."[34] Religious tradition and the parochialism of tribal ties had to be abandoned; emancipation required enlightenment and that in turn called for a liberation of the Jew from his people and their way of life. The dietary laws, for example, precluded fraternization and intermingling. Observing the Sabbath on Saturdays separated Jews from those who observed it on Sundays. Indigenous Jewish languages such as Hebrew or Yiddish precluded communication with the host culture. These and other "misguided" parochial practices had to go, as did the idea of a separate and Chosen People. Voltaire had after all predicted that the educated and enlightened among the Jews would join other intellectuals while those who refused to join would be absorbed in the dark swarm of undifferentiated masses.[35]

Undeniably, these trends toward secularization and democratization affected all people in the Occident. However, because the shape and character of Western secular life was built upon a foundation that was essentially Christian, Christians by and large did not have to abandon as much of their tradition and way of life as did the Jews.[36] But, as Jacob Katz has pointed out, matters were different for Jews. "The Jew faced a dilemma: should he succumb to the temptation of society-at-large if it involved accepting Christianity or remain a member of a socially inferior minority."[37]

To be sure, the process that led to this choice did not happen all at once. The winds of change that began as light breezes in the eighteenth century and ended up as tempests in the twentieth moved gradually eastward across Europe, arriving relatively late in Poland, Russia, and the pale of settlement where the great bulk of Ashkenazic Jewry had settled. Moreover, these changes were met in distinct ways by different communities; and, in any given place, reactions of all Jews were by no means all the same. An increasingly mobile Jewry was becoming increasingly differentiated in its response to the new conditions of Jewish existence. While German Jewry seems to many to have been the archetype for Jewish emancipation and enlightenment, the experience there was by no means the absolute paradigm for all other Jewish communities. Galician, Lithuanian, Russian, Hungarian, French, Dutch, Moravian, Bohemian, Italian, English, Scandinavian, and American Jews each had their own special and diverse responses to modernity.[38]

Although these different reactions and the circumstances that led up to them constitute an important concern for the historian who no doubt would want to be more careful about delineating and analyzing the complexity and nuances of the variations, we may for our purposes divide the reactions as falling, more or less, into three broad categories: *assimilation, acculturation,* and *contra-acculturation.*

At one extreme were those who chose to assimilate. While a complex process, assimilation may be defined operationally as a process in which strangers or newcomers so thoroughly learn the ways of the host society (which accepts them) that they become for most practical purposes indistinguishable from that host society. In the most extreme cases, the asssimilated—who commonly constituted a minority before they joined the mainstream—abandon or forget completely their original identity and patterns of culture for ways that are new.[39] Describing those Jews who took this option, people whom he calls "ex-Jews and other heretics," Isaac Deutscher suggests: "They all found Jewry too narrow, too archaic, and too constricting. They all looked for ideals and fulfillment beyond it."[40] Prepared to abandon their Judaism and the community that practiced it for the world outside, they decided to get out of the ghetto as swiftly and completely as they could. In words that epitomize this attitude Daniel Khvolson, a Lithuanian-born, Russian orientalist who studied in the university at Breslau and upon returning to Russia converted to Christianity, suggested that "it was better to be a Christian professor in St. Petersburg than to be a Jewish *melamed* [teacher] in the shtetl."[41] To such Jews who broke away from their tribal ties and the venerable authority of the tradition, there were in principle "no intermediate loyalties between the individual and humanity as a whole."[42]

But not everyone chose the assimilationist option. *Maskilim,* Jews who sought to embrace enlightenment (*haska-*

11

lah) and the opportunities of emancipation without necessarily abandoning their attachments to Judaism and Jewish life, opted for another alternative. In the parlance of sociology, *maskilim* could be described as promoting culture contact with the world outside the Jewish one. They advocated acculturation, the process by which "an individual achieves continuing competence in his culture," but not assimilation. [43] In practice, this meant learning to become literate in the language of the host society, moving beyond the local Jewish community, getting a university education, and perhaps pursuing a profession that was not, strictly speaking, bound up with Jewish concerns. It meant sharing in the values and some of the ethos of the non-Jewish world. Capturing the essence of this attitude, the eighteenth-century German Jew and *maskil*, Moses Mendelssohn, urged his fellow Jews: "Comply with the customs and civil constitutions of the countries in which you are transplanted, but at the same time, be constant to the faith of your forefathers." [44] Like other *maskilim* he aimed at social integration into the host societies without the social dissolution of the Jewish one. In a popular aphorism of the *haskalah*, the nineteenth-century essayist and Hebrew poet, Yehuda L. Gordon, suggested that the Jew "be a person when you go out and a Jew in your home." [45]

The option the *maskilim* selected engendered opposition. While to their traditional opponents the essential thrust of their action was to advance excessive movement away from Jewish parochialism, their assimilationist counterparts considered them still too powerfully bound to parochial loyalties. In time, however, many of the aspects of acculturation that the *maskilim* had sought to encourage were mandated by the state. This was particularly true in the sphere of education which became increasingly a matter of public rather than parochial control; the state, for example, demanded instruction in the language of the host country. And the demands of industrialization and modernization tacitly encouraged career patterns that required Jews to learn skills and acquire training beyond the precincts of the ghetto.

The *maskilim*—perhaps because they had been at the forefront of culture contact—were often caught up in the sweep of history, the powerful forces, and allure of the emergent new civil society. Many found more and more difficulty in holding fast to their Jewish ties. Numerous *maskilim* or their children—including Mendelssohn's—embraced the most extreme forms of assimilation.[46]

The ideal of the *haskalah*, however, did not disappear. It influenced a variety of other Jewish movements that sought to make their peace with the changing conditions of modern society without capitulating to complete assimilation. And its basic premise—that culture contact with the world beyond the Jewish one could be beneficial for the Jews (and for their host cultures)—remained influential (both positively and negatively) in much of what Jewish life became.

The *haskalah* and its ethos of acculturation affected diverse elements of Jewish life. For example, it set the stage for a renascent Hebrew and developing Yiddish literature that was to take its place in modern literature. By writing about contemporary matters in these ancient and time-honored Jewish languages, one could remain tied to Jews while also fostering links to contemporary society. In the sphere of political life, the *haskalah* nurtured in some (albeit a small minority at the outset) the idea of secular Zionism, a political ideology that merged Jewish nationalist aspirations with the modern notions of liberalism, socialism, and the nation-state. Not only could an individual Jew be like all other people, a Jewish state could become like all other states.

But the *haskalah* also affected religion. In the domain of religion, there were those who sought a successful acculturation to non-Jewish society and culture but something short of the extreme of total assimilation. They attempted to reach an accommodation with the host society through a process of compromise which minimized the strains and conflicts that came from being a Jew in a Gentile world.[47] Some of these Jews attempted merely to *re*-form Judaism, to make it fit in with the times. Aesthetic standards and refinements derived from the Protestant environment were applied to synagogue architecture, liturgy, and education. Functionally, this meant omitting parts of the traditional way of Jewish life that appeared irreconcilable with the new position of Jews. To take just the most obvious, the seemingly "unrefined" traditional service was replaced by the ostensibly more decorous worship, led by a voice-trained cantor and university-educated rabbi, who often chanted prayers and addressed the congregation in the vernacular rather than Hebrew and Yiddish. Perhaps more important, to many Reform Jews, no part of Jewish life seemed more irreconcilable with emancipation, enlightenment, and the acculturation they aspired to than traditional ritual practice. This, then, was the first aspect of Judaism subject to reform. Religion became for many reformers something separated from ritual praxis—a fundamental break with the prevailing creed of traditional Judaism where being a "good Jew" meant observing every *mitzva*, punctiliousness in observing the commandments and associated practices. To the reformed Jew, if "good Christian" was synonymous with "good person," so too was "good Jew," as long as excessive Jewish ritualism gave way to general moralism. The emphasis throughout, however, remained on entering fully into the mainstream of modern society and the host culture, but doing so as a reformed Jew.

Although less extreme than the Reform Jews, others—particularly in Germany and around the seminary founded in Breslau by Zacharias Frankel in 1854—sought acculturative "changes that were not in conflict with the spirit of historical Judaism," changes that "could be made validly in the light of biblical and rabbinic precedent."[48] These Jews who wished to be conservative in their reforming, and who came to be known at first as adherents of the "historical school of Judaism" and later simply as "Conservative" Jews, viewed Judaism as always having been a succession of changes. But while they continued to advocate changes, they had to balance within their ranks those who wanted to be boldly innovative as well as those who were ready to make changes only with the greatest reluctance and delay. Thus, for example, Frankel opposed the abolition of Hebrew as the language of Jewish prayer at the same time that he pressured those more traditional than he was in outlook to incorporate modern scholarship and the advances of contemporary culture into Jewish education.

And then in contrast to those who opted for acculturation in one way or another were those Jews who, repelled
by the values and ways of the world outside their own,
wished to contra-acculturate, "to stress the values in abo-
riginal ways of life, and to move aggressively . . . toward
the restoration of those ways."[49] In the face of culture contact—especially after the state laws mandated it—and
seeing how many of those who had sought to accommodate themselves to civil society had fared, these Jews
sought steadfastly to retain their tribal and traditional ties.
Wedded to yesterday and distrustful of what today or to-
morrow offered, they saw the acculturative trends of the
haskalah and the charm and substance of the non-Jewish
world as potentially harmful. Still attached to the idea of a
"chosen people," they repudiated pluralism.

This is not the place to review the full range—and there
was a range—of responses of traditional Jews to the processes of assimilation, acculturation, and reform.[50] Generally, those who would emerge as the most traditionalist Orthodox rejected as much as possible the attractions of the
host cultures to which ex-Jews flocked; while on the other
extreme the more modernist Orthodox—not unlike the
Conservative Jews of the historical school—sought to re-
tard the movement outward by demonstrating the capacity
of historic Judaism to harmonize its teachings with modern
conditions.

During the early years, however, "Orthodox" was the
term most often associated with the rejectionists of modernity, those traditionalists who supported contra-acculturation or at least a very decelerated acculturation to
Western society. As such, the term and in a sense the
movement is a product of the late eighteenth century,
when Jewish society, at the dawn of modernity, underwent
the loosening of the bonds of tradition and the emergence
of non-Orthodox tendencies and trends. It developed as a
direct reaction to what its adherents viewed as the assimilationist crises of emancipation and *haskalah* as well as re-
formist responses.[51]

Certainly, maintaining Orthodoxy in the situation of modernity, "to reaffirm the authority of tradition in defiance of
the challenges to it," was not the same as being *bound* by

15

tradition in a premodern world.[52] And herein lies the essential difference between contemporary Orthodoxy and premodern Judaism. Modernity, as Peter Berger has argued, is "a near-inconceivable expansion of the area of human life open to choices."[53] To embrace tradition in the situation of modernity thus meant that a person *chose* tradition as but one selection in the marketplace of ideas and life-styles. Accordingly, by the nineteenth century in Europe, even those who remained faithful to tradition did so as moderns. As Jacob Katz has explained, "[T]heir loyalty to tradition was the result of a conscious decision, or at the very least a stance assumed in defiance of a possible alternative suggested by the life style of other Jews. In contradistinction to the tradition-bound, therefore they should be called traditionalists."[54]

It is important to keep in mind that the most contra-acculturative traditionalists—those who sought self-segregation and hoped to consolidate, strengthen, and vitalize the influence of a totally Jewish environment, who "in order to protect their souls attempted to fence in their members and fence out the secular"—were the progenitors of Orthodoxy.[55] To some, including those who do not share the entirety of their point of view, they continue to "represent 'true Orthodoxy' in its purest form," and "all other forms are compromises and, therefore, less authentic."[56]

As we have suggested, not all Orthodox Jews totally rejected modern civil society. Some among them were willing to accept the externals and superficial patterns of behavior of the emergent civil society while (at least to themselves) deliberately rejecting many of the values and ideological assumptions of that world. They saw themselves unenthusiastically accepting the style but not the substance of contemporary life, particularly that part of the substance they regarded as conflicting with their conception of Judaism.[57]

At the same time, others who called themselves "modern Orthodox" accepted the substance of their host cultures and also tried inductively to create some synthesis of Judaism and contemporary civil society. They eschewed the implicit contra-acculturation of Orthodoxy—wishing to be *of* as well as *in* the host culture and contemporary society and refusing "to be identified with ghetto conditions"—but they would not abandon the Jewish attachments embedded in Orthodoxy.[58] They tried to find a way to remain true to what they understood as the demands of sacred tradition and parochial bonds, while avoiding the rejectionism and social insularity these foster. They sought to accept the authority of the past, while still maintaining some modicum of personal autonomy in an age that increasingly emphasized individual freedom. They tried to follow in a temperate way the path of culture contact embarked upon by the *maskilim,* valuing reason, science, and secular education; but by maintaining strong ritual and communal links to the traditional Jewish community, law and faith, they hoped to resist the assimilationist forces which had swept away their forebears. Those who did not find a way to synthesize the two worlds, often—as we shall demonstrate later in these pages—tried to compartmentalize the various worlds they inhabited: Jews at home, and largely indistinguishable from non-Jews when they went out.

Their's was an *adapted* acculturation. Adaptation is a process of acculturation where both "original and foreign traits are combined . . . with either a reworking of the patterns of the two cultures into a meaningful whole to the individuals concerned, or the retention of a series of more or less conflicting attitudes and points of view which are reconciled in everyday life as specific occasions arise."[59] In short, in their adaptation some Orthodox Jews sought to find a way of interpretively bringing together the two domains—the parochial and the cosmopolitan—in which they found themselves. They were not ready to absolutely reject either one. In fact, even though their primary commitments were to being Jewish—"Before heaven and earth we openly confess that were our Torah to demand that we abstain from everything going under the name of civilization and enlightenment, then without vacillation would we honor this demand, since our Torah is our faith"—they did not believe *au fond* that they would be forced to choose between being part of the host culture and remaining Orthodox Jews.[60] And if they had to choose, they would deal with those choices on a case-by-case basis as the specific needs arose.

The two directions of Orthodoxy can perhaps be summarized as follows. The contra-acculturative traditionalists are be characterized by several key features. Now, as always, compared to most other Jews, they are more attached to the past and emphasize its importance in their lives. They value stability and the status quo. They remain more tribalist and culturally insulated from contemporary culture than most other Jews, but (like everyone in the situation of modernity) not completely untouched by life outside the Jewish domain. Trying to remain attached to the parochial world of Jewish life and tradition, they are relatively punctilious in their ritual observance and tend to be more socially and politically conservative. They are as well more fervent and doctrinaire than most other Jews in their theology and beliefs. More often than not, they are willing to bow to religious authority to determine what should be done and how one should live life. And yet, because they live in a traditionalist rather than a tradition-bound circumstance, where authorities are chosen rather than given, they may not always agree on who that authority is.

Those more consciously acculturative in their orientation, on the other hand, tend to display the opposite characteristics. They are morally attached to contemporary life and culture with its future orientation and emphasis on change. Yet, as Orthodox Jews, they have adapted their acculturative tendencies so that they are as well bonded to the traditional Jewish past. "We are Orthodox Jews," Norman Lamm says, describing himself and these people, "who have . . . undergone the modern experience—and survived it; who refuse to accept modernity uncritically, but equally refuse to reject it unthinkingly."[61] Their adapted acculturation has inclined them to synthesize or compartmentalize their lives so that they can exist simultaneously in the parochial world of Orthodoxy and the more cosmopolitan one of modern America without feeling the constant pressure of inconsistency. They tend sometimes to be relatively lax or at least more permissive in their religious practices (although not nearly as lax as the bulk of non-Orthodox Jewry). They remain rather individualist

Table 1.1

Traditionalists	Modernists
Contra-acculturative/attached to traditional Jewish culture	Acculturative/attached to contemporary non-Jewish culture
Tribalist/parochial (do not mix with others)	Pluralist/cosmopolitan (mix with others)
Past orientation/stressing stability	Future orientation/stressing change
Punctilious observance/strict in attachment to *halacha*	Relatively lax observance/eclectic approach to *halacha*
Tend toward totalistic Jewish attachments	Tend toward a compartmentalization of Judaic and secular attachments
Accept traditional authority/ask the rabbi when in doubt	Incline toward personal autonomy/try to avoid asking the rabbi
Faithful (go to yeshiva)	Emphasis on reason and science (attend university)
Politically conservative	Politically moderate to liberal

and even eclectic in their willingness to accept religious authority, often preferring not to "ask the rabbi" but to interpret for themselves what Judaism demands of them. They are somewhat ambivalent about the major tenets of Orthodox doctrine and faith, while remaining committed to the world of reason and its handmaiden science. Although dedicated to their way of life, they are tolerant of pluralism in Jewish life. Finally, while conservative in many respects when compared to non-Orthodox Jewry, they are in contrast to the traditionalists relatively more liberal on political and social issues.

The differences between the two extremes are recapitulated in table 1.1.

In nineteenth-century Europe where these Jewish responses were first being articulated, all trends of Orthodoxy at first viewed modernity and immersion in cultural life beyond the Jewish one as inherently dangerous to the continuity of essential Judaism, as they understood it. The more traditionalist saw the absolute necessity of erecting high walls to fence out as much of modernity and the non-Jewish world as possible. Rabbi Moses Sofer, known as the Hatam Sofer and a major rabbinical influence of the last generation, perhaps articulated the rejectionist attitude most dramatically in his famous slogan: "The new is prohibited by the Torah." [62]

On the other hand, the acculturative tendency in Orthodoxy was perhaps most clearly represented by Rabbis Samson Raphael Hirsch and Esriel Hildesheimer and earlier Isaac Bernays and Jacob Ettlinger—to name but a few of the more prominent exemplars of this response. These were Jews who did not look upon the contact between Jewish and European cultures as lamentable. *Torah-imderech-eretz* (the Jewish way of life [torah] and timeless tradition in harmony with the times and the surrounding environment) was the motto of this group. [63] They remained certain of "the eternal newness and applicability of the Torah to any situation that might arise." [64]

These acculturative, modern Orthodox saw less of a conflict—though still one of significant dimensions—between the larger society's secularizing tendencies and their view of essential Judaism. As a result, they were prepared to accept greater involvement in the larger Western culture, albeit an involvement that was to be controlled and circumscribed. Recognizing that they were traveling in the direction of unrestricted acculturation and wary of assimilation, they were careful to distinguish themselves somehow from reformers and those *maskilim* who had been pulled too far away from the basics of Judaism as they, the Orthodox, understood it.

This led to political divisions, as when, for example, some German Orthodox under the leadership of Rabbi Samson Raphael Hirsch elected to secede from any Jewish communal organization that included the non-Orthodox. "For them, religion is valid only to the extent that it does not interfere with progress," Hirsch explained, drawing the distinction between reformers and his own brand of acculturative Orthodoxy; "for us, progress is valid only to the extent that it does not interfere with religion." [65] By and large, these acculturative Orthodox believed that either in style or in substance or in both they could enter the mainstream of history and their host cultures without sacrificing anything of significance in their Jewishness. They could pursue "a faithful adherence to traditional teachings combined with an effective effort to keep in touch with the spirit of progress."[66]

This required a careful balancing act. And the acculturative Orthodox had to be wary of making too many compromises. They were, and many would argue still are, always looking to their right wing to see whether or not they had gone too far. They could always count on the traditionalists to tell them when they had done so.

While a conviction of the adaptability and universality of Judaism seemed at first the essential element of this acculturative tendency in Orthodoxy, in time, as acculturation became more and more identified with other non-Orthodox trends, a number of those whose forebears espoused this philosophy came to see modern Orthodoxy as dangerous. "The modern Orthodox Jew has become deeply affected by the hedonism of Western man," as one rabbi put it.[67] To some this meant turning rightward and toward greater contra-acculturation, while to others it meant moving toward quasi-acculturation where substantive accommodations to modern life and culture were exchanged for stylistic ones.[68] Once again, as at first, Orthodoxy was caught in the tension between acculturation and contra-acculturation. How much to adapt and how much to preserve became, then as now, a matter of debate and some dissension.

Varieties of American Orthodoxy

These various trends and tensions marked American Orthodoxy as it emerged. Beginning in 1881, when "a self-conscious Orthodoxy" arrived with the first waves of the Eastern European Jewish immigration, and through the present, American Orthodox Jews have been divided between those who moved into acculturative directions— even with adaptations—and those who went the other direction.

In many ways, the early immigrants can be seen as inertially Orthodox.[69] Their practices and worldviews were largely carryovers of traditions from their European Jewish heritage. As long as they could be held onto with a minimum of resistance, they were maintained.[70] But when American and modern life began to buffet these traditions, the inertial attachments were insufficient to maintain Orthodoxies. These early Orthodox Jews had simply not had the chance to develop the ideological and institutional coherence and resistance characteristic of those volitionally Orthodox who, immersed in the situation of modernity, had *chosen* to be Orthodox, not simply slipped into it out of inertia. On the other hand, many of those Jews who migrated to America just before or in the aftermath of World War II came with a far more experienced, time-tested, worked-through, volitional Orthodoxy.[71]

This is not to say that the earlier immigrants did not make important contributions to Orthodoxy. They did. They built institutions and communities that guarded tradition and fostered ties among those who shared commitments to it. Thus in 1886, Yeshivat Etz Chaim which would mature into Yeshiva University was formed.[72] As earlier noted, in 1898, the main federation of Orthodox synagogue communities in this country, the Union of Orthodox Jewish Congregations of America, was founded. In 1912, young Orthodox Jews on New York's Lower East side who viewed themselves as undeniably American organized what would become one of the largest Orthodox synagogue movements, the Young Israel.[73] In 1922, the Hebrew Theological College of Chicago, which like Yeshiva University offered a primary emphasis on traditional Talmudic study but also provided opportunities for secular studies, opened its doors. By the eve of World War II, there were established several Orthodox American rabbinical associations. Many of those institutions continue to serve the contemporary Orthodox population.

There were numerous other important educational, congregational, volunteeristic Orthodox institutions that trace their origins to the early Orthodox immigrants. But the Orthodoxy of the mid-twentieth century "revitalized and transformed Orthodoxy's strength and orientation."[74] In many ways the tensions and lines of fracture which characterized Orthodoxy as it developed in Europe and had existed in nineteenth-century America were in this century engraved more deeply by the new immigrants and their offspring.

What are these lines of fracture? As already submitted, they were patterned by the clash between acculturative and contra-acculturative orientations, both of which from the beginning coexisted within Orthodoxy. In America, these antithetic tendencies expressed themselves institutionally and ideologically, creating what has come to be called popularly (both by insiders and outsiders to Orthodoxy), "right-wing" and "left-wing" Orthodoxy. The former generally became identified with the contra-acculturative orientation, and the latter was generally in favor of some adapted form of acculturation. Because right wing and left wing have political connotations that go far beyond matters of religion, and because they are not really descriptive, other nomenclature has come into use. Thus the right wing is sometimes called "traditionalist" or "ultra-Orthodox," while its counterpart is sometimes called "modern Orthodox" or, more recently, "centrist Orthodox."[75] Sometimes, as well, these various Orthodox groupings are identified by organizational affiliation since certain organizations have become emblematic of particular trends in Orthodoxy.

To understand these sorts of identifications, a review of the various groupings and trends as well as the organizations and institutions associated with them in American Orthodoxy will be useful here. While our purpose is not and cannot be to describe and define the multitude of Orthodox Jewish organizations, we do wish to sketch a brief map of Orthodoxy in order to better identify those Orthodox Jews who make up the people whom we have surveyed and about whom we shall be reporting in the pages that follow.

We begin, as did Orthodoxy, with the contra-acculturative groups. In America, perhaps the most important source of these Jews has been the yeshiva. Often an academy that separated its students from the lay community and therefore the pressures to acculturate to the wider world while it instructed them in the Talmud, Bible, and rabbinic sources, the yeshiva developed and nurtured an insular Orthodoxy that strived to be totalistic and uncompromising in its attachment to tradition.[76] Here the entire day and much of the night was spent immersed in review of ancient texts under the tutelage of revered rabbinic authorities. This was the traditionalist world *par excellence.* Thus both the founding of and attendance at yeshivas often served as a way of becoming aligned and identified with the contra-acculturative orientation. It is no accident that those Jews who sought to assert and safeguard their Orthodoxy in America did so by founding new yeshivas or transplanting European yeshivas here. We have already mentioned a number of such institutions which were founded by the early Eastern European immigrants.

Certainly, there were other such institutions established that sought (albeit as a latent function of their existence) to limit as much as possible the impact of contemporary American culture and values upon Orthodoxy. In 1926, Mesivta Torah Vodaath, begun as an elementary school in 1917, instituted itself as a place where religious studies and particularly Talmud would act to limit engagement with life in America.

These contra-acculturative institutional trends became more pronounced in the interwar period and grew even more in the forties. Indeed, a list of the yeshivas in America that generally eschew acculturative tendencies shows the earliest one, Torah Vodaath, founded in 1926, with most others founded between 1933 and 1949. This period saw the establishment of a number of yeshivas that would train a cadre of students who at best looked upon themselves as *in* but not *of* America. That is, they were willing to make necessary but inconsequential adjustments to American life as long as they could remain firmly ensconced within the precincts of Orthodox life and tradition. These students (all boys; girls were given a far more modest education) not only went to places like Torah Vodaath or Mesivta Tiffereth Jerusalem in New York but also to the Telshe yeshiva founded in Cleveland in 1941, Ner Israel founded in Baltimore in 1933, Chaim Berlin which in 1939 became an advanced yeshiva in Brooklyn, or Beth

Midrash Govoha in Lakewood, New Jersey, which began taking in students in 1943. Often students lived in these schools for nearly eleven months a year.

Summing up the outlook of these schools, Eliezer Berkovits, a contemporary American Orthodox rabbi who represents a contrasting acculturative tendency, suggests:

> They do not acknowledge that Jewish communities do live in the context of a secular civilization that confronts the Jew with innumerable intellectual, moral, and religious challenges. For them, Jews, even in the midst of the world, ought to and can encapsulate themselves—as it were. Jews should live in a spiritual ghetto of their own making. . . . It is not their aim to be contemporary. One might better say that according to them the source of all evil stems from being contemporary.[77]

Although Berkovits writes from—at the very least—a mildly antagonistic position on the other wing of Orthodoxy, he expresses what modern Orthodoxy often perceives as an essential feature of "yeshiva Orthodoxy": "a yeshiva that had secular and religious studies in one building was not good enough."[78] This contra-acculturative stance has often centered around the matter of secular education which is considered as a conduit via which culture contact with the non-Jewish world occurs. In essence, the yeshiva world often argues that "there is no intrinsic value in any knowledge outside of the Torah, that Torah is totally self-sufficient for a Jew's intellectual needs, that study or enjoyment of secular studies and culture is a waste of time, for all knowledge—religious and secular—is to be found in the Talmud," a view echoed by a leading rabbi of one of the yeshivas who is quoted as having said that "those who receive a secular education cannot express authentic Torah views."[79]

"In general, students at these schools are expected not to pursue any secular studies at colleges and universities."[80] While some do, often taking courses in night school, these efforts are viewed as unavoidable necessities which enable the young student to prepare to make a living. Yet secular education and the connection to contemporary secular culture which it implies are not viewed as having intrinsic worth.

In contrast to these yeshiva Orthodox stand the Orthodox of the day school. Although we shall have much more to say about day schools in subsequent chapters, we wish to point to them here as emblematic of a particular Orthodox type. The essential feature that distinguishes the day school from the prototypical yeshiva is its emphasis on secular education. This ideal is perhaps most succinctly articulated by David Berger (himself an Orthodox Jew who is a professor of Jewish history at Brooklyn College, a secular and public university) who submits, "Torah combined with secular learning . . . is one road to human perfection."[81] Rejecting the insularity of the yeshiva Orthodoxy, the day school Orthodox have sought to synthesize—or at the very least syncretize—secular and Jewish learning. As one modern Orthodox Jew expressed it: "[W]e will fuse the golden teachings of the days of old with the challenges that confront us as individuals and as a community in twentieth century America."[82] In less lofty and more practical terms, "the vast majority of parents whose children are enrolled in day schools expect their children to become professionals," something that will take advanced university training and all that implies.[83] They aspire to a relationship with the world from which secular knowledge emerges.

For those for whom the primary and secondary day school is the emblem of their acculturation, the officially integrationist Yeshiva University whose motto is *Torah U Madda* (Jewish learning and secular science) represents the higher educational counterpart to the insular contra-acculturative yeshivas.[84] Thus there are yeshiva Orthodox and Yeshiva University Orthodox who represent recognizably variant attitudes toward contemporary American life and culture.[85]

The two points of view can also be discovered in the rabbinical associations into which the Orthodox have organized themselves. In describing the various perspectives taken by the rabbis who populate these associations, Jeffrey Gurock speaks of *resisters* and *accommodators*. "The former," he explains, "have attempted to reject acculturation and disdained cooperation with other American Jewish elements, fearing that alliances would work to dilute traditional faith and practice. The latter have accepted the seeming inevitability of Americanization and have joined arms with less-traditional elements in the community."[86] Although the personalities and motives behind the origins of these various associations are complex and sometimes overlapping, by now the organizations have taken on symbolic significance, and membership in them serves as yet another way of identifying one's brand of Orthodoxy.

On the contra-acculturative side is the Agudath Ha-Rabbonim (sometimes referred to as the Union of Orthodox Rabbis).[87] Founded in 1902 "to improve religious instruction and seek only observant teachers in the *cheder* [religious school], organize careful records of marriages and divorces, war against 'orthodox' Sabbath violators in the marketplace, and establish an inspection system of *kashrut* and *mikvaot* [ritual baths]," it for a time largely limited its membership to European born and trained rabbis.[88] "The East European rabbi, who usually found his way into the ranks of Agudas Harabonim, attempted to ignore the essential challenge which this [contemporary American] reality posed."[89] As such, the Agudists established a reputation of being in but not of America. To a large extent the association has remained attached to essentially sectarian, Orthodox religious concerns.

Although there are a number of smaller and even more fiercely contra-acculturative rabbinical associations—including the Rabbinical Alliance of America, Hitachdut Harabbonim Haredim, and the Agudas Ha-admorim—in popular parlance they are often all lumped together under the banner of the Agudath Ha-Rabbonim. What they share in common is a strong commitment to promoting Orthodox Jewish religious observance above all else, even at the cost of ignoring or spurning contemporary American culture. They eschew dialogue or interaction with those more acculturative rabbis who do not share these commitments.

Like the rabbinical organization, the Agudath Israel, a lay organization, also has become identified among the Orthodox as "basically sectarian" and contra-acculturative.[90] Similarly, one may speak of a variety of hasidic organizations which by and large turn away from genuine engagement with American culture and society.[91]

At the other extreme of Orthodoxy, there is the Rabbinical Council of America. Founded in 1935 by American-born rabbis (many of them graduates of the Rabbi Isaac Elchanan Theological Seminary of Yeshiva University) who had been unable to find a place for themselves in the Agudath Ha-Rabbonim because their American ordination was considered inferior to some of the old-world degrees by which people qualified for the Aguda, the RCA became in time identified with what we are calling an adapted acculturative position.[92] "The RCA, unlike other Orthodox rabbinical associations, generally sought rapprochement, when possible, with non-Orthodox rabbis."[93] One of its leaders has written that "the R.C.A. in its half-century of existence, has literally created, nurtured and developed the modern Orthodox rabbi, as well as the modern Orthodox community, and has provided them with their philosophy, their structure, and their program."[94] While this claim may be somewhat grandiose, there is no question that to speak of an RCA rabbi and community is to connote modern Orthodoxy in the same way as to speak of the Aguda is to imply its opposite.

Other associations such as the Young Israel synagogues, which "consist mainly of college-educated, American-born, middle-class" Orthodox Jews or Mizrachi (which recently changed its name to "Amit") Women, the religious Zionist organization, likewise represent acculturative tendencies. On the other hand, Hadass synagogues (although primarily in Europe) or N'Shai Chabad—the Lubavitcher Hasidic women—are often associated with its converse.

When we look at the entire map of Orthodoxy, then, we find on the right wing the yeshiva people, the Agudists, Hasidim, and those in general who champion contra-acculturation. And when we look at the other side, we discover day school and Yeshiva University people, RCA, Young Israel, and Mizrachi adherents.

As any insider will be quick to point out, this map is still far too vague and general. Our study endeavors to go further. But first an important qualifier.

It is among the Orthodox Jews who have chosen an adapted form of acculturation—the so-called modern Orthodox—that we have done our survey and whom we examine. We do so because we are intrigued by their struggle to adapt acculturation, to be both Orthodox Jew and contemporary American. We want to see how they manage that. We also choose them as the objects of our study because the powerfully contra-acculturative Orthodox would after all, almost by definition, want to have nothing to do with a university-sponsored study such this one. But by largely excluding the right-wing people from our study—because they have in a sense excluded themselves—we have not completely eliminated their point of view.

Even among those whom we have labeled "acculturative," there remain traditionalists and contra-acculturative tendencies. That is, while the hallmark of these Orthodox Jews is the effort to find a way of bringing together the contemporary world and the traditional demands of Judaism through a variety of approaches, there are among them also those who, while remaining committed to acculturation, harbor doubts about the long-term advantages of this approach for the survival of Judaism. These latter Jews look with some yearning to the contra-acculturative option, even though they are not necessarily ready to altogether separate themselves from the contemporary world—at least not yet. So while our sample may not have the hard core contra-acculturative, Agudist, yeshiva, right-wing Orthodox, we suspect—and the pages that follow will show—that there are in our population some who may eventually choose to move rightward and away from the conflicts of acculturation. Indeed, many of these are people who, having gone through something of a yeshiva education, continue to feel attachments to that way of life.[95]

So we look at the acculturative Orthodox and find among them not only those who are drawn powerfully by the advantages of acculturation and who would adapt it only minimally to conform with the demands of their Orthodoxy but also their opposites. And between these two are those who distinguish themselves by "moderation," who remain convinced that they can be part of the modern world as long as they remain anchored powerfully to the tradition.[96]

The Sample, the Method, and the Pattern of Presentation

To draw our portrait of contemporary American Orthodoxy, we chose to survey approximately 1,000 people, the large bulk of whom identified themselves as Orthodox Jews. Our surveys presented respondents with dozens of statements asking them to express their alternative points of view (various degrees of "agree" or "disagree," "Opinion A" or "Opinion B," etc.). This procedure generally resulted in substantial and predictable differences among respondents.

The data were collected in 1979 and 1980. There is no comprehensive master list of Orthodox Jews in the United States. Instead, we were compelled to piece together a sample of Orthodox Jews from sources self-defined as Orthodox. We began by administering mail-back questionnaires to mailing lists supplied by an association of Orthodox professionals, an Orthodox periodical, a Young Israel synagogue in the Boston area, and a modern Orthodox synagogue in northern New Jersey. From these samples we collected 515 respondents in roughly equal number from all four sources. We then initiated a preliminary analysis of our data, modifying some conceptual points. As a result, we made some minor changes in the questionnaire, dropping a few items and adding some others. We then mailed the revised questionnaire to approximately 1,000 members of the Lincoln Square Synagogue on Manhattan's Upper West Side. The synagogue is a vital congregation with large numbers of young couples and singles, many of whom, it is thought, derive from non-Orthodox backgrounds and prior affiliations. After mailing questionnaires, we received completed responses from 490 people. These comprise the largest single source of the nearly 1,023 usable interviews.

Very traditionalist Orthodox Jews are—as we have acknowledged—almost totally unrepresented in our study.

Although we have some members of the Aguda in our sample, we have, as far as we know, few if any Hasidic Jews in our sample. This is because of the way we found our respondents and in part because of, as we have already explained, their insular ideology that makes many such Jews unwilling to participate in a study such as ours. Our best educated guess is that this type of Orthodox Jew represents about a quarter of the Orthodox Jewish population in America. However, while their point of view and behavior may be expected to be more traditional than the most traditionalist elements of our sample, we do not believe that they contradict the portrait we shall paint in these pages. Rather, they simply represent a more distinct boundary on one extreme of the group of Orthodox Jews. That is, everything we shall say about the traditionalists in our sample is likely to be true about those to their traditional right—only more so.

In other senses, our sample also constitutes a particular piece of the Orthodox universe. To assess some of the ways it is different, we may compare characteristics of our sample with those from the (self-defined) Orthodox respondents contained within the 1981 Greater New York Jewish Population Study.[97] Almost 30% of American Jews reside within the eight counties covered by the New York study; and, owing to their concentration in the five boroughs, Westchester, and Long Island, probably most American Orthodox Jews live within the study's region.

Comparisons of our Orthodox sample with the New York study's Orthodox subsample (see table 1.2) reveal substantial but theoretically consistent differences. The Orthodox sample that we analyzed is disproportionately young. Half the respondents were under thirty-five as contrasted with just a quarter of the New York area Orthodox; at the other extreme, just 10% of our respondents were elderly (sixty-five or over) as compared with almost a third (31%) of the New York group.

Second, and as a direct consequence of this age difference, many more of our respondents never were married, and far fewer were widowed than in the New York study sample.

Third, our sample is extraordinarily well-educated. Most

31

Table 1.2: Key Sociodemographic Characteristics of Two Samples of Orthodox Jews (%)

	Sample Used in this Study	Subsample from the 1981 Greater New York Jewish Population Study
Age:		
65 +	10	31
55–64	7	18
45–54	11	15
35–44	18	12
LT 35	50	25
	100	100
Marital Status:		
Men:		
Never Married	24	12
Married	71	75
Divorced/Separated	4	6
Widowed	2	7
	100	100
Women:		
Never Married	35	5
Married	50	73
Divorced/Separated	5	4
Widowed	10	18
	100	100
Education:		
Men		
Graduate degree	63	25
Bachelor's	20	25
Less	18	50
	100	100
Women:		
Graduate degree	50	12
Bachelor's	26	24
Less	24	65
	100	100
Income:		
Above $40,000	36	19
$20,000–$40,000	41	43
Below $20,000	23	39
	100	100

Note: Percentage totals have been rounded.

respondents had a graduate degree as compared with just a quarter of the Orthodox men in New York and an eighth of the Orthodox women; conversely, only about a fifth of our respondents failed to report a college degree as opposed to most New York area Orthodox Jews.

Fourth, consistent with the educational and age differences, our respondents earned higher incomes than those in New York. Over a third reported household incomes (in 1980 and 1981) of $40,000 or more as contrasted with less than a fifth of the New York–area Orthodox households. While mean reported income amounted to $39,000 in our sample, the New York Orthodox families reported an average of only $28,000 in 1981.

Fifth, as our analysis in Chapter 6 makes clear, the Orthodox in our sample are more ritually observant than are the self-identifying Orthodox in the Greater New York Jewish Population Study. This discrepancy is understandable for several reasons. Our sample is younger, more educated (in Judaic and secular terms), and consists almost exclusively of affiliated Orthodox Jews. If they are ritually more observant, we imagine (for reasons that will become increasingly apparent to the reader) they may well be more traditional than the general population of Orthodox Jews in other ways as well.

Yet, what is most interesting about the gap between our sample and the population study is that New York's Orthodox are, in turn, more ritually active than those outside the metropolitan area. Studies in other cities have located large numbers of relatively nonobservant Orthodox that are proportionally a greater segment of those who identify themselves as Orthodox than those so identified in New York Orthodoxy. If all this is so, then our sample is more observant (and in other ways traditional) than the full spectrum of American Orthodox Jews. In other words, not only does it fail to contain the most traditional, it also underrepresents the most modern. Since a central purpose of our study is to demonstrate patterned variation, the truncation of the right and the underrepresentation of the left actually embodies a conservative assumption. That is, insofar as we demonstrate variations across this slice of Orthodoxy, one can be sure of even greater variations across the full range of Orthodoxy from the most traditional right to the most modern left.

These differences are the direct and expected consequences of our sampling procedures. By eliciting the cooperation of affluent modern Orthodox synagogues and an association of Orthodox professionals, and by surveying readers of an Orthodox periodical, we were bound to obtain a sample that was decidedly upscale, one characterized by higher education and income as well as, it seems, by youthfulness.

These distinctive features of our sample ought not to be seen as drawbacks. Rather they ought to be seen as the direct and necessary outcomes of deciding to focus on Orthodox Jews who are inextricably in the situation of modernity. We chose to examine Jews who most forcefully experience the tensions of combining a commitment to the parochialisms of Orthodoxy with a life in the contemporary cosmopolitan world. We chose a population where practically all the faces of Orthodoxy are to be found. If anything, those who are younger, more educated, more affluent, and more single should confront the situation of modernity more immediately and repeatedly than their older, less upscale, and more family-oriented Orthodox counterparts. Their resolutions of the tensions occasioned by the pulls of American modernity and Jewish traditionalism lie at the heart of this investigation.

In considering our sample, the reader is perhaps tempted to object that we have not captured a perfectly representative population of Orthodox American Jews in our survey. In answer, we would reply that there is no perfectly representative population of Orthodox Jews in America. And the search for one is a chimera.

Several considerations make the construction of a perfectly representative sample of American Orthodoxy unrealistically costly, if not nearly impossible, even with considerable personnel and financial resources. One is the problem of definition. At the more modern end of the Orthodoxy spectrum, as we shall demonstrate throughout this book, are Jews who identify as Orthodox but whose ritual practice, religious faith, communal networks, and social attitudes would probably make them less than fully Orthodox in the eyes of many traditionalists. The boundary separating Orthodox from non-Orthodox Jews, then, is rather fuzzy. While we have chosen to adopt a broad definition of who is Orthodox—those who say they are Orthodox and belong to an Orthodox institution qualified for our study—we readily concede that others may regard this definition as overly broad.

At the other extreme, many contra-acculturative traditionalists—as we pointed out—are reluctant to participate in social surveys of any kind, especially those coming from the secular world of the university and investigating matters of religious belief and practice. As we have noted, the traditional end of our sample stops short of those highly insular groups whom we regarded as difficult if not impossible to survey via a university-generated, mail-back questionnaire.

But these problems aside, the most formidable obstacle to drawing a truly representative sample of American Orthodoxy entails the small size of the population. All of Orthodoxy—including the entire spectrum from the most modern to the most traditional—constitutes an extremely rare population group in American society. Jews comprise less than 3% of American households. Several local Jewish population studies suggest that Orthodox Jews comprise roughly 10% of American Jewry, implying that Orthodox Jews are less than .3% of the total American population.[98] It is clear that we could not, at reasonable costs, obtain a truly random and representative nationwide sample of the Orthodox universe, even with agreement on boundaries and the cooperation of the most traditional.

True, several local Jewish population studies—based as they most often are on random digit dialing—contain representative samples of Orthodox. But these studies, for obvious reasons, lack in-depth data on beliefs, practices, and attitudes which are critical for studying internal differences among Orthodox respondents. Instead of attempting the impossible (or inordinately expensive) or settling for the very limited information available in the methodologically rigorous local population studies, we opted for a reason-

able alternative: a sample drawn from merged lists of synagogues, periodicals, and organizations (described above),
institutions regarded as falling under the Orthodox rubric.

In light of the unrepresentative nature of our sample, we
were compelled to view our quantitative data quite skepti-
cally. Our own situation was very much unlike that of most
demographers who, for example, customarily take much
government census data at face value (although they too
know full well the measurement and sampling problems
inherent in such data). Indeed, social scientists working
with large and representative survey samples also can
have more confidence in their data than, in all candor, we
did in ours. In fact, in many large-scale surveys—cen-
suses, national public opinion polls, etc.—the data themselves are the "news"; researchers make important schol-
arly contributions by simply reporting vital statistics,
electoral preferences, or other such findings supported by
data appropriate to such claims. Our data is not like that.

Actually, we want to make clear from the outset that no
reader ought to walk away from the chapter on ritual practice with the idea that the percentages we cite there define
precisely the percentages of all ritual practices among all
modern Orthodox Jews in America. As we have conceded,
we cannot define precisely where Orthodoxy begins and
ends; and, even if we could, we could not obtain a perfect
(or even nearly perfect) sample of that population group.

Rather, throughout our analysis, we are careful to talk
only in broad terms of general relationships between Orthodox traditionalism and the several features of Orthodox
life that distinguish the more modern from the more traditional. To do so, we rely not only upon our data but also
upon our years of qualitative observation of Orthodoxy
and American Jewry as a guide and a check on the reliabil-
ity and validity of our quantitative analysis. Fortunately,
the broad patterns we uncovered comported quite well
with our initial understandings and our theoretical framework. To us, and we hope to other informed observers (Orthodox insiders or outsiders), the findings seem to be accurate and useful reflections of the population generally
referred to as "modern American Jewish Orthodoxy."

In short, the strength of our conclusions and the portrait that we have drawn by way of the survey data do not rest on the absolute authority of the quantitative data. We used the survey data to extend and refine our thinking; we hope they will be understood as illustrative of broad trend rather than definitive of precise details. We protest this much because we are well aware that numbers often give the impression of absolute accuracy and exactitude. Rather, we hope our description of American modern Orthodoxy will be seen more as a portrait than a photograph. And we believe the likeness of our portrait is a good one.

Our book is organized around four dimensions of the faces of Orthodoxy. These are: ritual observance, what insiders call "keeping mitzvas"; belief or *emunah;* communal bonding or *kehilla;* and social ethos and political worldview or, as insiders might put it, "finding one's *hevra."* Together these four dimensions will give depth to our comprehension of contemporary American Orthodoxy. Of necessity, we shall return to many of the points we have set out in an introductory way here. But when we return to these points, we shall frame them with the data we have collected from our survey and interviews with the people who made up our sample. They will flesh out the many faces of Orthodoxy in America. Out of them—of these Jews who try to adapt acculturation with the contra-acculturative tendencies of tradition, who try to be cosmopolitan and parochial or modern and orthodox—will emerge what we believe is an important story of the contact between two worlds which many believed were mutually exclusive.

2 *Mitzva:* Ritual Practices and Orthodox Jews

> Hasten to perform the easiest *mitzva,* and flee from
> all sin; for one *mitzva* will lead to another *mitzva,*
> and one sin to another sin.
>
> Ben Azzai, *Avot* 4:2

As we stated at the outset, Orthodox Jews are not all alike. Some—the "traditionalists"—have tried to keep contemporary society's influence strictly circumscribed, maintaining their strongest allegiance to the parochial way of the Jewish past. These are Jews who see the worlds of *halacha* (Jewish law—literally, "the way") and American life as mutually exclusive paths incapable of integration within the life of the individual.

Others, the so-called modern Orthodox, have tried to find a way of remaining linked both to the contemporary non-Jewish world in which they find themselves and to the traditions and practices of Judaism to which they remain loyal. For some this has meant little more than a nominal attachment to Orthodoxy, while for others it has meant a partial attachment to the demands of the tradition.

Yet despite the differences between the modernist and traditionalist trends of Orthodoxy, "they agree in making the symbol of the Torah, representing the element of continuity, primary to Judaism and central to their definition of a Jew."[1] "Torah-true" Jews—as many of these people refer to themselves—bind themselves to the demands of the Torah such that "when confronted with a contradiction between a *halachic* statement and a sociological trend or scientific 'truth,' Torah, as it has always been understood, must prevail."[2] That is, in principle all Orthodox Jews share an ideological commitment to the way of tradition and are shaped by observance of the ritual and the *halacha.*

They share as well a dilemma: being attached to a life guided by Jewish law or *halacha* while also locating themselves in the situation of modernity, they must find a way to come to terms with these often antithetical realities.

They must discover a means of coming to terms with worlds that are sometimes in collision or at least in contention with each other and each of which makes comprehensive claims upon them.

Precisely how that accommodation is shaped, the nature of the compromises made, and the boundaries of flexibility is what we have tried to decipher in our research and intend to describe in this account. From this effort will emerge a sense of how people come to grips with tradition in the contemporary context, how modern Orthodox Jews cope with and commonly resolve the tensions of simultaneously living in different worlds.

The Centrality of Ritual Practices: Counting *Mitzvas*

Our governing research strategy throughout this work has been to compare and contrast the various streams of American Jewish Orthodoxy, to learn about the convergencies and divergencies among them. The problem is to find the lines of fracture among these groups. There are various ways of going about this task. Certainly the tools of social science can be used. Yet, even before beginning, it is important to qualify our use of the term "groups." There are, as we shall demonstrate, marked differences among the streams of Orthodoxy, and these differences are often readily acknowledged by Orthodox Jews themselves. However, the "groups" (a more precise although awkward term would probably be "subgroups") we shall investigate are less distinct communities than they are different regions or clusters or streams in the traditionalist-modernist flow of Orthodoxy.[3]

With this qualifier in mind, we could define the groups or streams solely in terms of their theological beliefs. Hence, the most unswerving in their commitment to particular fundamental tenets of Orthodox Jewish faith (such as belief in God, confidence in revelation at Mount Sinai, or conviction about the coming of the Messiah) would comprise the traditionalist wing. Those who identify themselves as Orthodox but who largely reject or are at best uncertain about these beliefs would make up what we would call the "nominally" Orthodox. Finally, those who affirm the truth of the theology and doctrine but with significant ambivalence would define a modern Orthodox center.

Alternatively, in a similar fashion, we could measure social involvement. Here we would argue that those who find themselves in a segregated Orthodox community, with most of their friends Orthodox, who feel most close and similar to other Orthodox Jews, and who belong to Orthodox institutions above all others would be the traditionalists; those most integrated into American host society while still maintaining some tenuous links to Orthodoxy would be the nominals. Those at intermediate levels of social segregation (or integration) would be the centrist Orthodox.

In fact, we decided to use neither measures of theological beliefs nor communal involvement to define our groups. Our principal reason for rejecting these alternatives is that measurement of either turns out to be difficult and relatively inexact. First, "belief systems have an existence that is independent of the individual who experiences the commitment" to them.[4] Second, as Fackenheim has argued, one "cannot measure the depth of religious commitment."[5] And with regard to social ties, both the degree of involvement and the strength of communal bonding are difficult to articulate.

We chose instead to define the three Orthodox groups— the "traditionalists," "centrists," and "nominals"—in terms of ritual practice, what insiders call "the observance of *mitzvas*." Aside from the methodological and research advantages of such clear-cut criteria, we felt that we had good substantive reasons for preferring ritual practice— *mitzvas*—over beliefs and social ties as a starting point. Most critically, Orthodox norms strongly emphasize practice and the carrying out of *mitzvas*. Historically, for those who would be called "Orthodox," practice was always crucial.[6] An age-old Talmudic doctrine asserts, "A man should always perform the *mitzvas* even if he does not believe in them, since by doing so he will come to believe."[7] Because ritual observance was considered capable of generating belief and not vice versa, the former was considered primary.

41

The Orthodox Jew *believed* in doing *mitzvas*. This approach, as leading Orthodox Rabbi Walter Wurzburger explained to his coreligionists, "encouraged the performance of good deeds [i.e., *mitzvas*], even if prompted by ulterior motives. . . . on the ground that, eventually, the habit of performing good deeds may gradually transform our mentality and ennoble our character to such an extent that we may reach a level of religiosity where the good deed is inspired only by the sublime desire to serve God."[8]

This ethos of praxis has apparently become an integral part of the taken-for-granted reality of Orthodox Jewish life. As one Orthodox Jew, responding to a question about the role of belief in his life, expressed it: "It's interesting that when an outsider talks or thinks about Orthodoxy, he tends to emphasize belief. From from the inside, we are more concerned with practice. I don't even know whether my wife and I agree on belief."[9]

The emphasis on the ultimacy of practice grows out of the conviction that the purely religious attitude of faith must be placed in a framework of consistency, regularity of conduct, and authority. These in turn emancipate the observant from the need to contrive their behavior *de novo* each time they are faced with a life decision. Second, it provides them with limits and determinate goals, the reaching of which offers some sort of gratification. There is simple satisfaction in carrying out prescribed ritual practices precisely. Although this concern with Jewish praxis leaves some room for debate about the ultimate goals of Jewish life and the genuine way to "serve God"—an ambiguity some modern Orthodox have sought to exploit in their continuing efforts at doctrinal reinterpretation—it became a keystone of all varieties of Orthodox life. Adherence to *halacha*, the normative pattern of observances and ritual practice, constitutes the explicit element of Orthodox Jewish belief. Through it not only sentiments but actions are shared.

The centrality of ritual practice is also apparent in the extraordinary attention Orthodox Jews pay not only to their own ritual practice but also to that of their neighbors, friends, and kin.[10] Insiders easily locate themselves and others on the traditionalist-modern continuum by noting performance of key indicator rituals in conjunction with an implicit standard of ritual observance. They know, for example, that Jews who fast on the minor fast days of the Jewish year or those who refuse to eat even kosher foods at the homes of nonkosher (i.e., nonobservant or non-Jewish) friends belong to the traditionalist wing of Orthodoxy. Similarly, they can readily surmise that those who fail to obey the *halachic* prohibitions on the use of electricity on the Sabbath, or who dine in nonkosher homes, or who fail to fully and properly observe some of the major and minor holy days are, if Orthodox, less than completely traditional and perhaps little more than nominally Orthodox. It is not because these particular observances are the most doctrinally important that they are so utilized but because they indicate a pattern of ritual behavior usually consistent with a particular religious profile.

Between the ritually very active traditionalist and the relatively nonobservant nominally Orthodox lies a complex center. As we shall soon show, this central stream is populated by individuals who live in the crosscurrents between the extremes. Here, perhaps most clearly, the antithetical character of the intersecting ways of life makes itself felt. The people who live in these crosscurrents between the modern and traditional, the rational and enchanted, the cosmopolitan and parochial themselves vary considerably in several aspects of Jewish identity and commitment. They also, however, consistently differ in several crucial ways from their Orthodox counterparts on both sides.

The Center and the Extremes:
Boundary-setting Rituals

To get beyond generalities, and in order to more sharply define the streams among the Orthodox, we devised a questionnaire whose purpose was to provide a portrait of those American Jews who call themselves Orthodox. Our questionnaire asked respondents about a wide range of Jewish ritual practices. Some of these are in fact observed by many, if not most, American Jews; others are practiced by very few, primarily by the traditionalist Orthodox. We could have chosen to classify our respondents in terms of not some but all the available ritual practices. Counting how many rituals each respondent performed, we would then define the traditionalists as those observing all or almost all of the rituals, the nominals as those practicing relatively few, and the centrist modern Orthodox as those performing a middle range of ritual practices.

But we rejected using all the available ritual questions to construct an index of Orthodox traditionalism since doing so would have precluded our further examining variation in ritual practice among Orthodox Jews. One of our key research questions—the one we address in this chapter—is to discover which rituals in fact typify traditional Orthodox Jews, which characterize both traditional and centrist modern Orthodox, and which are practiced by all three Orthodox groups. By using only a few (rather than all) indicator rituals to define the three groups, we can still examine how the observance of other rituals—the ones outside the index—varies across Orthodoxy.[11] In this way, the various groups could be seen more vividly, and the apparent monolith of Orthodoxy would give way to a more accurate view.

With this strategy in mind, we first separated the Orthodox ($N = 665$) from the non-Orthodox ($N = 358$; total $= 1,023$). Respondents were asked whether they saw themselves as "Orthodox," "Conservative," "Reform," or something else. Only those who answered "Orthodox" qualified for inclusion in one of the three Orthodox groups. That is, even if by practice, belief, and affiliation someone would appear to qualify as an "Orthodox Jew," we were not ready to so identify him or her if the person was not ready to be self-identified as Orthodox.

Throughout this study, our non-Orthodox subsample serves to provide a vivid contrast to the Orthodox respondents. We claim that the differences between our Orthodox and non-Orthodox respondents represent but a small section of a continuum that, in simplified terms, runs from the most modernist Reform to the most traditionalist Orthodox. Several studies have documented the patterns of Jewish and modern involvement that distinguish Orthodox from Conservative or Reform Jews. In broad strokes, the

Orthodox outscore Reform Jews in ritual practice, religious belief, ethnic embeddedness, social conservatism, and attachment to Israel, with the Conservatives reporting intermediate scores.[12] Thus, in contrasting the Orthodox in this study with a group of tradition-leaning Conservative Jews, we are in effect minimizing the distinctions between Orthodox and non-Orthodox; the gaps are even smaller when we realize that we will focus on the differences between our non-Orthodox and the least traditional Orthodox, those we call "nominally" Orthodox. That differences nonetheless will be found between even these nominally Orthodox and the traditional-leaning non-Orthodox, we think, highlights the special character and definition of Orthodoxy. In actuality, of course, the differences in the Jewish population between the typical Orthodox and the typical non-Orthodox are far greater than those we find here between the nominally Orthodox and the "right-wing" Conservative Jews.

Among the self-defined Orthodox, we constructed our index by counting the practice of seven indicative observances. Two deal with the observance of the dietary laws, three with the Sabbath, and two others with fasting. While substantive reasons for selecting these rituals will become clear as we go on, the methodological ones can be stated simply at the outset. Jewish law makes distinctions between men and women, wed and unwed, among others. Any index that sought to compare levels of observance would in great measure have to mute these distinctions. Accordingly, we chose rituals for our index that by and large pertain to both single and married, both men and women equally within the Orthodox normative system. We assigned points for each ritual observed: those who observed all the rituals would get the most points, while those who observed the fewest would get the least points. In this way we could define an index of observance and categorize Jews in our sample more precisely.[13]

To be sure, some insiders and those familiar with the rituals of Judaism might argue that other practices than those we chose are far more important from an ideological, historical, and religious point of view. We have no argument

45

with that. Nevertheless, what makes a ritual a good indicator is not necessarily the same as that which makes it religiously central. It is possible, in fact, to look at certain behaviors which in and of themselves may not be ideologically crucial but which reveal (or predict) much about the overall pattern of religious observance. Thus, to draw an analogy, if a man always wears a tie to match his shirt, this practice alone does not make him a fastidious dresser. It is likely, however, that persons who care enough to always match ties and shirts will also care about the aesthetics of the rest of their appearance. With this qualifier in mind, we may now consider the items in our index.

The first of these was *fasting on the tenth of Tevet*. Although the origins of the ritual of fasting are obscure, there is no doubt that it is among the oldest Jewish practices.[14] While historically there have been a variety of reasons associated with this ritual—for example, as a means of having requests fulfilled by God, as a form of repentance and humbling, as a sign of mourning, as an expression of otherworldly asceticism and accompaniment to ecstatic visions—contemporary Jews for the most part view fasting as an institutionalized religious obligation (into which they may or may not succeed in channeling their spiritual feelings) rather than a spontaneous spiritual expression. That is, they generally do not fast simply when the spirit moves them but fast instead on those days set aside by the biblical injunction and rabbinic tradition. There are three categories of such fasts: (1) fasts decreed in the Bible or instituted to commemorate biblical events, (2) fasts decreed by the rabbis, (3) private fasts.

The Day of Atonement, Yom Kippur, is the only fast that is mentioned in the Five Books of Moses, and as such it has an importance beyond any other such day. Three other fasts commemorate ancient assaults against Jerusalem and the Holy Temple there. They include the ninth of the Hebrew month of Av (*Tisha B'Av*), a day of national mourning for the destruction of the First and Second Holy Temples in Jerusalem; the seventeenth of the month of Tammuz, a commemoration of the breaching of the walls of Jerusalem by the ancient infidel conquerors; and the tenth of Tevet, in memory of the first siege of Jerusalem by the Babylonian

46

king Nebuchadnezzar. There are as well two other yearly fasts: the third of Tishrei (*Tsom Gedalia*), in memory of the slaying of the Jewish patriot Gedalia and his associates by the rulers of Babylon; and the fast of Esther on the thirteenth of Adar in commemoration of the Jews of Persia being saved from genocide. There were in addition to these days rabbinic traditions of fasting, including the *BeHaB* fasts of consecutive Mondays and Thursdays.

While the laws and customs pertaining to fasting are voluminous and complex and need not be discussed here, it is important to note that among the fasts noted above only Yom Kippur and Tisha B'Av are considered "major" fast days. While the former is generally considered more important than the latter and is associated with far more spiritual activity, both nominally require one to fast a full twenty-five hours (from the evening of the previous day to nightfall the next). The seventeenth of Tammuz, tenth of Tevet, third of Tishrei, and Fast of Esther nominally require fasting only from dawn until nightfall, hence their common characterization as "minor."

Jews are most likely to fast on major fast days and least likely to fast on the others. Moreover, among those most likely to fast on these days, adult men predominate (children under the age of thirteen are not required to fast by law, and women are often excused from fasting more than a part of the day by custom). Among the least observed of the minor fast days is the tenth of Tevet. Accordingly, on our index, men received a point for fasting the entire fast day; women qualified if they fasted only part of the day.

A word of explanation is in order about the differing standards for men and women. As already noted, Jewish law places varying obligations on men and women. For the most part, men are expected to observe more of the commandments while women's obligations tend to be more elective. As such, to take on an obligation where none exists—as is often the case among observant women—may be seen as a greater act of devotion than simply to fulfill a standing obligation—the case for men. In the case of fasting, we found empirically that women who fasted only part of a day were in a sense evaluated (within the community) so as to equate them with men who fasted a full

47

day. The question of whether a woman is obligated to fast is a complex one in Jewish law. Pregnant women or nursing mothers are generally exempt from such obligations. The weak and infirm (in the past often—rightly or wrongly—a condition attributed to women) are likewise exempt. Accordingly, even though all others were expected to fast, a folkway evolved among many Orthodox Jews that provided women greater latitude than men in deciding whether or not to fast. Indeed, in many respects (i.e., other rituals, beliefs, social segregation or integration) women who fasted part of the day were similar to men who fasted a whole day. Our inquiries within the Orthodox community about this equation yielded answers that confirmed it. It is as if many Orthodox Jews were saying that someone who has the choice of whether or not to fast and *chooses* to do so needs to do only half as much to get the same credit as someone who has the obligation to fast a full day and does so. Our index reflects this.

A second of our indicator observances was *fasting on Tisha B'Av*. Since this is one of the "major" fast days which is seldom observed punctiliously outside the Orthodox community, we expected it to be a useful discriminator not only within the Orthodox community but between it and outsiders. Men who fasted the entire fast and women who fasted at least a part of it were awarded one point in our index.

Among the Orthodox, the mandate to observe the dietary laws, to keep kosher, is essential. Three of the next indicator ritual observances pertain to the matter of keeping kosher, the fulfillment of Jewish dietary laws. Here, as with fasts, we do not propose to set forth all the nuances and rationales underlying these observances. It is enough for our purposes to point out that the mandate to eat only kosher (i.e., religiously approved) foods is traced by believers to Scripture and outlined in precise detail in rabbinic sources. These include numerous prohibitions, including one against eating any animal that does not both chew its cud and have a cloven hoof, any fish that does not have fins and scales (including crustaceans), birds of prey, and almost all insects. They include as well an injunction against eating any meat that has not been slaughtered and prepared according to the strict dictates of Jewish ritual. The dietary laws, moreover, prohibit the mixing of meat or meat-based products with any dairy ones; a prohibition that extends to the mixing of utensils, pots, and dishes that are used for meat with those used for dairy foods. Some rabbinic opinions suggest that dishes only acquire a "meat" or "dairy" character when the food in them is hot. Cold foods, this argument runs, may come in physical contact with vessels of all sorts, even nonkosher ones, without coming into *legal* contact with them. Nevertheless, this sort of contact is not encouraged, and separate sets of dishes for milk and meat products are commonly required.[15]

As one might expect, laws as complex and varied as these inevitably lead to a variety of interpretations and debates about what does or does not qualify as kosher. For the most part these matters are handled by virtuosi—adjudicators (*poskim*) or committees of scholars among the Orthodox—who decide what is or is not permissible. At the same time, however, norms and customs make their way into lay observance and form a kind of "recipe knowledge," which constitutes "what everybody knows." This recipe knowledge "supplies the institutionally appropriate rules of conduct" for everyday life.[16] Normally, Orthodox Jewish recipe knowledge is linked to lay interpretations of rabbinic dicta and biblical injunctions. Nevertheless, like all folk wisdom, it is not as precise and standardized as the legal codes. Thus it may happen that what everybody knows is not always what according to the law everybody is supposed to do. The result of this may be that, while people remain loyal to the strictures of the law in principle, it is possible to extract principles of behavior from their conduct that are not, strictly speaking, identical with the formal law.[17]

Distinctions between recipe knowledge and formal laws of behavior abound in connection with the dietary laws. Those who are familiar with both codes of conduct, as are many Orthodox Jews, are often acutely aware of the contradictions between the two domains. They also know what everybody does and must choose the "everybody" they wish to join in their observances.

Among the dietary law observances we used as indicators is *refraining from eating cold salads at the home of a non-kosher friend or acquaintance.* As noted, some opinions would view eating such salads as technically in line with the letter of dietary law, if not altogether in its spirit. The coldness of the salad suggests no legal contact is being made with the nonkosher vessels in which the food is served. But, as some Orthodox Jews would argue, there are possibilities that in a nonkosher home and on such dishes small morsels of nonkosher food might inadvertently be consumed. Moreover, commensalism with those who do not keep kosher may imply and lead to other prohibited behavior. It may also implicitly sanction the legitimacy of not keeping kosher if the friend is a Jew, a tolerance that those wholeheartedly embracing the tradition are hardly likely to allow themselves. After all, the person who believes in the strict interpretation of the law cannot "believe anything 'with all [his] heart' without a sentiment of pity and even of horror for those who believe [and observe ritual] differently."[18]

Accordingly, one who refrains from eating a cold salad in the home of a nonkosher friend, even where the pressures exist for maintaining friendship through the sharing of food, would be answering to a different demand, one regarded as religious in origins. In our index those who thus refrained received a point.

In this same line of reasoning was another indicator ritual observance: *refraining from eating warm kosher food cooked at the home of a nonkosher friend or acquaintance.* As one might guess, some Orthodox Jews choose to interpret dietary laws in a lenient fashion or to disattend them by eating permissible food cooked with and placed upon nonkosher utensils and dishes. To be sure, the recipe knowledge of Orthodoxy draws distinctions between the cold salad eaters and the warm food eaters, marking the latter as relatively more lax in their ritual observance. Accordingly, those who declined to interpret dietary laws in such a lenient fashion, who refrained from eating warm kosher foods cooked at nonkosher friends' or acquaintances' homes received a point on our index.

Finally, in line with these laws was the indicator of *maintaining two sets of dishes and utensils, one for meat meals and another for dairy meals.* As earlier noted, this is one of the fundamental prerequisites for observing the dietary laws. Along with buying meats only from a kosher butcher, it is one of the most important ways to signify one's home as "kosher." Moreover, it requires significant economic and instrumental effort. Not only must one own two sets of dishes, one also must be scrupulous about keeping them separate. While we did not ask respondents about the extent of their effort at maintaining the separation between the dishes, an effort that may vary within the world of those who have a kosher home, we were satisfied that simply keeping two sets of dishes indicated a modicum of observance. Accordingly, those who did so received a point in our index.

The last two of our indicator observances pertain to the observance of the Sabbath. Many Orthodox Jews consider the observance of the Sabbath, what insiders call being a *shomer Shabbos* (literally, a Sabbath observer), as the single most important indicator of a person's level of commitment to the tenets of Jewish law. In the day-to-day folk wisdom of Orthodox Jewish life, if one is a shomer Shabbos, many other ritual behaviors may be assumed on his or her part. And if one is not, then the observance of all other ritual laws is suspect. As Abraham Joshua Heschel put it: "What *we* are depends on what the *Sabbath* is to us."[19] It is as if the observance of Sabbath was the key to all other elements of ritual life.[20]

There are a variety of practices prohibited on the Sabbath, all flowing from the biblical commandment to "keep" and "remember" it by resting and refraining from particular labors during it. These are all related to what the Talmudic rabbis determined were the thirty-nine fundamental labors that were prohibited by the Bible. Of these labors (all of which were in one way or another carried on in the building of the holy tabernacle [as detailed in Exodus 30–32]), perhaps the best known is the making of fire. Orthodox rabbinic authorities have concluded that the use of electricity in general and the "kindling" of lights—even electric ones—in particular are included in this prohibition. Thus anyone who turns lights on and off on the Sabbath would be transgressing a fundamental prohibition. To be sure, this does not mean that those observing this injunction necessarily sit in the dark. Contemporary Orthodox Jews commonly use timers and other electronic devices that are preset to turn lights on and off on the Sabbath. In this way they can have light while still adhering to the prohibition against turning lights on and off. In our index, therefore, those who always *refrain from turning lights on and off on the Sabbath* score a point.[21]

Although there is no commandment that specifically prohibits Jews from "going to work on their job" on the Sabbath, the various strictures pertaining to the Sabbath clearly imply that such an activity is not allowed. After all, the original occasion of the Sabbath in Genesis marks God's taking a day off from His job. Most people (religious functionaries and physicians engaged in life-saving activity excluded) have jobs that require them to carry on a whole array of practices not allowed on the Sabbath. Hence, for them such a job would be prohibited on that day. Accordingly, those who *refrain from "going to work on your job" on the Sabbath* scored a point on our index.

Both empirical and substantive reasons have led us to choose these particular indicators of Orthodoxy. Empirically, we found wide variations in the frequencies of performance. Two of the practices—fasting on the tenth of Tevet and refraining from eating even a cold salad in a nonkosher home—were observed very infrequently in our sample. (The proportions were only 42% and 35%, respectively, among all our Orthodox respondents.) Similarly, the Tisha B'Av fast, refraining from turning on and off lights on the Sabbath, and refraining from eating warm foods in a nonkosher home were observed with about the same modicum of frequency among the Orthodox (81%, 82%, and 74%, respectively). Virtually all those who called themselves "Orthodox" kept the last two practices (not going to work on the Sabbath = 94%, and two sets of dishes = 96%). Thus we can speak of "hard" and "easy" criteria of Orthodoxy. To qualify as traditionalist Orthodox Jews on our index, respondents had to pass hard as well as easy tests; they had to observe (i.e., score a point on) all seven rituals. Those we called centrist Orthodox performed most (four to six) of the rituals; that is, they passed moderate to easy tests. Finally, those whom we defined as nominally Orthodox performed a minority (one to three) of these rituals (and others) but nevertheless still identified their denominational identity as Orthodox.

Table 2.1 permits a clearer understanding of how we defined the three groups of Orthodox Jews and, by implication, how we constructed the ritual observance boundaries separating them.

As noted above, traditional Orthodox Jews, by definition, perform all rituals. The centrist modern Orthodox differ from them primarily in their failure to perform the two least popular practices (the Tevet fast and eating no cold salads in nonkosher homes). Only about half the centrist modern Orthodox fasted on the minor fast day, and as few

Table 2.1: Seven Ritual Practices Used to Construct the Orthodoxy Index by Orthodoxy (%)

	Orthodoxy			
	Non-Orthodox	Nominal	Centrist	Traditional
Fasting on the tenth of Tevet:				
Men				
(whole day/part day)	0/ 2	3/18	53/26	100/0
Women				
(whole day/part day)	0/ 1	0/ 0	15/27	66/34
Fasting on Tisha B'Av:				
Men				
(whole day/part day)	7/19	31/34	95/ 3	100/0
Women				
(whole day/part day)	8/17	29/34	78/18	100/0
No cold salads at non-kosher friends' homes	6	5	20	100
No warm "kosher" foods at nonkosher friends' homes	8	16	79	100
Two sets of dishes	54	80	99	100
Never turns on lights on Sabbath	2	18	92	100
Never goes to work on Sabbath	47	70	97	100
Approximate N	358	110	410	145

as 20% claimed that they do not eat cold salads in non-kosher homes. (Clearly, they must fail to meet at least one of these "hard" tests, otherwise they would probably qualify as traditionalist Orthodox.) These two practices, then, are the most decisive rituals in the index for separating the traditionalists from the centrists.

While divided on the two "hard" rituals, nearly all the centrists qualified on all the other rituals. Thus, almost every one of the centrist men reported fasting the entire Tisha B'Av, and a similar overwhelming number of the centrist women fasted at least a part of the day. Almost all of the centrist modern Orthodox "never" turned lights on the Sabbath on or off. Similarly, nearly every one of the centrists never went to his or her job on that day, and they all kept two sets of dishes. A substantial majority did not eat warm kosher foods in nonkosher homes.

The two most widely observed practices on table 2.1—not going to work on the Sabbath and keeping two sets of dishes—at once help to separate the nominally Orthodox from the non-Orthodox as well as from the rest of the Orthodox. Observance of these two practices is virtually universal among the traditionalists and centrists. However, among the nominals—those who at the very least call themselves Orthodox—there is a noticeable minority who may work on the Sabbath or who may have no separate dishes. Nevertheless, they are more likely to observe these practices (70% vs. 47%, and 80% vs. 54%) than those who do not call themselves Orthodox.[22]

In short, the vast majority of centrist Orthodox respondents never worked on the Sabbath, had two sets of dishes (one for meat and one for dairy), fasted on Tisha B'Av (and possibly although not necessarily on the tenth of Tevet), did not turn lights on and off on the Sabbath, were unlikely to eat warm foods in nonkosher homes, although they would eat cold salads there. Hardly any nominally Orthodox Jews fasted on the tenth of Tevet, refrained from eating foods in nonkosher places or turning lights on and off on the Sabbath. Most fasted to some extent on Tisha B'Av (although a plurality did not fast a whole day), and large majorities did not work on their jobs on Sabbath and had two sets of dishes.

Finally, we may discover how the non-Orthodox differ from these Orthodox groups in terms of the rituals reported in table 2.1. Few non-Orthodox (even the most traditionally inclined non-Orthodox who entered our sample) observe fast days other than Yom Kippur; most eat forbidden foods in nonkosher homes; and most freely turn lights on and off on the Sabbath. However, roughly half of these (most of whom in our sample belong to an Orthodox or Conservative synagogue) observe the more popular practices of refraining from Sabbath work on the job and maintaining meat and dairy dishes. (Clearly, most non-Orthodox American Jews fail to observe these practices,[23] but even when compared with those who do to some extent, like those in our sample, there are differences between them and the Orthodox.)

We make no claim for the inviolability of these distinctions. In fact, we suggest quite the opposite by drawing upon sociologist Paul Lazarsfeld's concept of "the interchangeability of indices," the idea that several indices can perform more or less as well as one another in distinguishing people along a spectrum.[24]

Our selection of questions may strike some as arbitrary—others could do as well; moreover, the location of our intergroup boundaries is also somewhat arbitrary. One may certainly raise or lower the criteria of observance that demarcate the traditionalists from the centrist modern Orthodox, or the centrist from the nominals. That judgment largely depends upon the size of the sample and the distribution of respondents over the traditionalist-modern continuum. Moreover, those who may be relatively traditionalist in one community or sample may be fairly modern in another context, and vice versa.

We fully appreciate the element of arbitrariness, therefore, in distinguishing among Orthodox subgroups. We still contend, however, that studying differences among these groups is both possible and fruitful. Even though our ritual-based distinctions may seem arbitrary to some, we shall show that they are nevertheless associated with all sorts of consistent, and therefore meaningful, variations. They include still other rituals, theological beliefs, and social insularity as well as political and social attitudes. In

Table 2.2: "Strictness" of Orthodoxy (Self-evaluated) by Orthodoxy (%)

| | "Would you characterize yourself as . . . Orthodox?" | | | |
| | Orthodoxy | | | |
	Non-Orthodox	Nominal	Centrist	Traditional
Strictly	2	10	50	90
Fairly	5	64	46	10
Slightly	20	23	4	0
Not	73	3	0	0
	100	100	100	100
N	176	107	404	142

fact, if we do admit to a degree of arbitrariness in our definitions of these various Orthodox types, whatever differences we do find among them are that much more impressive in light of the crude techniques available for distinguishing varying levels of Jewish Orthodoxy.

Validation by the Respondents

One immediate way of confirming the lines of cleavage we have distinguished is to turn to the respondents themselves and see whether or not they agree with our evaluations. Accordingly, we asked them to reckon their own degree of Orthodoxy with the question: "Would you characterize yourself as 'strictly Orthodox,' 'fairly Orthodox,' 'slightly Orthodox,' or 'not Orthodox'?" As table 2.2 demonstrates, the respondents' evaluations do indeed accord with our own. The way we identified their level of Orthodoxy on the basis of the seven rituals was by and large consistent with the way they ranked themselves.

Nearly all of those our index called "traditionalist Orthodox" deemed themselves "strictly Orthodox." At the other end of the spectrum, hardly any of those we judged nominally Orthodox referred to themselves as "strictly Orthodox." Most called themselves "fairly Orthodox."

Perhaps most interesting of all is the fact that those we defined as the center of the modern Orthodox stream turned out to be divided in the way they viewed themselves. Some saw themselves to be more like their traditionalist counterparts, while others considered themselves tending the other way. The proportion who characterized themselves as "strictly Orthodox" (50%) is about halfway between that of the other two Orthodox groups. Moreover, these respondents are split virtually down the middle between the self-avowed "strictly" and "fairly" Orthodox.

Finally, as one might well expect, the vast majority of those who gave a non-Orthodox answer on denomination also characterized themselves as "not Orthodox" on the strictness-of-Orthodoxy question. Of those, however, who did not do so, almost all judged themselves "slightly Orthodox."

The close correspondence between the respondents' own evaluations and our ritual-based classification suggests something about the respondents and our classification. About the respondents, it says that all members of the Orthodox community—as well as those who stand close to but outside of it—know full well what is expected of the Orthodox Jew. To be sure, the point of reference for determining whether one is "strictly," "fairly," "slightly," or "not Orthodox" may shift from person to person or community to community, so that what is considered, for example, "strictly Orthodox" for one is only "fairly Orthodox" for another. There seems to be a reasonable degree of consensus, however, at least about ritual norms. (And, as we demonstrate in later chapters, that understanding of expectations extends to other domains as well.)

With regard to our classification, the correspondence with self-evaluations shows that we have captured in our index a reasonable representation of social reality. In other words, the respondents agree there are varying degrees of Orthodoxy. In essence, they agree in general terms with the ways in which we have divided them. Moreover, those divisions have consequences for many areas of religious and secular life, not the least important of which are other rituals from the index.

57

The Hierarchical Structure of Ritual Practice

Previous studies of American Jewish religious behavior have documented what cultural natives and insiders well understand: there is a hierarchical structure to ritual observance.[25] Very simply, not every ritual commandment is practiced with equal attention and regularity. Not only do the frequencies with which certain rituals are observed vary considerably, but particular observances are commonly linked to one another in predictable ways. Jews who observe the "hard" rituals (e.g., refusing to ride, spend money, or use electricity on the Sabbath) are almost guaranteed to perform the "easy" and most popular ones (e.g., lighting Hanukkah candles, going to a Passover seder, or fasting on Yom Kippur). Conversely, Jews who fail to perform the "easy" practices are highly unlikely to carry out the "hard" ones. Hardly anyone who eats ham sandwiches in contravention of Jewish dietary laws simultaneously observes laws prohibiting work-related activities on the Sabbath. As a result of these sorts of linkages we may speak of a hierarchy of ritual practice among American Jews, including the Orthodox.

TRADITIONALIST ORTHODOX JEWS

Accordingly, we would expect to find a similar structure to ritual practices among Orthodox Jews. Here, however, we are dealing with those observances most American Jews find "hard." Indeed, few of the non-Orthodox practice these rituals. In the hierarchy of practice we would expect that almost all traditionalists would observe all the ritual items found in our survey. Sometimes the logic is quite direct and obvious. Since traditionalists (by our definition) fast on one of the minor fast days, they should also fast on all the others; since they refrain from eating even a cold salad in a nonkosher home, there is no reason to believe that they would do so at a restaurant. But we would also expect the traditionalists' observance to extend beyond the domain of just those rituals that are conceptually proximate to those embodied in our operational definition of a traditional Orthodox Jew. We would expect their observance to extend to areas further afield such as dress, ritualized text study, synagogue attendance, Sabbath observance, and the so-called Laws of Family Purity which among other things require regular immersions of the menstruating wife in a *mikveh* (ritual bath).

In fact, table 2.3 demonstrates nearly universal compliance by traditionalists with all these areas of ritual practice. These Jews are, of nothing else, consistent in their relatively punctilious observance of *mitzvas*.

Among traditionalists, 95% or more of the men fast not only on the tenth of Tevet (the observance contained in our definition of a traditionalist) but *also* on the three other minor fast days: the seventeenth of Tammuz, the third of Tishrei (also called "Tsom Gedalia"), and the Fast of Esther. Similarly, among the women, nearly all observe the fast at least a part of the day, in line with long-established custom. Clearly, observing one of these minor fast days implies observance of all the others as well.

Again, much as expected, the traditionalists' compliance with the strictest interpretation of the dietary regulations is almost universal. All buy meat only from kosher butchers and report that they do not eat warm kosher foods in nonkosher restaurants, while almost all refrain from eating cold salads in nonkosher restaurants.

Their observance of the Sabbath is also nearly universal. Nearly everyone reports never doing housework or watching television on that day; all of the men and a substantial majority of the women claim that they usually attend Sabbath morning services. In fact, almost all the men report they usually attend all three Sabbath services (Friday evening, Saturday morning, and Saturday afternoon) in accordance with the formal demands of Jewish law.

Significantly, as we suggested and as any insider would anticipate, the punctilious observance of the traditionalists extends to areas far removed from those explicitly contained in our operational definition of Orthodox traditionalism. Virtually all of the traditionalists claim that the woman of the house uses the *mikveh* (ritual bath) and almost all the men study sacred texts weekly, and 90% usually do so on the Sabbath—in line with their respective *halakhic* obligations.

Table 2.3: Ritual Practices by Orthodoxy (%)

	Orthodoxy			
	Non-Orthodox	Nominal	Centrist	Traditional
Fasting (whole day/part day)				
Seventeenth of Tammuz:				
Men	0/4	5/18	60/26	99/1
Women	0/2	3/13	21/31	80/20
Tsom Gedalia:				
Men	0/3	5/15	53/21	95/3
Women	1/1	0/0	15/27	66/27
Fast of Esther:				
Men	2/5	8/22	63/21	97/3
Women	2/6	5/17	31/33	77/23
Yom Kippur (whole day only)				
Men	78	97	100	100
Women	84	91	98	100
Kashrut				
Buy only from kosher butchers	56	81	100	100
No warm foods in nonkosher restaurants	13	24	81	99
No cold salads in nonkosher restaurants	6	8	23	91
Sabbath				
Never do housework	30	70	93	96
Never watch television	8	34	92	99
Attend Sabbath morning services (usually/sometimes):				
Men	25/47	59/38	93/5	100/0
Women	18/53	51/37	70/24	75/23
Attend all three Sabbath services (usually/sometimes)				
Men	4/20	23/43	61/32	95/4
Women	4/7	18/25	10/34	9/37
Other Practices				
Woman regularly goes to *mikveh*	3	26	79	99
Studies texts weekly (usually/sometimes):				
Men	14/34	30/35	62/33	90/10
Women	6/32	23/49	35/45	30/68

Table 2.3: Ritual Practices by Orthodoxy (%) (*Cont.*)

	Orthodoxy		
	Non-Orthodox	Nominal	Centrist	Traditional
Sabbath				
Usually studies texts on Sabbath:				
Men	28	56	81	94
Women	17	60	56	67
Man keeps his head covered "on the street":	3	22	71	100
Man wears tzitzis (inside/ outside shirt)	2/0	19/0	73/2	85/15
Married woman covers head in public	0	5	34	91
Synagogue attendance				
Men:				
Daily	1	9	26	66
More than once a week	6	21	39	28
Once a week	15	28	26	4
Women:				
Once a week or more	15	28	57	48

Perhaps the most telling pieces of evidence of the traditionalists' commitment to Orthodoxy come from those practices that visibly distinguish the Orthodox Jews from their contemporaries. All of the traditionalist respondents report that in accord with religious custom the man of the house keeps his head covered (i.e., with a hat, or a skull cap [*yarmulke*]) and that he wears *tzitzis* (fringes, sometimes called *arba kanfos*), a fringed undergarment mandated in the Bible.[26] Only among the traditionalists do we find a sizable proportion (15%) of the men who in accord with a relatively recent religious custom wear their fringes outside their shirt where it may be made easily visible and

61

where it acts as a more public emblem of their contra-acculturation and fidelity to traditional Orthodoxy.)

Traditionalist women also are distinguished from their contemporaries in that, in line with a religious custom that traces itself back to biblical and Talmudic sources,[27] over nine out of ten report that the (married) woman of the house covers her hair in public (either with a kerchief ["*tikhl*"], wig ["*shaytl*"], or hat). It was only during the last century in Europe that the custom for married women to cover their hair became stylistically developed. In the present day, however, it is a firmly established practice among traditionalist Orthodox Jews—something our survey confirms.

In short, there are no rituals in our survey where the traditionalist Orthodox (who are, in essence, operationally differentiated from the other Orthodox in terms of just two practices: refusal to eat cold salads at the homes of non-kosher friends and fasting on the tenth of Tevet) depart from traditional norms.[28]

CENTRIST MODERN ORTHODOX

Compared with the traditionalists, the centrist modern Orthodox, while substantially complying with many if not most ritual norms, nevertheless display markedly lower rates of observance in certain areas. One difference between these two types of Orthodox Jews concerns the observance of the minor fast days. Rates of fasting among the centrists are about thirty to forty percentage points below those of the traditionalists. Moreover, as potentially private rituals—whether one is or is not fasting is not immediately apparent—the fast days are vulnerable to disattention and dissembling. That is, one can continue to identify himself as both Orthodox (i.e., a faster) and modern (i.e., a nonfaster) at once. (It is well noting that modernity generally shuns acts of self-abnegation such as fasting.)

Although individuals must choose whether to fast or not, the group as a whole can choose both—and does. About half fast on the minor fast days and half do not.

Similarly, the centrists are more likely to deviate from the traditionalists in their patterns of compliance with the dietary laws. Only about four out of five will not eat warm nominally kosher foods in nonkosher restaurants. The discrepancy with respect to cold salads is even greater. Less than a quarter of this group refrains from eating cold salads in nonkosher places of dining compared with 100% of the traditionalists. Clearly, the moderns are aware of the nuances of religious law and the distinctions drawn between hot and cold foods. Although they remain attached to the concept of keeping kosher (virtually all of them, e.g., keep two sets of dishes and buy meat only from a kosher butcher), they are more compromising in both regards than are the traditionalists, and they are significantly more accommodating to modern norms of eating anywhere and with anyone when they believe the law provides some latitude, some discretion for individual decision making.

A similar pattern can be discerned in the case of Sabbath prayer service attendance. The centrist modern Orthodox men attend the synagogue on Sabbath mornings almost as often as the traditionalists (93% vs. 100%). However, they are substantially less likely to attend all three services (61% vs. 95%). Here, as with fasting and observance of the restrictive dietary laws, the more demanding the practice, the greater the discrepancy between the traditionalists and moderns.

Centrist Orthodox women attend Sabbath services as often as traditionalist ones. At first glance, this seems curious. In other respects, these more modern women tend to exhibit lower rates of ritual observance than their traditionalist counterparts. They are, for example, much less likely to fast a whole day on the seventeenth of Tammuz (21% vs. 80%) and less likely to use the *mikveh* (79% vs. 99%). Insofar as rituals are concerned, thus, we might therefore expect lower service attendance rates among these modern Orthodox women. In America, however, the Sabbath morning service has become the *sine qua non* of communal bonding, the most public occasion of displaying one's identity as a member of the Orthodox community. And thus while these women may lag behind their traditionalist counterparts in their ritual fervency and involvement, they are nevertheless less likely to accept the traditionalist norm which de-emphasizes female obligation (and reaffirms female frailty) to participate in such communal activities as Sabbath morning prayer. As if to display their conviction that they can participate equally with the men, they come to the synagogue on Sabbath. To be sure, centrist women may not come for precisely the same reasons as their traditionalist sisters (although we have no way of knowing this from our data), but they *do* come.

These centrist modern Orthodox differ from the traditionalists in numerous other ways. The men are significantly less likely (by about twenty-five to thirty percentage points) to study Jewish sacred texts on the Sabbath, to keep their heads covered on the street, or to wear fringes. As noted, the women are less likely to use the *mikveh*. Consistent with earlier findings in connection with "hard" observances and those that separate them from the non-Orthodox world, only about a third as many of these centrist Orthodox wives are willing to keep their hair covered in public as their traditionalist Orthodox counterparts do (34% vs. 91%).

And yet, when they compare themselves with the nominally Orthodox and all those to the less or nonobservant extreme, many of the centrists see themselves as being "strictly Orthodox"—and so identify themselves. Nevertheless, looking to the more observant traditionalists they assume, in the words of one: "We probably don't come up to specs."[29]

NOMINALLY ORTHODOX

Just as centrist modern Orthodox are substantially less observant than the traditionalists, so similarly nominally Orthodox Jews are less ritually active than the centrists. Aside from fasting on Yom Kippur, there are no rituals where rates of observance among the nominally Orthodox even approach those among the centrists. For example, about fifty percentage points separate the two groups' rates of fasting on minor fast days; hardly any nominally Orthodox fast an entire day on those occasions. Only about a fifth of the nominally Orthodox men keep their heads covered in the street (i.e., in public) or wear *tzitzis*, whereas two-thirds to three-fourths of the centrists do.

Hardly any nominally Orthodox refrain from eating cold salads in nonkosher restaurants; and only a quarter, as opposed to the vast majority of the centrists, refrain from eating warm kosher foods in such places. Although a large majority of the nominally Orthodox do not do housework on the Sabbath, and a plurality of the men and women usually attend Sabbath morning services, these figures are substantially lower than those found among the centrists.

Even greater variations in Sabbath observance can be found between the two groups. Thus, the use of television on the Sabbath points up a crucial distinction. Whereas almost all the centrist respondents report never watching television on the Sabbath, only a third of the nominals made such a claim. Apparently, those who identify with Orthodoxy but reside on its marginal wing have adopted an approach to the Sabbath in which it remains a special day but not necessarily in traditional terms. Even as they faithfully attend synagogue services on Sabbath morning (perhaps for many of the same reasons of communal bonding that their more observant counterparts do), they watch television before and afterward. That is, Sabbath may be viewed by these Jews as a family day set aside for rest, relaxation, some synagogue attendance, and the contact with other Jews that it brings about and affirms, and leisure as symbolized perhaps by the use of television.

While the nominally Orthodox perform ritual practices less often than other Orthodox groups, the religious behavior of the nominal women is especially noteworthy. Among the centrists and traditionalists, women fast, study Jewish texts, and attend synagogue services much less often than comparable men. These patterns are in keeping with traditional sex-linked differences in normative expectations. As noted earlier, the discrepancy between the sexes is smaller among the centrist modern Orthodox than among the traditionalists; but among the nominals these sex-linked differences in ritual practice disappear almost entirely. Nominally Orthodox women fast on minor fast days, study sacred texts, and attend Sabbath services almost as often (or as seldom) as their male counterparts. At the same time, nominally Orthodox women are much less likely to use the *mikveh* (only about a quarter do) than the centrists (more than three-quarters do) or traditionalists (virtually all do). Thus, relative to their more observant peers, the nominally Orthodox women have substantially departed from traditional norms in an area such as the use of the *mikveh* where there are special obligations for the Jewish woman, but they have maintained a relatively higher level of observance in areas that are traditionally male obligations (i.e., fasting, studying, and public [synagogue] prayer). Clearly, as we move to the religious left, not only does secularism increase but so too does sexual egalitarianism, as evidenced in the similar levels of Jewish practice among the nominal men and women.

Though more observant than the mainstream of American Jewry and therefore willing and able to call themselves "Orthodox," these people, when measured against other Orthodox Jews, are—as the data here and in the rest of our report affirms—Orthodox in name but not as clearly so in other respects. Or, to put the matter more simply, the nominally Orthodox diverge most dramatically from normative Orthodox practice in the relative laxity of their observance.

THE *NON-ORTHODOX*

The non-Orthodox in our sample, although considerably more observant than most American Jews, still perform rituals substantially less often than do all the Orthodox Jews. Hardly any of the non-Orthodox fast on the minor fast days. None of their married women covers her hair in public, and almost none of their men keeps his head covered on the street or wears fringes. Nearly all will eat salads or heated kosher foods in nonkosher restaurants. Few regularly study sacred texts, and few refrain from watching television on the Sabbath. Indeed, on that day only small fractions refrain from housework. Finally, few attend Sabbath morning services with regularity—25% for the men and 18% for the women.

The only area where we find substantial compliance with traditional law and custom among these non-Orthodox are those where substantial numbers of American Jews generally are observant: Yom Kippur fasting, and the practice of buying meat only from a kosher butcher. By way of comparison, in the New York area, for example, two-thirds of adult Jews reported fasting on Yom Kippur, and over a third of all Jewish households claimed to buy meat only from a kosher butcher.[30]

But the high frequency with which the non-Orthodox in our sample observed these rituals does not negate the low rates at which they performed the other practices relative to the Orthodox groups. This finding demonstrates the existence of a distinctive set of ritual practices which serve to set apart all varieties of Orthodox from the remainder of American Jews.

Sociology versus *Halacha:* Explaining Variation in Ritual Observance

While the foregoing discussion has focused on different patterns of practice among Orthodox Jews of varying degrees of ritual observance, we have yet to concentrate on a correlative issue: the rituals themselves, and why some are more readily observed than others. The centrist modern Orthodox, an intermediate group floating in the cross-currents of the universal and the particular, the two worlds they inhabit, offers an ideal locus in which to study ritual observance variation. They obviously exercise discretion in choosing which ritual commandments they follow and which they choose to ignore. When they ignore certain religious obligations, most undoubtedly do so while being generally aware of the ritual requirements incumbent upon the traditional Jew. In addition, most centrists are "natives," thoroughly socialized into Orthodox culture and society and thus know what is expected of them. Many, in fact, have friends or family from the more traditionalist wing to their ideological right and have need on occasion to conform their behavior according to its more stringent demands. In light of these conditions, then, why do many—if not most—centrist modern Orthodox Jews choose to puruse a course of what seems, at the very least, to be the violation of selected religious prescriptions?

We may ask this question in its obverse as well. Since many of the centrists are also intimately connected through ties of family and friendship with the more marginal, nominally Orthodox Jews who hold out an implicit model of religious life which incorporates laxity in and disattention to certain ritual practices, why do the centrists shun that model and instead continue to be more punctilious in their observances of certain rituals? In short, we ask, why and how does the center exist?

This question is very much like the one raised repeatedly by sociologists and historians who have studied the effects of modernization upon tradition, wondering if and how the two could coexist, and trying to describe the point of their intersection. More specifically, it is also the question at the heart of the experience of postemancipation Jews, many of whom sought to balance the demands of citizen status in the host culture with commitments still felt toward the parochial obligations of Judaism.

Nevertheless, even though they sought to enter civil society with their Jewish identities intact, they often found it necessary to modify their religious behavior with an eye to social acceptance. Practices that severely inhibited integration—or at least appeared to do so—were those that modernizing Jews most readily abandoned. The dietary restrictions, for example, stood as a barrier to socializing between Jews and other citizens; prohibitions on Sabbath work came to have severe economic consequences for Jewish workers and their employers; and the intensive study of Talmud—a uniquely Jewish sacred text—only served to underscore and therefore in the eyes of some perpetuate Jewish distinctiveness and foment anti-Jewish prejudice. These were practices whose observance declined.

Explaining the decline of Jewish religious practices in America, the social historian Ben Halpern has articulated this point when he explains that "anything which is closed off and private—any collective intimacy shared only by those of the same . . . origin and not basically accessible to others . . . is certainly permissible in the . . . ghetto, but it signifies an unwillingness to be integrated into the real America."[31]

On the other hand, reinterpretation, "the process by which old meanings are ascribed to new elements or by which new values change the cultural significance of old forms," became the order of the day for those Jews who sought, in the words of Rabbi Abraham Isaac Kook, "to make the old new and the new holy."[32] They held onto those practices which could be reinterpreted to ostensibly comport with or which could be understood and accepted by the host culture. Those they could not reinterpret or explain, they sometimes changed, or at the very least kept from public view. "Be a man in the street and a Jew in your home," the Jewish poet and essayist Y. L Gordon had argued.

Sociologists Marshall Sklare and Joseph Greenblum succinctly spelled out five conditions which lead to the retention of certain Jewish rituals:

> The highest degree of retention will occur when a ritual: (1) is capable of effective redefinition in modern terms, (2) does not demand social isolation or the adoption of a unique life style, (3) accords with the religious culture of the larger community and provides a "Jewish" alternative when such is felt to be needed, (4) is centered on the child, and (5) is performed annually or infrequently.[33]

In some ways, centrist modern Orthodox Jews repeat this pattern of using social acceptance criteria similar to those once used by Jews first emerging from the ghetto. Trying to remain neither remote from nor untouched by the host American culture, they—more than most non-Orthodox Jews who also try to be both Jewish and American—reinterpret, compartmentalize, and sometimes modify their Jewish existence in the light of contemporary patterns of culture even as they place great emphasis on their ties to Orthodox beliefs and practices. In the street, as it were, they pass as normal Americans, cosmopolitans. In their homes, the parochial Orthodox Jewish community, they remain traditional Jews. Each setting—the American cultural street and the Jewish community home—requires some display of belonging. And as they have done all this, these Orthodox Jews have at least tacitly broadened the limits of what is acceptable and expectable Orthodox Jewish behavior.[34]

Our investigation leads us to suggest that frequencies of ritual observance among the Orthodox in general and among the centrists in particular reflect three sorts of influences: (1) religious meaning, that is, the import of the rituals within the traditional culture and heritage; (2) communal control, that is, the ability of the parochial Orthodox community to enforce and reinforce the performance of certain practices; and (3) social influence, that is, concern about social acceptance in the larger (host) society and culture. Insofar as some practices are more observed than others, they may well be so because of variations in their religious, communal (i.e., the *Orthodox* community), and social (i.e., American society) implications. To put matters most simply, we argue that the chances that a given ritual will be observed increase if the ritual is religiously meaningful; if it is subject to the sanction of the Orthodox community; and if it does not serve to segregate one psychologically, culturally, or socially from other Americans. Certainly, all this is the case only among those Orthodox Jews who choose to align themselves to some extent with American culture and society. To discover how, in fact, ritual performance varies within modern Orthodoxy, read down the centrist column of table 2.3. As noted earlier, relative to the nominally Orthodox, the centrists have largely retained a number of practices; and relative to the traditionalists they have in effect largely abandoned or refrained from taking up some others. Among those practices in which the difference between centrists and traditionalists is greatest and which the former are least likely to perform in contrast to the latter, we find: refusing to eat cold salads in a nonkosher restaurant, daily attendance at the synagogue by men, and covering the hair by married women in keeping with traditional Jewish customs of modesty.

Failure to keep these practices may be explained in terms of the previous discussion. All symbolize or induce social segregation. Moreover, all are religiously ambiguous: they derive from what may be perceived as a discretionary portion of religious law and custom. A cautious reinterpretation of the law does not quite forbid eating cold salads with nonkosher utensils and dishes in a nonkosher eating establishment. Nevertheless, traditionalist, insular Orthodox Jews find eating even technically kosher foods in a non-kosher milieu troubling in several respects. Their very presence in such a place might easily and erroneously convey a message to the unsuspecting Jewish observer that the Orthodox approve of eating not just permissible salads but all foods in this particular place. Second, their presence in such a place may imply a sanction of being in such a non-Orthodox setting. Thus, while eating cold salads in a non-kosher restaurant may not technically be a transgression of the letter of the law of keeping kosher, it is for the traditionalist a transgression of its spirit.

Most centrists (and—as we shall see—nominals) who move readily into non-Orthodox precincts prefer not to forego this open passage to the world outside the parochial one. They wish to be able to, among other things, dine with those who do not keep the Jewish dietary regulations—not *because* they transgress these laws but *in spite* of it. They therefore prefer in this case to adhere to the letter of the law while eschewing its social consequences.

Similar considerations apply to daily attendance in the synagogue. This constant reminder of sectarian and ghettoized existence is perhaps difficult to bear by those who look to make their ways into the outside world. So if they pray daily, centrists do so at home and in a hurry, on their way out.[35]

As for the covering of heads by married women, the religiously based requirements for this practice are reinterpreted by the centrists (to say nothing of the nominals) as being ambiguous at best and more likely discretionary. Like refusing to eat in nonkosher places, or going to the synagogue daily, the wearing of such coverings is seen as serving to sharply differentiate and ultimately segregate the Orthodox from all others. Consequently, few of the centrist married women and only a tiny fraction of the nominally Orthodox keep their heads covered, allowing for what they believe is easier entry into American society. (Those centrist women who do wear head covers often wear stylishly coiffured wigs which are unrecognizable as wigs to the untrained eye. This is a far cry from the obvious peruke worn by Orthodox women with more insular pro-

clivities. And even traditionalist women who choose on occasion to pass into the outside world—e.g., for economic
reasons—often trade their kerchief head coverings which
mark them as obvious outsiders for wigs that look like no
head cover at all.)[36]

Committed to a life partially set apart by virtue of their
espousal of Orthodoxy and certain mandatory practices
which accompany it, the centrists—like other modernists—seek whenever possible to mitigate their segregation. Where discretion seems possible, where the Jewish
law appears to allow for latitude in the direction of assimilation into the host culture and contemporary life patterns,
Orthodox Jews tending toward modernity move as much
as possible into the world outside the strictly Orthodox
one. Or put baldly and simply, where *halacha* has apparently failed to stake out a position, modernity rushes in to
make its claims.

The data on synagogue attendance and on observing minor fast days reflect how centrists inhibit being embraced
by the intensely parochial Jewish life—inhibitions that
nonetheless fall considerably short of what most other
American Jews choose. For example, they all display the
use of fall-back options rather than total avoidance of the
practices some of them choose to avoid. As already noted,
virtually all traditionalist men "usually" attend all three
Sabbath services. Centrists, however, are much less likely
to "usually" appear at all three; only a slim majority do so.
But practically all the rest—about a third—do so "sometimes." There are none who say they "never" go, as there
are among the nominals and the non-Orthodox.

A comparable pattern appears with regard to behavior
on minor fast days. Almost all of the traditionalist men fast
a whole day on the minor fast days; and very few fast only
a *part* day on these occasions. Among the centrists, however, whole-day fasting is much less frequent, though still
a majority do so. Here part-day fasting is much more common, typifying about a quarter of the centrists.

In both of these cases—synagogue attendance and fasting on the minor fast days—relative to the traditionalists
from a fifth to a third of the centrists have simply adopted
a lower frequency or shorter duration with which they at-

tend to certain Jewish practices. That they claim to under-
take these activities "sometimes" or "part of the day" demonstrates that almost all remain at least aware of their
religious commitments. But it also demonstrates that there
are other factors in their lives that curtail their involvement
and perhaps their commitment.

There are communal controls at work here, too. The
norms of Orthodox culture, particularly among the centrists, demand male attendance at the main Sabbath service on Saturday morning; this is a kind of "touching base
with the community." But the communal expectations of
attendance are effectively relaxed with respect to Friday
evening or Saturday afternoon services. Here, as long as a
significant quorum is present (one usually smaller than the
turnout on Sabbath mornings), the community seems satisfied.[37] Similarly, as noted earlier, fasting can be a private
act with relatively little opportunity for public display. One
who does not fast or who fasts only part of a day does not
publicly challenge the tenets of Orthodox Jewish practice.

All this changes when fasting becomes a part of behavior
in public. Under these conditions, people are more likely
to fast than if their behavior were to pass unnoticed by others in the community. Indeed, of the minor fasts, the Fast
of Esther alone is tied in with such public behavior, followed as it is by a communal assembly in the synagogue
which large numbers of people commonly attend: the
Purim celebration and the recitation of the Scroll of Esther
which immediately follow it. At this gathering, those who
have fasted a full day may conceivably publicize their fasting either in conversation or by other signals (notably, an
emphasis on weakness such as sitting at points in the service when standing is normal, or by facial expressions emphasizing their pallor). We are thus not surprised to find
that of all the minor fasts, the Fast of Esther is one on
which the greatest majority of centrist men fast. Yet, even
here, the fast itself, carried on silently while the centrists
are off carrying on their modern lives, is among a significant minority only a partial involvement.

The interplay of traditional religion, concern with acceptance by the larger society, and communal norms is well
illustrated in a group of observances where the centrists

deviate even less substantially from the standards maintained by the traditionalists. Roughly three-quarters of the
centrists keep their heads covered in public; the same proportion wear *tzitzis* (albeit always under their shirts and
out of public view), and about the same number of centrist
wives regularly immerse themselves in a *mikveh* in accord
with the demands of Jewish law. Recall that practice of
these activities is universal among the traditionalists.

What is interesting about these centrist proportions is
that they both exceed those of other ritual practices discussed, and yet they are less than those of the traditionalists. In each case, we should wonder why the practice of
this ritual has remained as high as it has but still remains
lower than the traditionalist rate.

Consider the covering of the head first. Heads may be
covered in a variety of ways, the most common of which
for Orthodox Jews are hats and skull caps (*yarmulkes*). The
former, in principle, could be worn without distinguishing
its wearer as anyone special. In fact, hats do mark the Orthodox Jew, especially in American society where people
by and large do not wear hats. *Yarmulkes* serve to unmistak-
ably distinguish the Orthodox male from the non-
Orthodox.[38] Since wearing one is akin to making a public
statement about one's attachment to the Orthodox community, failing to wear one may be symbolically understood as an opposite assertion. The principal inhibition to
wearing a *yarmulke* publicly, then, is that it creates a subtle
but overt barrier between the Orthodox and others, both
non-Orthodox and Gentile (precisely what its champions
desire). The male who wears one expresses solidarity with
his fellow Orthodox while marking himself as something
of an American outsider. Hence, there is at once a social
cost and a communal reward in wearing a *yarmulke*.

The modernists among the Orthodox increasingly prefer
the *yarmulke* to the hat. It is as if the *yarmulke*—especially if
it is one of the small knitted type modernists favor rather
than the large, old-fashioned black velvet or gabardine—is
not as stigmatizing as a hat in hatless America. As Jews
have generally come to feel more at ease in expressing their
distinctiveness in a contemporary America whose growing
ethnic consciousness has led to a tolerance for symbolic

expressions of such ethnicity, they have begun to wear *yarmulkes* more in public. That is, as social cost has decreased, the rate of *yarmulke* wearing has increased. Younger centrist Orthodox are more apt to keep their heads covered in public than their older counterparts.[39] But the meaning of that covering may not be the same as that which it had for earlier generations. The older man whose head is bare may in many ways be more traditionalist in his outlook and behavior than is his son who wears a little knitted *yarmulke* atop his contemporary haircut and, along with faded blue jeans and a tee shirt, may be sporting an obscene message. Today, however, that little head cover worn by the young has become the cultural *sine qua non* among the Orthodox for all but the nominals.

The wearing of fringes by men and attendance at the *mikveh* by wives are both relatively well-shielded from public view. As a result, they have few consequences for social integration. At the same time, they are viewed as religiously essential. The command to wear fringes is one of which no Orthodox Jew can claim to be unaware. Several times a day men probably recite the prayer in which the scriptural injunction to wear such fringes is repeated: "The Lord spoke to Moses, saying: Speak to the children of Israel and tell them to make for themselves fringes on the corners of their garments throughout their generations. . . . You shall have it as a fringe, so that when you look upon it you will remember to do all the commands of the Lord, and you will not follow the desires of your heart and your eyes which lead you astray."[40]

Clearly, the symbolic and religious significance of *tzitzis* stands at the intersection of belief and ritual practice. It is meant to restrain unbridled desires and remind a Jew of his obligations and presumably the connection they engender. Accordingly, wearing fringes has become a kind of symbolic medallion of membership in the Orthodox fraternity. And indeed, wearing them so that they are visible has been a way of flaunting one's capacity for turning away from the attractions of the outside world. Keeping them under one's shirt is a way of muffling that restraint without forgetting or denying it altogether.

Going to the *mikveh* also is a practice high in religious

75

and symbolic significance for Orthodox Jews. Jewish law has a great deal to say about the sexual conduct of married couples. The Babylonian Talmud devotes the full tractate of *Niddah* to it, and there are as well lengthy passages dealing with the subject in other volumes.[41]

The woman goes to the *mikveh* at night, unobtrusively, according to Jewish law. No one but the wife and her husband need know; the functionaries at the bath are expected to be discreet. The outside world need never know that she observes this ritual, and commonly it does not. To be sure, the user of the *mikveh* may interpret the meaning of her practice in any way she chooses: in traditional religious terms as a divine commandment, in symbolic terms as a dramatic reenactment of her own bodily rebirth, in psychological terms as a way of renewing her husband's and her own sexual appetites, and so on.[42] But the act itself is viewed as doctrinally essential while entailing little social cost. It is therefore performed by most centrists.

The matter of Jewish study, the ritual review of sacred texts, also may be looked at in order to see the extent to which American social factors have made inroads on religious and communal ones. The importance of such ritual study for Judaism cannot be overestimated. "Although Judaism has for generations derived its identity and justification from books—the book or scroll, more than the picture or statue, became the preferred emblem of the diaspora Jew—the influences of the outside world, the exigencies of physical survival, and the imperatives of involvement in modern civil society have over the years turned Jews away from the traditional house of study. *Lernen*, a spiritual meditation on and lifelong review of Jewish books, became exchanged for learning, an intellectual acquisition of knowledge, and for earning, economic and material survival."[43] For Jews engaging in ritual study, the precise sacred texts are not as important as the act of studying. Yet, while most Jews do not *lern*, many Orthodox Jews reinforce their active and symbolic ties to sacred texts (and to one another) by engaging in a regular review of them.

Generally, as with other ritual activities, the stronger one's traditionalist tendencies, the more often he becomes engaged in *lernen*. While the obligation to study is a constant one—"You shall meditate upon it day and night," scripture commands (Joshua 1:3)—the press of everyday life has in many cases led many Orthodox Jews to set aside the Sabbath for this and other specifically Jewish activities. In the choice between reading the newspaper and the Talmud, the former all too often gets picked while the latter remains on the shelf.

As expected, almost all the traditionalist men claimed to engage in some study of Jewish texts. Conversely, only about a quarter of the non-Orthodox men made such a claim. (Since our non-Orthodox were a relatively conservative lot, this figure is probably far higher than the general Jewish average.) Among the nominally Orthodox men, slightly more than half made claims about the constancy of their Sabbath study, while the centrist men had an enormous majority (but still fewer than the traditionalists), asserting that they regularly study Jewish texts on the Sabbath.

Among a majority of all types of Orthodox men, Jewish study—at least on the Sabbath—is apparently expected behavior. At the same time, however, there is a clear drop in such involvement as one moves away from the traditionalists. Indeed, one might argue that increasing marginality from traditional Jewish concerns and involvement, or, expressed another way, the attraction of the non-Jewish world, diminishes involvement in ritual study. Among the Orthodox there are still powerful bonds to the ways of tradition and (as we shall show in a later chapter) communal ties to other Orthodox Jews, and hence a majority engage in some Jewish study.[44]

Childbearing Variations among the Orthodox

Before concluding this chapter on *mitzvas*, we would do well to examine the performance of one final act which in some contemporary eyes falls outside the purview of religious activity strictly defined but one that—as many Catholics and fundamentalist Protestant groups have amply demonstrated—is quite closely connected with religious commitment. We speak, of course, of fertility patterns.

Table 2.4: Childbearing Variables by Orthodoxy (%)

| | Orthodoxy | | | |
	Non-Orthodox	Nominal	Centrist	Traditional
Number of children:				
Married, 35+ years old	2.0	2.1	2.9	4.2
Married, 18–35 years old	1.1	0.7	1.5	2.1
Wrong to limit number of children	9	14	27	60

The biblical injunction in Genesis (1:28) to "be fruitful and multiply" is a norm central to the Orthodox community. But not only is there a distinctive religious/symbolic significance attached to bearing and rearing children, there are other aspects of cultural significance as well. Like other groups, Jews have had a past of high fertility. Their adaptation to the modern world meant that they, like other Western groups, would diminish their fertility and adopt the lower fertility ideals of middle-class society. For Orthodox Jews, however—as for similar religious groups—involvement in the religious community meant attachment to a pronatalist, high fertility heritage.[45]

Accordingly, we would expect Orthodox traditionalism to be associated with childbearing. In table 2.4 we present data relating to the number of children born to those married respondents over and under thirty-five years of age. We also present there the responses given to the question whether or not it is wrong for a couple to voluntarily limit the number of children they will have. It is not surprisingly that we find that within age categories the traditionalists have had more children than the centrists, who in turn exceed the nominally Orthodox. Among those over thirty-five, when childbearing may be assumed to have been largely though not totally completed, the nominally Orthodox birthrates only slightly exceed those of our sample of non-Orthodox.

Among the older group, reading from right (traditionalists) to left (non-Orthodox), we find the mean number of children declining as follows: 4.2, 2.9, 2.1, 2.0. The younger adults (under thirty-five) exhibit a similar pattern: 2.1, 1.5, 0.7, 1.1. Evidently, the more traditionalist Orthodox not only have more children throughout their lives but they have them earlier. Since we know from considerable previous research that Jews are highly efficient at avoiding unwanted pregnancies (they are adept at contraception), we can infer that the different Orthodox groups are having different numbers of children precisely because they so choose.[46]

More evidence to this effect can be gleaned from the results pertaining to the question of the advisability of voluntarily limiting the number of one's children. There are small increases in the proportions opposing this view as we move from the non-Orthodox (9%), to the nominal Orthodox (14%), and to the centrists (27%). When we reach the traditionalists, the figures jump dramatically to upward of 60% who believe that it is wrong to limit childbirths. Clearly, traditionalist Jews at least in theory are the most pronatalist among the Orthodox.

The traditionalists' actual birthrate, however, although highest of all Jews, constitutes clear evidence that they do practice some form of birth control. A mean of 4.5 number of children may be found among those traditionalists over thirty-five who claim to oppose limits on childbearing (data not shown on table). But "natural fertility" rates, where there is no contraception, are far higher.[47] Obviously, even the Orthodox traditionalists in our sample have adapted to the contemporary norm by practicing some form of contraception despite their stated support of high fertility ideals.[48]

A general conclusion to be drawn from these results is that even those who in other respects qualify as traditional Orthodox have adjusted their behavior—such as in the case of childbearing—to the modern world more readily than they have changed their attitudes, at least toward contraception. At the very least, lip service to ideals seems in this case to outlive their practice.

Conclusion

The essential lesson to be derived from this discussion of ritual variation within modern Orthodoxy is that religious/

symbolic issues, communal ties, and social factors all play important roles in determining ritual performance. Or to put the matter more simply, even with regard to *mitzva* observance one must look beyond Judaism to comprehend what is going on in the lives of Orthodox Jews.

Such an examination reveals that contemporary Orthodox Jews are not, as some—perhaps looking at them from the distance of mainstream American life—have claimed, a world apart but are rather similar in varying degrees to other American Jews in their desire to be both Jewish and American, both parochial and cosmopolitan, particular and universal. They are all, in one way or another, in the situation of modernity. Moreover, as one moves away from the traditionalist stream, one discovers that practices that inhibit this process of modernization and Americanization but are of perceived low religious/symbolic importance are disattended, and even the so-called important *mitzvas* show some effects of Orthodox cultural dualism.

The Orthodox (most of whom are *not* traditionalists) certainly do not ignore altogether the demands of religion and Jewish observance. There is no doubt that they *are* different in important respects from other kinds of Jews and from non-Jews in America. Yet, as we have seen, to understand their *mitzva* behavior, we need the perspectives of sociology, for what they do or do not do is not explained only by their religious sensibilities and proclivities. Being part of a community in which ritual observance is a matter of public concern, they find religious motivations underpinned by communal obligations. They perform or fail to perform certain ritual acts not only out of religious sensibility but also out of communal responsibility and in answer to social expectations. Thus it is a community—albeit one with several streams—that is being studied here and not simply a religious option.

Seeing that ritual practice is affected by factors other than religion—even among the Orthodox—naturally makes us wonder whether matters of belief are also subject to social and cultural factors. Just as the ritual and other behavior of centrist Orthodox Jews, the largest stream of our sample, stand somewhere between those of their traditionalist and nominally Orthodox counterparts, so too we would expect to find similar patterns in other areas as well. And just as the study of ritual practice—*mitzvas*—pointed to tensions of modern Orthodoxy, so too will an exploration of beliefs elucidate the ways in which the Orthodox in general are like or different from other American Jews. It is, therefore, to belief—*emunah*—we now turn.

The Religious Faith and Fervency of Orthodox Jews

There is almost no such thing as a perfectly orthodox believer.

Jean-Marie Guyau,
The Non-Religion of the Future

As the previous chapter demonstrated, Jews
who identify themselves as Orthodox by no means share a
single set of ritual practices or codes of behavior but rather
can be divided into at least three groups: those who are
strictest in their observance—people we call "traditionalists," those who are Orthodox mostly in name and who are
rather lax in practice—people we call "nominally Orthodox," and those (by far the largest number of Orthodox
Jews in our sample) who fall between these two extremes—those we call "centrists."

In light of the variations in practice, one should not be
surprised to discover that the same sort of variation exists
among the Orthodox with regard to belief. Simply put, not
all Orthodox Jews share the same degree of faith (what in
Hebrew is sometimes called *emunah*) in certain fundamental creeds and central teachings of traditional Judaism.

Some might find it hard to believe that so-called Orthodox Jews could be anything less than absolutely certain of
their belief in God, the immutability of His Torah, the coming of the Messiah, and other essentials of Jewish faith.
After all, belief in these and other principles like them is
daily reiterated by many Orthodox Jews in their daily prayers. Moreover, the life of observant Orthodox Jews, as has
already been suggested in the previous chapter, demands
significant attention to a wide variety of practices—some
of which entail considerable costs of time, energy, and
money, while also setting one apart from the larger culture
or at least precluding social intimacy with non-Jews and
even the vast majority of non-Orthodox Jews. One might
therefore reasonably expect that such practices should be

supported by some equally strong commitments in matters of faith.

That, however, is just the point. Just as there is variation in practice—even among those who call themselves Orthodox—so we discover there are variations in matters of faith. And these variations, we will show, coincide quite closely with those in practice. Simply stated, just as we found there was room under the cover of Orthodoxy for some differences in adherence to *mitzvahs*, so we shall find the same sort of differences in attachment to principles of *emunah*.

As we have already stated, traditional Judaism emphasizes practice over theology. In the course of a lengthy interview about his Orthodoxy, one man reacted to a question about matters of faith by pointing out that when he explained to his children why he and their mother never emphasized belief in their Orthodox upbringing, he said: "We never taught you that you were supposed to believe this or that. We taught you what to do." When asked about the role of belief in her Orthodox upbringing, yet another women explained: "It never occurred to me to ask myself whether I believed in what I was doing. . . . We don't talk about belief; we live." Finally, talking about prayer in his life, one Orthodox Jew confessed: "You know, for a whole year I couldn't *daven* [pray] with *kavannah* [devotion]," meaning that while he carried on the ritual practice of prayer, he did so without the devotional belief that is strictly speaking supposed to accompany it. Indeed, unlike the word *mitzva* which is both meaningful and commonly employed by Orthodox Jews to refer to their ritual activities, the term *emunah*, while comprehensible to most Orthodox, is not commonly heard or used—so much does faith remain an unspoken and implicit matter of Orthodox Jewish life.

How it is possible for people to disattend belief is a question that we cannot hope to answer within the framework of this paper. Suffice it to say here that the evidence suggests that it is possible. Moreover, Orthodox Jews do not appear to be the only ones who act without immediately referring their behavior to belief. Indeed, as Professor Martin Marty has reported, ". . . the same sociological surveys that find the majority of Americans professing belief in God and affiliating with church and synagogue find only a minority expressing any interest in theology or concurring with their church's major ethical positions."[1]

That Jews (or anyone) could act one way and believe another (or not believe at all) is at least partially explained by the fact that, to affect the daily lives of people, the import of a religious message or belief must be capable of being routinized. This process of concretization in which the religious belief is finitized and translated into a series of rituals (either verbal or gestural or both) may ultimately lead to a separation of the belief from the act which was once meant to point to it. Moreover, because matters of belief are interior dispositions that remain relatively hidden from view while practices are often part of public behavior, they can more easily be dropped without incurring a change in one's position in the society of the religious. Belief, once routinized and made concrete in the form of ritual practice, may devolve into formalism. While genuine faith supporting actions is often assumed, there is no way that it can be easily assured. Indeed, in the mind of the religious believer, it is precisely God—and not man—who can know the mediations of one's heart and character of one's devotion. Accordingly, where matters of faith are concerned, religion and its defenders must unceasingly defer to God (or human conscience) for enforcement.

Thus, while all religions aim to control belief above all else, they often settle for a display of belief through the carrying out of ritual, the latter being far easier to observe and enforce as well as to fulfill.[2] In effect, this means that at any particular moment or for any period, practicing Orthodox Jews can entertain serious doubts about one or another fundamental Jewish belief, ignore it, or remain altogether oblivious of it while carrying out traditional practices. Thus, for example, three Jews may wear *tzitzis* (ritual fringes) but only one does so primarily because he believes that it is a God-given command, while another does so (out of his shirt) because he wants to identify himself as an Orthodox Jewish male, and a third may do so out of custom or habit. And for most, such practices probably

85

reflect some amalgam of beliefs, social considerations, and habituation.

Often, as sociologist Allie Dubb has pointed out, ". . . religious practices are modes of Jewish identification rather than expressions of religious feeling" or faith.[3] Hence, we should not be surprised if some Americans (including American Orthodox Jews) carry out ritual practices in order to indicate something about who they are rather than because of certain theological positions. They may act in a relatively observant manner—to demonstrate, perhaps, their alignment with a particular community (a point we shall elaborate in a later chapter)—without at the same time feeling attached to particular supporting creedal beliefs which would seem to be associated with these practices. Some analysts have defined such Judaism as "Ortho-*prax*" (with the emphasis on practice) as distinct from Ortho*dox* (with the emphasis on doctrine or belief).

While Jews calling themselves Orthodox may thus certainly deviate from normative religious belief, we nevertheless anticipate that the more ritually observant would deviate less. In other words, for quite obvious reasons, those who more carefully observe more traditional practices should, all things being equal, more readily report fervent acceptance of and support for various expressions of fundamental religious doctrine (even if in the course of their everyday religious lives they do not often refer to matters of faith).

Not only do we expect to uncover consistent variations in belief patterns among the three groups of Orthodox Jews and a non-Orthodox control group which we inserted into our sample for comparative purposes, we also expect to find that different expressions of traditional beliefs will occur with different frequency among diverse groups. In other words, while we expect different groups of Orthodox Jews to have varying beliefs, we also would expect that, even where these different groups share a common belief, there are variations in the degree of fervency to which they share that belief. While it is difficult to measure the fervency of a belief in an individual—that is, by and large, an internal matter—unanimity of a belief in a group can be defined as maximum fervency, while varying degrees of divergence of support for an article of faith might be called something less than absolute fervency. For example, if only a third of the members of a particular group hold a belief which *all* the members of a second group hold, we can safely say that the first group less fervently believes in that article of faith than the second. Moreover, if half of a given group believes one thing and the other half believes its opposite, we may say that *the group* is perfectly ambivalent or torn on this matter (although this does not presume that any given individual feels so divided). Finally, since our questions generally offered a range of alternative responses (strongly agree, agree, undecided, disagree, and strongly disagree), we can find instances where respondents groups differ in their tendency to provide the most extreme and unqualified or more moderate and qualified responses, providing another indication of fervency of belief.

In what follows we shall be particularly interested in learning precisely which tenets or expressions of religious belief are matters of consensus for all varieties of Orthodox Jews and which serve to most sharply differentiate the modern from the traditional wings. Finally, we will see if there is a relationship between varieties of belief and those of practice.

Central Tenets of Orthodox Jewish Faith

While we do not presume to review nor did we try to measure adherence to all the central tenets of Orthodox Jewish faith, we did focus upon three that are basic and that empirically have become shibboleths of Jewish commitment for many Orthodox Jews. These are that (1) God definitely exists, (2) the Torah was revealed by God to Moses at Sinai, and (3) there is a Messiah and he will come

To be sure, much has and more could be written about the centrality of these beliefs to Judaism. It is not our place to make this case. We can, however, point to no less an authority than Maimonides, the influential and revered medieval Jewish philosopher, commentator, and exegete, whose thirteen principles of faith sum up the essentials of

a Jewish credo. Seven of these assert the definite existence of God (as creator, solitary in His omnipotence, incorporeal, eternal, the object of worship, omniscient, and the source of all human reward and punishment). Another identifies a belief that the entire Torah was revealed by God to Moses at Sinai. Finally, a belief in a Messiah who will someday come is also cited as essential.

While one might perhaps be tempted to suggest that these Maimonidean principles of faith are marginal, a look in almost any prayer book used by Orthodox Jews reveals that they are repeated as part of the Jew's daily morning prayers. The famous Ten Commandments begin with assertions of God's existence; and divine revelation at Sinai is supposed to be the key spiritual event in the formation of the Jews as a people, while a belief in the Messiah is central to the idea of redemption which is repeated in countless places in Jewish tradition. One would be hard-pressed, therefore, to find an Orthodox Jew who was ignorant of these formal articles of faith or totally unaware of their importance.

Table 3.1 presents results from questions we asked that focus on these three articles of faith. As one might expect, the traditional group was nearly unanimous in concurring with these statements, while the centrist modern Orthodox were only slightly less prepared (but, still, they *were less prepared*) to endorse these views (between 82% and 88% of them did so). Support for these beliefs, however, was considerably less frequent among the nominally Orthodox. Only three-quarters of them affirmed their belief in revelation at Sinai; only five-eighths could say that God "definitely" exists, and only a bare majority agreed that there was a Messiah who would come. The largely right-wing Conservative Jewish control group (our non-Orthodox) gave even less support for these views: only about half "definitely" believed in God or in revelation at Sinai, and only about a third believed in the coming of the Messiah.

Orthodox insiders, as well as many outside observers, many well be surprised at these survey findings and their implications. They suggest the presence of sizable minori-

Table 3.1: Belief in Central Tenets of Judaism by Orthodoxy

	Orthodoxy			
	Non-Orthodox	Nominal	Centrist	Traditional
Would you say that God exists?				
Definitely	50	63	85	97
The Torah was revealed by God to Moses at Sinai				
Agree strongly	13	31	54	83
Agree	37	43	34	13
Total	50	74	88	96
There is a Messiah and he will come				
Agree strongly	7	23	50	85
Agree	24	31	32	11
Total	31	54	82	96

ties of fairly observant Jews who identify themselves as Orthodox and yet who nevertheless have significant doubts about some of the very basic tenets of belief. In broad terms, we can see from the table 3.1 that about one centrist modern Orthodox Jew in six and about a third of the nominally Orthodox harbor uncertainty about these crucial articles of faith. That is, as one moves from the traditional Orthodox group to the less observant counterparts, the fervency of the groups' beliefs declines.

At first, only relatively small differences seem to separate those falling in our centrist category from those we call "traditionalists" in their overall concurrence with the statements on revelation and the Messiah. A closer inspection of the data in table 3.1, however, reveals a crucial distinction between the two groups. The traditionalists were far more likely than the centrists (83% vs. 54% and 85% vs. 50%, respectively) to "agree strongly"—rather than merely "agree"—with the two statements. While only about half the centrists strongly agreed that the Torah was revealed by God to Moses at Sinai and that there was a Messiah who would come, five out of six of the traditionalists did so. The latter group was obviously more fervent in its beliefs. We shall see similar patterns in our analyses of our respondents' faith in a personal and active God and of their belief in the applicability of ancient religious law.

An Active and Personal God

Writing of the importance of the belief in a personal and active God, the author of the venerated, medieval Judaic text, *Sefer Ha-Chinuch,* remarks: "The root of this commandment needs no explanation [for] it is known and revealed to all that this belief is the foundation of religion, and he who does not believe in this denies the essence and has no portion among or privileges of the Jews" (25:1). Maimonides in his Sefer Ha-Mitzvot lists a faith in God, in His activity and involvement in daily life, as the premier belief of Judaism. More recently, the great nineteenth-century German Orthodox rabbi, Samson Raphael Hirsch, wrote that "not the knowledge of the existence of God, but the acknowledgement of God, as *my* God [is] . . . the foundation of a Jewish life."[4] Clearly, there can be little if any doubt that Jews who claim to hold on to an Orthodox belief would be unlikely to admit publicly, as did one non-Orthodox man, that "as for God—he was a very distant relative who never visited us anymore, in business for himself."[5] Believing Orthodox Jews, as shown in table 3.2, affirm that the God to whom they pray frequently intervenes in everyday life to favor those who need His help.

Table 3.2 presents results from five questions in our survey that pertain to the issue of God's involvement with people in a personal, everyday way. We asked respondents their views on the statement: "God plays a negligible role in everyday life." As one might expect, almost all traditionalists rejected this view, as did a similarly high number of the centrists. However, only slightly more than half of the nominally Orthodox Jews and less than half of the non-Orthodox control group disagreed with the statement.

If we look more closely at the results, moreover, we see even more—a repetition of a pattern we discovered earlier. When asked whether they "disagreed" or "disagreed strongly," the traditionalists overwhelmingly "disagreed

Table 3.2: Beliefs in an Active and Personal God by Orthodoxy

	Orthodoxy			
	Non-Orthodox	Nominal	Centrist	Traditional
God plays a negligible role in everyday life:				
Disagree strongly	11	26	48	70
Disagree	37	31	32	17
Total	48	57	80	87
If a person won the lottery, did he do this with God's help?				
Yes	24	27	67	90
Which person is likely to be more successful: one whom God favors or one who makes his own plans and efforts?				
God favors	5	11	26	53
Both equally	38	43	53	37
Total	43	54	79	90
Which was more important in the recovery of a gravely ill child—Prayer or medical care?				
Prayer	3	8	14	29
Both	48	51	69	66
Total	51	59	83	95
God will punish those who transgress His commandments:				
Strongly agree	4	7	25	60
Agree	21	32	38	32
Total	25	39	63	92

strongly" (70%). Most of them were quite certain they believed in a God that did *not* play a negligible role in everyday life. But the centrists, those who seek to be faithful to the Jewish ways and beliefs of the past while being neither remote from nor untouched by the contemporary world of reason and secular values, were torn. Less than half "disagreed strongly." As for those who were at most nominally Orthodox, only about a quarter could strongly disagree with the notion that God plays a negligible role in everyday life. Clearly, the fervency of faith in the activity of God's role grows distinctly more modest as one moves away from those who by their ritual observances qualify to be called "traditionalist Orthodox."

The extent to which this belief in an active, involved God extends to various spheres of life can be seen in three questions we asked on how the respondents would explain winning a huge amount in the lottery, success in life, and the recovery of one's gravely ill child. In each instance, we asked respondents to contrast either the efficacy or likelihood of divine intervention with other, rational (contemporary) explanations for happy outcomes—such as luck, hard work and planning, or medical care. In all three instances, the traditionalists more than the centrists, and the centrists more than the others—nominally Orthodox and the non-Orthodox—were prepared to affirm their belief in divine intervention.

Specifically, we asked, "Suppose a person won a million dollars in the lottery, would you say he did this with the help of God?" Almost all of the traditionalists gave an affirmative reply, as did two-thirds of the centrists, and only about a quarter of the nominally Orthodox and the non-Orthodox.[6]

The other two questions—regarding the recovery of one's sick child or who succeeds in life—offered a choice of three response alternatives. One affirmed the predominant role of God, a second affirmed a rational (and contemporary secular) alternative, while a third referred to both options "equally" influencing the occurrence of favorable events.

Thus we asked, "Which person is likely to be more successful?" The choices offered were: "One whom God chooses to favor," "One who carefully plans his own existence and then makes every effort to carry out those plans," or "Both equally." Obviously, the first and last answers incorporate some notion of divine intervention in contrast with the second choice which excludes such an idea. Consistent with our earlier findings, nearly all of the traditionalists and over three-quarters of the centrists gave God a role in the child's recovery, while only slightly more than half of the nominally Orthodox and less than half of the non-Orthodox did so. We find roughly the same sort of response to our question on whether "the best possible medical care" or fervent prayer were more important in the recovery of one's gravely ill child. Again, almost all the traditionalists and an overwhelming number of the centrists gave responses reflecting some divine intervention (either prayer was more important than medical care or both were equally important) in contrast with the second choice which excludes such an idea. Among the nominally Orthodox and the non-Orthodox, the figures were much smaller, hovering around the 50% mark.

Although traditionalists and centrists largely concurred in affirming some divine role, a closer look at the data reveals that the former were much more likely to give credence to the answer reflecting a *predominant* divine role over the rational alternative (i.e., believing that prayer was more important and that one who succeeds is one whom God has chosen to favor). Of all groups, the centrists were most likely to endorse the equivocal, bivalent point of view. Over half answered "both equally" in the who-will-succeed question, and over two-thirds did so in the prayer-versus-medical care one. Not ready to completely abandon the credibility of divine explanations, they were nonetheless also not prepared to deny totally the efficacy of modern medicine or rational planning.

The centrists' preference for the bivalent alternative, one which affirms both the modern and rational along with the traditional God-oriented world symbolically reflects their dual commitment to both these domains. Relative to their traditionalist counterparts, they find it slightly more difficult to assign exclusive or predominant weight to divine intervention over more rational means for achieving successful outcomes. Yet, relative to those who were less or non-Orthodox, their faith was clearly more marked—that is, compared to most other Jews, our centrists hold great faith in God.

There is no quick explanation for this dualistic stance. One obvious possibility is that insofar as Orthodox Jews have embraced the worldview of modernity, they have moved away from a belief in God. As sociologist Peter Berger submits: "It is safe to say . . . that modern consciousness is not conducive to close contact with the gods."[7] Yet insofar as they remain attached to religion through their

93

Orthodoxy, they retain a devotion to the belief in God's existence and omnipresence. People who stand in both the modern and the Orthodox worlds are forced in some way to accept the worldviews associated with each—even when they are in conflict.

A second possible explanation for the dualistic stance of centrist Orthodoxy has to do with their desire to explain themselves to a contemporary cosmopolitan world which they partially inhabit but which does not share all their conceptions and beliefs. It may be that these Orthodox have so long tried to comprehend and articulate their "Orthodox Judaism in conceptual terms that are comprehensible to a non-Orthodox Jew" that in the process they have acquired some of his ways of looking at the world.[8] This means that at least in part they have experienced an erosion in their faith and an undermining of the "plausibility structure" that supports that faith.[9]

The last indicator of belief in divine activism which we summarize in table 3.2 concerns the belief: "God will punish those who transgress His commandments." Clearly, those who believe in divine intervention in everyday life may be expected to believe as well in reward and punishment by that God both here and in the hereafter. Consistent with this expectation, the traditionalists were nearly unanimous in their agreement with this proposition. While nearly two-thirds of the centrists expressed support for this idea, their numbers are significantly lower—although not nearly as low as among the nominally Orthodox, where a little over a third agreed, and the non-Orthodox, of whom only a quarter agreed that God would punish those who transgress. Again, looking more closely at the results, we find that the traditionalists were the ones who most readily endorsed the most fervent answer; 60% of them "agree strongly" with the proposition versus only 25% of the centrists. When centrists concurred with this principle, they were more likely than the traditionalists to simply "agree" than to "strongly agree."

While there is no quick explanation to be provided here, one is, however, tempted to recall that the centrists—as moderns—have come in contact with a plurality of worldviews. As Peter Berger says, "Modernity pluralizes both institutions and plausibility structures."[10] As moderns, centrists are, at least to some extent, committed to a world-view that presumes rationality, which suggests, as sociologist Max Weber said, ". . . there are no mysterious incalculable forces that come into play."[11] Accordingly, discovering that they (or others) have transgressed without being manifestly punished by God, they are—as moderns—hard put to be certain God is keeping a tally on people, rewarding or punishing them here and now. But then as Orthodox Jews they still give some credence to the hereafter, and rewards and punishments there remain to be experienced. Moreover, as Orthodox they do not presume to fathom all of God's mysterious ways. So the centrists hedge their bets, agreeing that God will punish those who transgress His commandments but not *strongly* agreeing with that proposition. For the centrists, "imprecision is expanding."[12]

The traditionalists, as we have seen by this unambiguous and relatively precise belief in God, are obviously more comfortable with divine mystery—to the truly religious, "a God comprehended is no God."[13] Consequently, they are perhaps less burdened by doubts even when they can see transgression occurring without immediate punishment. Put simply, the traditionalists appear to have more devotion to faith, while their less observant counterparts have been captured by reason.

The Modern World and *Halacha*

We would expect that those who are most certain about the central tenets of traditional Judaism and who have a stronger faith in the ongoing active intervention of God in everyday life will also display the greatest commitment to time-honored Jewish religious law (*halacha*). That is, they will *believe* in the efficacy and importance of strict Jewish observance. We, therefore, examine next the feelings of Orthodox Jews regarding the relevance and applicability of *halacha* to life in the contemporary world.

If *emunah* or faith is the implicit element of Orthodox

95

Jewish consciousness, *halacha* (Jewish law—literally, "the way") and adherence to its ritual injunctions may be said to constitute its explicit manifestation. Through it, not only sentiments but actions are shared. It objectifies the subjective religious moment and roots one in the real world of specific times and places. It "constantly demands from man that he translate his inner life into external facticity" and "provides the objective basis upon which the individual must build his own personal quest for holiness."[14]

As already noted, the Orthodox have always insisted on the dominance of *halachic* practice over even the deepest held faith. While faith was crucial, the rabbis believe that devoted practice within the strictures of *halacha* was deemed capable of generating that faith more easily than vice versa. Repeatedly, the rabbis comment in the Talmud, Codes, and even in the homilies, tales, and proverbial sayings that Jews should obey the injunctions of the law and observe the ritual practices even in the absence of total faith in them for by doing so they will come to believe.[15] Moreover, these commanded practices (*mitzvas*) are not explicitly dependent upon the comprehension of their spiritual purpose. Indeed, as Rabbi Isaac Aramah, the fifteenth-century exegete said, in words echoed by many traditionalists, "The Torah deliberately hid the reason of certain *mitzvas* in order that every person should recognize that every *mitzva* in the Torah has a hidden motive beyond reason." The clear implication is that Jewish belief requires that one act in accord with the law even before fully comprehending its motive force.[16] Among the Orthodox, this principle is encapsulated in a well-known epigrammatic phrase: *halacha le-Moshe mi Sinai* (*halacha* to Moses from Sinai). This means that, while reasons for a practice may sometimes be obscure or opaque, the law (the *halacha*)—which must be obeyed—was established by God in revelation of Moses at Sinai. The centrality of the belief in revelation at Sinai has already been noted. What needs to be added here is that the Orthodox believe that, on the occasion of that revelation, God presented Jews with the *halacha*, the way to live their lives.

The previous chapter already pointed out that so-called centrist Orthodox Jews accept the fundamental legitimacy of the *halacha* (even if they are somewhat equivocal about its divine origins) but at the same time remain convinced that they have an obligation as contemporary beings to separate the eternal from that which is temporally rooted in a particular historical or cultural epoch. Accordingly, centrists are ever searching for ways to reinterpret and thereby integrate the demands of Torah (religion) and its *halachic* aspect with contemporary life. As such, they retain a "perennial faith in the capacity of traditional Judaism to harmonize its timeless teachings with modern conditions."[17]

But while such a declaration may be relatively easy to subscribe to, the realities of life often make the integration of the claims of modernity and those of Orthodoxy difficult to reconcile. Conflicts can and sometimes do occur. For example, as moderns, centrists are part of the contemporary rational world in which action not clearly based upon reason is hard to justify. Sometimes, however, they discover certain demands of the *halacha* that appear to challenge the rules of modern order and rationality. As moderns they feel moved to drop that which seems unreasonable and out of tune with the times and place; but as Orthodox Jews they believe they are required to carry out *halachic* practices even if they fail to see the reason in them.

One option for handling them would be to abandon one of the worlds in conflict in favor of the other. Those who give up Orthodoxy or those who leave the modern world in favor of an insular traditionalism choose this option. Centrists, and to an extent those who while lax in observance still identify themselves as Orthodox, by definition do not.

For those Orthodox Jews located between the extremes of traditionalist insularity and non-Orthodox integration,[18] two other possibilities exist. First is that of the possibility of reinterpretation. Here they carry out a series of rationalizations and intellectual transformations in which old and new are shown to be continuous. In Peter Berger's formulation of this practice, "modern consciousness becomes the ultimate criterion of all religious affirmations."[19] *Halacha* only appears at first glance to be out of tune with the times ("the old shall be made new"). A closer reading either of the Jewish law or of the realities of the present reveals—they would argue—no conflict after all. And where there is a conflict, there is need to develop Jewish law ("the new shall be made holy") to meet the demands of the age, of course without compromising either. In the words of one modern Orthodox rabbi, Eliezer Berkovits: "There are certain fundamental requirements of [modern] life which *halacha* cannot ignore and without whose adequate satisfaction *halacha* itself becomes impossible."[20]

Reinterpretation and *halachic* development, however, require a relatively high degree of religious virtuosity and expertise. Most centrists look to their rabbis for these sorts of ideological calisthenics and innovations. While they wait for the rabbis to reinterpret and reconstruct the *halacha*, many tacitly choose another option. They compartmentalize. Simply, or more precisely with an unconscious sophistication, they learn to be *inattentive* to conflict by means of a kind of conceptual dimming of the lights in the one world while they move in another, and vice versa. This is not an outright denial of the conflict but rather an inattention to it. Thus, they accept certain *halachic* demands even though by doing so they seem to contradict another pattern of their lives. As Peter Berger puts it, people "just keep themselves very busy," too busy to become bogged down by the contradictions of their lives.[21]

We tried to uncover the lines of this reinterpretation and compartmentalization of *halacha* and the modern world first by shining light upon the points of conflict through a variety of questions. These are not necessarily issues that Orthodox Jews consciously grapple with in their everyday existence; as noted, they are "too busy" for that. But these are nevertheless questions that stand at the core of what Orthodox Jews do and how they live their lives, for the answers to the questions reveal some of the ways they have found to handle the conflicts of their lives as Orthodox Jews in a world that appears antagonistic to such Orthodoxy. Table 3.3 presents the results.

To be sure, these questions seemed particularly troublesome to those Jews who had selected the option of inattention. It forced them to stop "being busy" and to pay atten-

Table 3.3: Belief in Halacha by Orthodoxy

	Orthodoxy			
	Non-Orthodox	Nominal	Centrist	Traditional
The modern world is too complex to be ruled by Torah:				
Strongly disagree	10	27	57	84
Disagree	41	39	35	13
Total	51	66	92	97
Halacha must sometimes be ignored because of life in the modern world:				
Strongly disagree	5	18	49	84
Disagree	29	37	38	12
Total	34	55	87	96
One should not follow the Torah in blind faith:				
Strongly disagree	4	7	17	45
Disagree	15	25	29	29
Total	19	32	46	74
One should give alms because the Torah commands it or it's kind to do:				
Torah	5	15	25	51
Both	51	65	67	47
Total	56	80	92	98
I am not a "sinner" even if I transgress Jewish law:				
Strongly disagree	3	4	16	49
Disagree	10	20	33	26
Total	13	24	49	75

tion to these issues. But when someone has succeeded in dimming the lights, he does not take kindly to someone else embarrassingly turning them on. Indeed, many of our respondents who because of our questions had to come face-to-face with their religious decisions felt a need to keep explaining to us (or themselves) their reasoning, to define the lines of their reinterpretations more fully than a questionnaire such as ours allowed. Many questionnaires were appended with explanatory notes or requests for follow-up telephone calls. A number of people contacted us to explain why they chose the answers they did and why those choices needed further elaboration. Generally, it was those we characterize as "centrists" who wanted to add the most.

"Do you mean by your questions that the world should be ruled 'completely' by the Torah? Aren't there matters about which the Torah is silent?" one respondent commented, for example.

"The Torah itself demands that *halacha* be ignored under special circumstances," argued another, and therefore even if one expressed agreement with the proposition he was still to be considered a believer.

"Faith is by definition 'blind,'" added another, while suggesting that therefore the question itself could not adequately measure his or anyone's faith and that his real faith was far greater than what would be measured by an instrument such as ours.

The first two questionnaire items placed the conflicts in baldest terms. We asked respondents the extent to which they agreed with the statements: "The world has become too complex to be ruled by Torah," and "Jewish law, *halacha* must sometimes be ignored because of the hardships it may create for those living in the modern world."

As with many of the questions whose answers were reported in the earlier tables in this chapter, we discover a familiar pattern. The traditionalists and centrists largely concur in expressing answers that generally affirm a religious orientation (in this case, disagreement with the statements). The traditionalists, however, are distinguished from the centrists in their marked tendency to express their point of view with greater fervor and certainty. With regard to these statements, they opted overwhelmingly for the "Strongly Disagree" response category. The centrists, on the contrary, were apparently not always absolutely certain that they could find a way to bring together "the timeless, fixed, normative world of sacred law and the fluid, ever-changing, concrete social condition."[22] They appeared to believe—at least to some extent—along with other moderns that what the contemporary rational world "refuses to grant to religion is not its right to exist, but its right to dog-

matize upon the nature of things and the special competence which it claims for itself for knowing man and the
world."[23]

Meanwhile, in a pattern reminiscent of earlier results,
smaller majorities of the nominally Orthodox agreed with
the two more observant groups; and even fewer of the
non-Orthodox disagreed with these two statements.

As suggested above, adherence to *halacha* demands from
the modernist, at least at times, suspension of the rules of
contemporary reason in order to maintain a strong commitment to the virtue of living, according to time-honored
(and sometimes rationally opaque) religious precepts. In
light of this conflict, as noted, the modern Orthodox Jew
strives to uncover a way to reconcile the two, hoping to
find that the Torah can be in tune with reason and modernity. Against this background, it should come as no sur-
prise that the centrist modern Orthodox respondents differed with their traditionalist colleagues over the
statement: "Generally, one should not follow the dictates
of Torah in blind faith." Almost half strongly disagreed
with this view, thus saying—in no uncertain terms—that
one should generally follow the Torah's dictates in blind
faith. The centrists, however, more prone to claim that
modern rationality not only does not have to come into
conflict with the Torah but can actually help the modern
Jew appreciate and understand it, were much less dis-
posed to endorse *without qualification* the proposition that
the Torah should be followed in blind faith. Only 17% did
so. Needless to say, hardly any nominally Orthodox or
non-Orthodox showed any unequivocal support for the
blind faith proposition.

This is not to say that the nontraditionalist Orthodox
were completely unable to countenance the idea of blind
faith. After all, nearly half of the centrists and almost a
third of the nominally Orthodox found that they could
agree in one way or another with this proposition. And
while that is considerably less than the three-quarters of
the traditionalists who found a way to admit to the possibility of blind faith, it is still measurably more than our
non-Orthodox respondents and, presumably, the general
population. One may speculate on the reasons for this ele-

ment of concordance with blind faith as having something to do with the accepted principle of *chok* (or decree) in Jewish law. The *chok* is that law that requires observance even though no clear reason for it has been given by the Torah. While there are many laws that qualify as *chok*, perhaps the best known are those associated with *kashrut*, the Jewish dietary laws. For all of the reasonable explanations that have been offered over the generations for these statutes, the fact is that there are none given by the Torah itself. Rather, once decreed, these laws must be followed in blind faith. Since we have already seen that among the most frequently observed rituals by all Orthodox Jews are those pertaining to the dietary laws, we know that many—if not most of our respondents—probably realize that they in fact *do* follow at least some of the Torah in blind faith. Thus, it would be hard for them all as a group to totally disavow this kind of behavior in principle. Accordingly, even though there are differences between traditionalist and nontraditionalist Orthodox, in no case did an entire category of Orthodox Jews disavow completely the idea that one should follow the Torah in blind faith.

The different normative emphases of traditionalists and other categories of Orthodox Jews is further illustrated in the results from our question on why "a person should give alms to the poor." Our question provided three choices for an answer: (1) the Torah commands it, (2) it is the kind thing to do, and (3) both equally. Traditionalists may be expected to more readily endorse a response that looks no further than the sacred text for legitimation of action ("the Torah commands it"). The non-Orthodox may be expected to offer a contemporary secular-ethical reason ("it is the kind thing to do"). But those Orthodox who are less observant than the traditionalists may—on the basis of their past responses—be expected to prefer to hedge their bets as it were and give the relatively equivocal response ("both equally"), which implies the notion of a harmony between the ancient sacred law and contemporary morality.

To be sure, there are some complications in this question that need sorting out. By and large, we may expect that Jews who live in America, where assumptions are made about the ethical rectitude of Judeo-Christian religious demands, and Orthodox Jews who harbor a faith that the Torah is a morally virtuous document will likely approach a question such as the one we have asked here with the presumption that the Torah would naturally ask people to do what is kind to do. And thus, only those who aggressively choose to assert the predominance of the Torah's demands over all other reality would select the response that they give alms (only) because it is commanded by the Torah.

Indeed, a slim majority of the traditionalists gave the fundamentalist answer, and hardly any responded with the purely secular-ethical response. That 51% of these American Jews found it unnecessary to go beyond the Torah to find a justification for giving alms is particularly noteworthy. On the other hand, we should not be surprised that even among the traditionalists nearly as many respondents also chose the "both equally" option.

When we consider the centrists and nominals, we discover, however, that a greater proportion of these Jews needed to go beyond the text. Only 25% and 15%, respectively, were satisfied to use the Torah as the predominant source for their almsgiving. Relatively far greater proportions of them needed recourse to morality beyond the boundaries of the Torah; about two-thirds of each of the other Orthodox groups gave the equivocal answer. Meanwhile, non-Orthodox respondents were split between the equivocal answer and the secular-ethical reply; only 5% said they gave alms because "the Torah commands it."

In the answers to the alms question, by answering "the Torah commands it" most traditionalists affirmed the primacy of religious tradition over secular morality and public opinion. At the other extreme, the non-Orthodox were most prepared to endorse a publicly popular and exclusively secular basis to moral action by answering that "it is the kind thing to do." Those between the two extremes try to maintain the congruence of secular and religious moral authority, implicitly denying a conflict and that one has to choose between the two.

The foregoing discussion has highlighted the differences between the traditionalists and other Orthodox Jews, suggesting a hierarchy of *emunah* in which, as a whole, traditionalists tend to believe the most fervently while centrists and the nominals are respectively less believing and less fervent in their beliefs Nevertheless, it is useful to recognize that most Orthodox Jews in our sample accept, albeit—as we have tried to show—with varying degrees of fervency, the notion that ancient sacred law (Torah, *halacha*) makes legitimate claims upon them. Both traditionalists and centrists (the bulk of the Orthodox Jews we have questioned) overwhelmingly agree in one way or another (as do two-thirds of the nominally Orthodox) that the Torah can rule over conduct in a complex world, and majorities agree that *halacha* should not be ignored in modern times. Similarly, most Orthodox Jews we surveyed believe (again, albeit to varying degrees) in the imminence and transcendence of God. So while Orthodox Jews are not monolithic in their religious beliefs, all these Jews *are* surely "more Orthodox" in those beliefs than those Jews who do not identify themselves as Orthodox.

From the previous chapter, we have established a hierarchy of ritual observances among the Orthodox. From this chapter we begin to see a hierarchy of religious belief. But how, we wondered, did these Jews look at themselves? Were they all equally satisfied with the correctness—even righteousness of their behavior?

To find out, we asked our respondents whether they agreed with the proposition that "I do not think of myself as a 'sinner' even if I transgress the dictates of Jewish law." We supposed, to quote sociologist Jean Marie Guyau, that "nothing can oblige [a person] to follow the dictates of reason to the bitter end, if he believes that the instant he calls certain dogmas and certain authorities in question he is committing a sin." [24]

Those who disagreed with this proposition in effect affirmed the traditional religious position that violating Jewish law is identical with sinning. As we would by now expect, the proportions of respondents who disagreed varied sharply among our four groups. Traditionalists most readily disagreed; three-quarters of them saw themselves as sinners if they transgressed the dictates of the law. There is some irony in this since, judging from their level of observance, we would suppose that, according to the strict dictates of Jewish law, they probably were the least likely of our sample to transgress.

About half of the centrists and a quarter of the nominally Orthodox—as opposed to only a small fraction of the non-Orthodox—could see themselves as sinners. Apparently the more you sin, the less likely are you to see yourself as such. Transgressions bring with them the self-conceptions necessary to sustain them. Or, perhaps certain self-conceptions are conducive to what the observant consider transgression. In either case, the less observant our respondents were, the less likely they were to see themselves as sinners.

Looking at the more extreme responses, this pattern is even more striking. The number of traditionalists who gave the most committed answer ("strongly disagree") far exceeded the number of centrists who answered in the same way (49% vs. 16%). Indeed, the extreme answer among the traditionalists matched the total number of centrists who either disagreed strongly or simply disagreed. And among the nominally Orthodox—those whose observances and beliefs are modest in the extreme—only a mere 4% strongly disagreed.

Clearly, there are a number of matters involved here about which we can only speculate. For example, one is tempted to conjecture about feelings of guilt. Could one say that traditionalists are far more likely to feel guilty (seeing themselves as "sinners") when they do transgress, precisely because, judging from their responses, they transgress least often? Centrists and nominally Orthodox Jews, who apparently feel less like sinners when they transgress, may perhaps be feeling that a good Jew need not obey every jot and tittle of the *halacha* and yet can still feel like a good person (i.e., not a sinner). As Jacob Katz remarked, "The old type [traditionalist] sinner accepted rebuke and was prepared to make amends by repentance; the new type of sinner refused to repent."[25] Once transgression has been integrated into a style of life, the routine of emotional adjustment requires that one rationalize or at least ignore its negative character and accept the legitimacy of one's actions. That is, the more one breaks the law, the less he is likely to feel as if he is sinning.

How is one to understand this inverse relationship between feeling like a sinner and behavior or beliefs that are not constrained by the dictates of Jewish law and observance? Here Mary Douglas offers some guidance when she argues that where "there are no overreaching doctrines of sin and atonement . . . , the idea of the self is free from social constraint."[26] That is, when people do not feel like sinners, they feel freer to express themselves, to choose for themselves what it is they wish to do. Simply put, free-thinking and freedom of action—the hallmarks of the age in which we live—are the opposite of traditional religion. At least these days it would appear that to sin is in.

Theological Boundaries

In Chapter 2 we divided one Orthodox group from another on the basis of selected ritual practices and demonstrated wide-ranging differences and, indeed, an implicit hierarchy in patterns of observance. Similarly, in this chapter, we have uncovered a series of boundaries and an implicit hierarchy of belief within Orthodoxy and between it and non-Orthodoxy. That is to say, we have found that even in the largely unspoken and often taken-for-granted domain of theology (which outsiders might have assumed would be constant for all those Jews who call themselves "Orthodox") there are undeniable divisions among the faithful.

From all appearances, the variations among groups in matters of faith are not rigid or absolute but rather matters of relative difference and interpretation. As a consequence, it would be insufficient—if not misleading—to simply list principles of faith applicable for one group and not for another. Instead, we wish to demonstrate that the variations on belief are as much, if not more, a matter of fervency rather than content. Some people believe more strongly while others do so with less conviction.

Table 3.4 largely demonstrates that proposition as it summarizes the stances of the four groups (non-Orthodox, nominally Orthodox, centrist, and traditionalist) toward eleven statements of religious faith, all of which were treated earlier in this chapter. These statements were selected simply because the questions permitted both moderately traditional and extremely traditional replies. In other words, eight of the items allowed one to "agree" or to "strongly agree" (or "disagree" and "strongly dis-

Table 3.4: Mean Percentages with Moderately Traditional and Extremely Traditional Responses to Eleven Questions on Religious Belief, by Orthodoxy

| | Orthodoxy | | | |
	Non-Orthodox	Nominal	Centrist	Traditional
Moderately traditional responses	32	40	45	28
Extremely traditional responses	6	16	34	63
Total	38	56	79	91

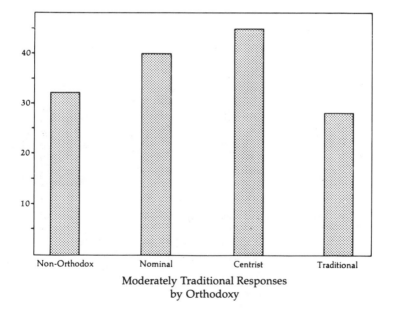

Moderately Traditional Responses
by Orthodoxy

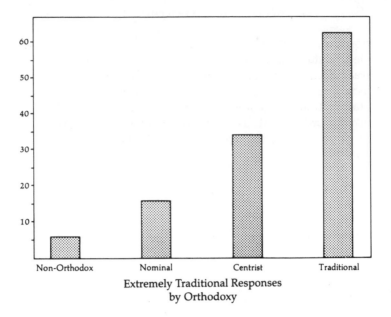

Extremely Traditional Responses
by Orthodoxy

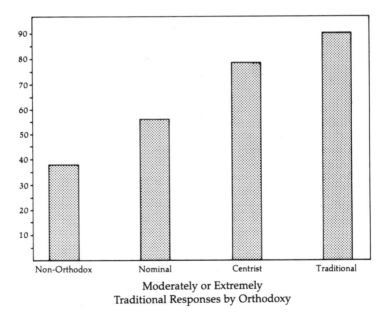

Moderately or Extremely
Traditional Responses by Orthodoxy

agree"). The other three posed a choice between traditional and modern replies (i.e., finding God's favor or personal planning, choosing prayer or seeking medical care, following the dictates of the Torah or the demands of kindness). We regarded the "both equally" replies for these three questions as expressing a moderate affirmation of traditional belief, and the unqualified responses (God, prayer, Torah) as indicating the extreme affirmation of traditional belief.

Table 3.4 presents the average (or mean) percentages giving moderately or extremely traditional responses across the eleven items for each of the four Orthodoxy groups.

The eleven (abbreviated) items (and moderate/extreme responses) summarized in the table include the following:

1. The Torah was revealed by God to Moses at Sinai (agree/strongly agree).

2. There is a Messiah and he will come (agree/strongly agree).

3. God plays a negligible role in everyday life (disagree/ strongly disagree).

4. Which person is likely to be more successful: one whom God favors, or one who plans and makes efforts? (both equally/God favors).

5. Which was more important in the recovery of a gravely ill child: prayer or medical care? (both equally/ prayer).

6. God will punish those who transgress his commandments (agree/strongly agree).

7. The modern world is too complex to be ruled by Torah (disagree/strongly disagree).

8. *Halacha* must sometimes be ignored because of the modern world (disagree/strongly disagree).

9. One should not follow the Torah in blind faith (disagree/strongly disagree).

10. One should give alms because the Torah commands it or because it's the kind thing to do (both equally/Torah).

11. I am not a "sinner" even if I transgress Jewish law (disagree/strongly disagree).

Across the four groups, the proportions expressing moderately traditional views are far more similar than are

the proportions with extremely traditional religious beliefs. The percentage with moderate beliefs peaks among
the centrists (at 45%) and is lowest at the two extremes
(32% among the non-Orthodox and 28% among the most
traditional). On the other hand, the proportion with extremely traditional beliefs climbs dramatically from the
non-Orthodox to the traditionalists. Hardly any (6%) of the
non-Orthodox have, on average, extreme beliefs, as compared with a small number (16%) of nominals, a third
(34%) of the centrists, and a clear majority (63%) of the traditionalists. In other words, as we move from group to
group in a traditional direction, the average percentage
with extremely traditional beliefs doubles (more or less)
with each transition.

If we add the moderate and extreme proportions, we
find the fraction of each group that at least accepts the
statements of belief, whether with a moderate or extreme
affirmation. In doing so, we find that the differences between groups are in the anticipated direction: concurrence
with traditional beliefs grows with traditional observance.
However, the differences between groups are not anywhere nearly as sharp or as dramatic as when we consider
only the proportion with extremely traditional views.

This circumstance leads us to infer that members of two
adjacent groups (such as traditionalists and centrists) are
indeed very likely to concur on the content of their beliefs.
After all—to take the centrists and traditionalists as an example—almost as many of the former as of the latter (79%
vs. 91%) at least assented in a moderate fashion to the
eleven items (on average). The critical distinction between
groups, however, is not so much in the content of their beliefs as in their fervency. To pursue the example, almost
twice as many traditionalists as centrists gave extremely
traditional answers on the eleven belief questions.

One way to interpret these results is to suggest that in
addition to marking themselves off via a set of ritual practices (as shown in our previous chapter), Orthodox Jews
may distinguish themselves and their religious ardor by
means of the fervency of their faith. That is, articles of faith
and their expressions may be more than matters of theol-

ogy; they also may serve the social function of being boundary markers.

Conclusions

The overall results reported in this chapter imply that if one compares two Orthodox Jews with close but not identical patterns of ritual observance, the two—if asked—will probably agree generally on most theological matters. That is, they will, at least in the realm of expressed beliefs, be undeniably Orthodox. Where they will most differ will be in the *certainty* and *fervency* of their beliefs. The more observant Orthodox Jew will probably express greater confidence in and fervor for a wide range of religious beliefs than his or her less observant counterpart.

As we have shown in this chapter and the previous one, Orthodoxy in America (if not elsewhere) consists of a package of interrelated items. Here we discovered how and to what extent the more ritually observant are also more certain and fervent about many fundamental religious beliefs, how their *emunah* matches their observance of *mitzvas*. The commonly held belief in some quarters that Orthodox Judaism is largely *only* Orthoprax is denied by our findings. A fervent belief does indeed often accompany maximal practice. Whether the latter is dependent on the former or simply associated with it, we cannot say. That they coexist and vary in parallel fashion seems demonstrated.

All of these findings lead us to wonder whether or not there is a social and communal component in this Orthodox package. That is, do people who observe the same *mitzvas* and share the same *emunah* also share the same *kehilla* or community? This question will be addressed in Chapter 4.

4 Kehillah: Orthodox Insularity and Community Boundaries

> With us Jews the individual doesn't exist; it's the community that counts.
>
> Chaim Grade

Survival versus Integration

As noted earlier, since the late eighteenth century, after generations during which Jews by and large lived in separate and isolated communities, Western societies began to open themselves to Jewish participation. Jews were gradually transformed "from barely tolerated individuals and communities into full-fledged citizens."[1] The parochial Jewish community found its way—often at great cultural expense—into the outside host society.[2] The historian Joseph Blau comments, "These last two hundred years might be described as the time in which the Jews have come out of the ghetto and into the world."[3]

By way of their passage out of the ghetto, many Jews moved from a position of temporal and cultural remoteness and entered Western society in body and in spirit, acquiring much of the local knowledge and taking on its way of life. From then on, with every change in the host societies and cultures came parallel changes in Jewish life. Accordingly, for example, as the nineteenth-century occidental world moved increasingly toward secularization and universalism, so too did many Jews.

Insofar as Jews retained an attachment to some degree of Jewish identity, they faced a particular dilemma. How were they to enter society on an equal footing with others and still preserve some aspects of their group ties and cultural differentiation? This dilemma was sharpened by many European thinkers and policymakers who made the dissolution of Jewish group ties an explicit condition of admission into the larger society. Others, perhaps more tactful, be-

113

lieved that admission of Jews as full participants in the larger society would promote the eventual disappearance of many aspects of Jewish group distinctiveness—in particular, those elements most alien to Western (European or American) culture. Jews, it was believed, had to make a decision. Should they succumb to the temptation of acculturation and its more extreme ramification, that is, assimilation, even if it involved accepting Christianity or some secularized variation of it? Or should they remain true to their traditions and continue as members of a socially inferior minority?

Several Jewish ideologies or worldviews arose in response to this new challenge which, in effect, appeared to offer acceptance for assimilation. Large numbers simply accepted the offer of emancipation and inclusion in return for abandonment of all parochialism and Jewish sectarianism.

Another type of Jewish response rejected the possibilities of assimilation. Among these, and central to our discussion here, were—as we pointed out in Chapter 1— those contra-acculturative Orthodox who rejected many of the cultural demands and social consequences of emancipation and argued that isolation was necessary for Jewish survival. "To perpetuate ourselves in spite of the tremendous forces making for the disintegration of the Jewish type," ran one such argument, "we need the consolidating, strengthening, vitalizing influence of the Jewish environment."[4] Simply put, these people essentially claimed that "a Jew is a Jew when he is with other Jews," because assimilation meant "the suicidal extinction of Jewish being."[5] To such Jews, emancipation was perceived as "a mistake, a curse, not a blessing, because it led the Jews to renounce their special status as eternal strangers and to secularize their lives."[6]

Not only did Jews as a people have to be segregated, but so too—some of those who rejected the trends of assimilation suggested—did Judaism. They rejected the concept of a "Judeo-Christian culture," of a continuity between what they considered to be polar opposites, and argued instead—in the words of a contemporary version of this position—that "to view Judaism within a foreign context

is to strip Judaism of its vital force, if not completely to cas-
trate it."[7]

In America, where the possibilities of assimilation in an
essentially open society were perhaps greater than anywhere else, these contra-acculturative isolationists tended,
as much as possible, to keep themselves separate from the
surrounding culture. They established many of their own
institutions and neighborhoods; they often spoke among
themselves and whenever possible in Yiddish rather than
in the English vernacular.[8] And when they built their academies of higher Jewish learning, their yeshivas, they made
"a deliberate attempt to isolate their students from American life."[9] It was, for example, no accident that the Beth
Midrash Govoha Yeshiva in Lakewood, perhaps the
preeminent institution of Orthodox learning in America,
was located in a rural New Jersey town far from any indigenous Jewish community. The basic premise among the
isolationists thus remained—as we noted earlier—that "if
the Jewish community is to survive, it must become more
explicit and conscious about the incompatibility of integration and survival," and in order to perpetuate itself in
America it must "reject the value of integration."[10] A recent
statement by Rabbi Nisson Wolpin, editor of the Orthodox
magazine *Jewish Observer*, perhaps comes closest to articu-
lating the current version of this ideal: "It is far easier . . .
to accept all aspects of modern culture in an indiscriminate
embrace, ironing out apparent contradictions with self-
congratulatory sophistries and apologetics, than to be on
the alert constantly, disclaiming more than accepting. It requires a good deal more courage to reject what is so attrac-
tively accessible in our free society, on the grounds that it
does not measure up to an objective standard, than to accept it and join in. Acting in this manner involves the risk
of sounding a negative note and projecting an unattractive
anachronistic image. But," he concludes, "this has always
been the price of Jewish survival."[11]

Between these extremes of assimilationism and contra-
acculturative isolationism were a spectrum of Jewish
groups who rejected the validity of a forced choice between
group survival or integration into the larger society.[12] In
Chapter 1, we referred to them as Jews who have chosen

the acculturative option. At the conservative end of this spectrum but in the liberal wing of their own order were those who in time came to be referred to as "modern Orthodox Jews." Their ideological heirs fall mostly—but, as we have seen, not exclusively—into the centrist and nominally Orthodox categories in our sample.

As we indicated earlier, modern Orthodoxy's principal social thinkers (primarily rabbis in nineteenth-century Europe and twentieth-century United States) argued in favor of a principle that did "not look upon the mingling of Judaism with European [read: non-Jewish] culture as a deplorable and unalterable condition."[13] Describing these Jews, among whom he counts himself, President Norman Lamm of Yeshiva University said, "For us, the study of worldly wisdom is not a concession to economic necessity. It is *de jure*, not *de facto*." Such a perspective, he went on to explain, "issues from a broad *Weltanschauung* or world view rather than from tunnel vision."[14] These Orthodox very simply took an optimistic view of the survival versus integration dilemma, even as they argued that they should indeed escape the ghetto as Jews, with their own spiritual treasures intact. The challenge confronting them was, in the words of Ephraim Sturm, executive director of the Young Israel movement, "to separate the eternal concepts of Torah from those things which were products of Europe and its self contained Jewish community."[15] They sought, again to quote Rabbi Lamm, to "be receptive to new ideas, honest questions and novel situations," because they believed that "the Jew can deal with his surrounding environment on Torah terms and shape the conditions of life accordingly."[16]

In their relative willingness to admit that they were making changes or compromises with the modern world, even the most modern of the Orthodox, however, differed from proponents of other Jewish more acculturative worldviews that were also optimistic about the feasibility of reconciling the twin impulses of surviving as a group and integrating into society. Unlike the latter, the Orthodox remained—as noted in previous chapters—in principle bonded to *halacha*, even if what it demanded of them was a rejection of modern values and life-styles. To be sure, as also indicated earlier, few of the modern Orthodox believed things would ever have to come to that; they remain convinced instead that they can be in and of the modern world without sacrificing their rootedness and attachments to Orthodox Jewish life and its strict demands.

With respect to integration with the non-Orthodox, the centrist modern Orthodox have for a long time remained between those on their traditionalist right and those non- or nominally Orthodox coreligionists on their modern left.[17] They looked at the former as too insular and hence too ready to surrender the shaping of modern Judaism to those with less than adequate commitments to the true religious heritage. And they considered the latter as, at best, well-intentioned; but also misguided, sometimes heretical, and inadequately committed to Jewish authenticity and distinctive group survival in the modern, open society.

The two alternative polar approaches to the survival/integration dilemma—one demanding near-total self-segregation; the other allowing for complete integration—have exerted competing influences upon American Orthodoxy. Both the community and individuals have resolved the dilemma differently over the years. In the late 1950s, the 1960s, and even into the early 1970s, for example, many modern Orthodox rabbis, institutions, and thinkers advocated an open approach tolerant of Jewish pluralism, which at the same time allowed those Orthodox who wished to make their way into contemporary American society. This attitude encouraged a kind of Jewish cultural pluralism and discouraged sectarian divisions. Some rabbis who took this point of view cautioned their followers not to accuse their non-Orthodox counterparts of "heresy." One said that "the use of [such] epithets and the levelling of sanctions [against the non-Orthodox] are counterproductive." And he added that "such words and actions are tantamount to an admission of intolerant mindlessness at worst and religious insecurity at best."[18]

Thus, modern Orthodox rabbis frequently joined their Reform and Conservative counterparts in such interdenominational bodies as the Synagogue Council of America and various local boards of rabbis. Several Orthodox day schools which emphasized high achievement in secular studies along with commitment to religious studies gained prominence in Orthodox circles. And many Orthodox made their way into walks of life—from medicine to law to big business to academia—which had heretofore been considered beyond the pale of their existence.

At the same time, the modern Orthodox also retained links and a concomitant rapport with traditionalists on their right wing. Sir Immanuel Jakobovits, chief rabbi of the United Kingdom, explained the connection as follows: "The perimeters of both circles [the modern and the traditionalist Orthodox] intersect to provide a considerable area of common agreement and joint endeavor, ideologically as well as organizationally." [19] Often they supported the same causes—increased aid to yeshivas and day schools, for example—and shared the same institutions. Indeed, the Orthodox modernists sought not only a *modus vivendi* with their traditionalist counterparts but also "a recognition that both schools of thought may be needed, together with the rivalries between them, to maintain the momentum of orthodox ascendancy." [20] That is, the centrists were ready to support the legitimate claims of their orthodox right as long as they in turn would grant the legitimacy of a centrist way of life. Those who had accepted an adapted form of acculturation wanted the approval of those who tended toward contra-acculturation.

By the late 1970s, however, that "momentum" had taken on a life of its own. Traditionalists were beginning to gain an ideological ascendancy among the Orthodox. Indeed, they had never really accepted many of the adaptations and reinterpretations and what they considered the "compromises" of the modernists. Moreover, cooperation between modern Orthodox and non-Orthodox waned. In the face of the chaotic 1960s, which were judged to be caused by noxious forces in the non-Jewish world, some Orthodox rabbis and their congregants began to argue against openness. In the words of one: "Tolerance, acceptance, and the opportunity to join as equals in an alien society have proven to be dangerous and debilitating, eroding Jewish observance and destroying Jewish identity as time passes." The period of the liberal swing in orthodoxy seemed to be coming to an end. The traditionalist voice that argued for separation from American culture and society was becoming louder and bolder. Often it led the nontraditionalist Orthodox to express their liberal and tolerant pluralist convictions in whispers.

Several theories have been advanced for this rise, real or apparent, of the voices of insularity and segregation. Some have argued that it was a part of the general "resurgence of ethnic consciousness of the early seventies . . . [which] helped to give [traditionalist] orthodox Judaism a certain legitimacy, an aura of glamour and authenticity lacking in other Jewish religious expressions which, by the emerging standards of the times, seemed to many to be hopelessly . . . bland."[22] Indeed, in their swing to traditionalism and ethnic pride, some Orthodox Jews while appearing to be going back to their own ways ironically followed trends in the general American society which also was turning more conservative and sectarian. Suddenly, the conservative tendency that always remained embedded in Orthodoxy became far more appropriate to the times. Against the background of that notion, there seemed no point in making peace with those who would dilute the genuine Judaism (which the most traditionally oriented Orthodox always believed was in their safekeeping). The idea that the preservation of ethnicity is a barrier against alienation and anomie was easily translated by some Orthodox Jews into the argument that adherence to a strict, aggressively contra-acculturative and Jewish observant life was a bulwark against the ills of alienation and anomie, the legacy of the 1960s. Moreover, few Orthodox Jews forgot that their movement was born out of rejection and contra-acculturation.

Another contributing factor, no doubt, was the institutional maturation and growing affluence of Orthodoxy. At one time, Orthodox Jews had few institutions whose success in America they could point to with pride. By the late seventies, many of those institutions, particularly those of the post–World War II era when a large immigration of Orthodoxy to America occurred, had a few decades of success. The once substantially less affluent Orthodox were now richer, with a generation university educated like their Reform and Conservative Jewish counterparts. Using their newly acquired resources, social status, communal power, and ethnic pride, Orthodox Jews built large numbers of yeshivas, synagogues, *mikvehs*, and other highly visible institutions. The kosher symbol (U) of the Union of Orthodox Jewish Congregations appeared on all sorts of major food products. All these were tangible and undeniable evidence of Orthodox success which simultaneously fostered a sense of self-sufficiency.

The more affluent Orthodox community began to support thousands of full-time Talmud students, young men who would spend a few years of intensive study in yeshivas or *kollels* (postgraduate academies of higher Jewish learning).[23] A celebration of Jewish study was held at Madison Square Garden in the early 1980s and beamed all over the world via cable television. Traditional Jewish study had become a legitimate part of the American landscape, and Orthodox Jews pursued it and the cultural baggage carried along with it vigorously. Not only traditionalist Orthodox but also their more modernist counterparts devoted years to intensive Jewish study—*lernen*—in the yeshiva. Among modernists, the practice of sending young men (and more and more women as well) to a yeshiva (usually in Israel) after their high school years and before entrance into college became a firmly established pattern in Orthodox life during the late 1970s and early 1980s (about two-thirds of Orthodox teenagers have been to Israel by the time they enter college as opposed to perhaps only 15% of non-Orthodox teens).[24] After their studies, these young people from the yeshivas returned to Orthodox communities as highly learned lay people as well as religious virtuosi and thus have come to exercise a significant influence on the tenor of their congregations and communities. As a result of their exposure to traditionalist rabbinic instructors in an isolated setting, their views often tend toward theological conservatism and social insularity, both hallmarks of yeshiva life, as we suggested in Chapter 1.[25]

Finally, and in some measure as a result of these developments, the Orthodox developed a self-image and reputation as being largely exempt from the demographic problems commonly thought to endanger the survival of non-Orthodox Jews. With regard to intermarriage, divorce, birthrates, and assimilation, the Orthodox appeared to themselves and others as far more vital and secure. The Orthodox were not losing their young to assimilation as many had supposed they would.[26] The fact that visible numbers of nonobservant Jews were choosing to "return" to the Orthodox way of life only served to reinforce their confidence.[27] Thus, during recent decades, insularity and separation once again seemed to grow and create boundaries not only between Jew and non-Jew but between the Orthodox and other Jews as well.

Orthodox Boundaries

What is the nature of these boundaries? Where are they drawn and how sharply are they defined? In our analysis we try to assess the extent to which Orthodoxy today is associated with insularity and segregation or with openness and tolerance. We continue to focus on those in the center of our sample of Orthodoxy. We seek to understand the particular tensions they experience in connection with their participation in a community set apart to some extent from the larger American society, on the one hand, and differentiated from the insular traditionalist Orthodox community, on the other. By comparing them with their counterparts to the right and to the left, we can learn, if only by inference, about the competing attractions that pull at them.

Our analysis will revolve around three dimensions of orientations toward a reference group: the cognitive, the affective, and the behavioral. In common parlance, these correspond to three broad questions. What do I think of and how do I perceive the group? How do I feel toward the group? What do I do (or think should be done) with, to, or for the group?

We expect that relative to their counterparts to the left the more traditionally observant Orthodox should be more sectarian and think of themselves as more similar to Orthodox than to other Jews, feel closer to the Orthodox, and be more actively involved in the Orthodox formal and informal community. Similarly, those nominally Orthodox might be expected to display the opposite configuration; while those in the center would be divided on these matters, trying to hold onto dual loyalties and ties.

We also look at the rhetoric surrounding issues of parochialism and cosmopolitanism. The more modern Orthodox have argued that involvement both in the Orthodox community and in the larger society are theoretically reconcilable, that there is such a creature as what we call the "cosmopolitan parochial," someone who can live in the local parish or particular community but still be a cultural citizen of a far more encompassing reality. In contrast, we shall show that, as already noted, traditionalists continue to suggest that integration inevitably promotes assimilation and the concomitant erosion of group survival.

Intergroup Friendship

Of the several ways to assess the extent and nature of identification, commitment, and involvement with the Orthodox community as against non-Orthodox Jewish and non-Jewish alternatives, one of the most crucial areas is that of friendship relations.

Like other moderns who consider themselves to be part of a universal humanity, modern Orthodox Jews have also declared that they can be friends with anyone, including the non-Orthodox Jew and the Gentile.[28] We asked our respondents whether or not they agreed with this sentiment (see table 4.1). Large majorities of Orthodox and non-Orthodox Jews agreed that "an orthodox Jew can be a close friend with Jews of all degrees of observance." At least three-quarters of the non-Orthodox, even more of the nominally Orthodox, and most of the centrist Orthodox agreed or strongly agreed as did three-fifths—a clear majority—of the traditionalists. The principle of amicable ties, a basic feature of modern pluralist societies, was intact even among the putatively insular Orthodox.

Looking closer at the figures, however, we can see some other messages embedded in the results. We discover that the two groups at the extremes, those who are farthest from each other—the non-Orthodox and the traditional-

Table 4.1: Friendship Measures by Orthodoxy

	Orthodoxy			
	Non-Orthodox	Nominal	Centrist	Traditional
An orthodox Jew can be close friends with Jews of all degrees of observance:				
Strongly agree	33	39	41	24
Agree	45	46	47	46
Total	78	85	88	70
An orthodox Jew can be close friends with non-Jews:				
Strongly agree	22	23	24	9
Agree	43	50	46	35
Total	65	73	70	44
How many of your close friends are orthodox?				
All	0	7	13	46
Most	3	29	62	50
How many of your close friends are not Jewish?				
None	27	26	46	67

ists—although generally affected by the pluralism characteristic of the modern situation, were least likely to support the optimistic view that suggested friendship was possible across Orthodox lines. Not only were relatively fewer of them ready to agree in any way with the statement, they were substantially less likely to "strongly agree." While roughly 40% of the nominally and centrist Orthodox strongly agreed they could be close friends with all types of Jews, no matter what their observance, only a third of the non-Orthodox and a mere quarter of the traditionalists answered with such conviction.

Indeed, the people in the middle, centrists and the nominally Orthodox, those who believe in principle that they can bridge the distance between the ties they have to the groups to the right and left of them, display the strongest agreement about the possibility of such ties. For if they were not to do so, they would in effect be expressing doubt about the possibilities and prospects of their own existence. We think they do so because they have the greatest investment in this position. As those standing on the bridge between the traditionalist Orthodox and non-Orthodox worlds, with friends (as we shall show) in both, they need to believe that that bridge is steady and secure. To believe otherwise, to not believe you can move in either direction freely, is to admit to your own isolation. Modern Orthodox Jews are apparently not ready to concede this.

We asked a similar question about the potential for friendship with non-Jews. Although in response we found the same pattern of higher numbers of those in the center agreeing than those on the extremes, the numbers agreeing in one way or another were lower across the board when compared to the previous question on friendship with nonobservant Jews.

While we can only speculate on the reasons for these lower figures, two general reasons suggest themselves. First, although American pluralism and its ethos of integration encourages friendly ties across ethnic and religious ties, the history of Jewish relations with non-Jews—particularly in the last generation—has been fraught with hostility. This has been a time when those relations deteriorated from "prejudice to destruction."[29] And while anti-Semitism remains largely dormant (some would say, absent) in American life, echoes of it still resonate in Jewish consciousness, particularly among those who are so clearly identified as Jews as are the Orthodox. These reverberations of hostility toward Jews may be loud enough to somewhat erode the optimism about the possibility of ties between Orthodox Jews and non-Jews.

Data from recent national surveys of American Jews supports this explanation when it indicates that about two-thirds of all Jews report that they are concerned about American anti-Semitism.[30] Moreover, anxieties about anti-Semitism are more prevalent among Orthodox and Conservative Jews than among Reform and nondenominational Jews. On an index measuring such anxieties, over 45% of the Orthodox scored high as did 44% of the Conservative Jews, but just 31% of the Reform and 28% of the respondents with no denominational identification did so.[31]

Second, for reasons suggested by the discussion of Orthodox Jewish practice and its creation of instrumental ties among Jews, even the most modern of Orthodox Jews cannot but experience greater distance from non-Jews than from their fellow Jews. They simply spend more time intimately tied to other Jews.

Thus, while we find evidence of optimism about the possibility of Orthodox Jewish/non-Jewish ties with between 65%–73% of three categories of respondents agreeing in one way or another with the statement that "an orthodox Jew can be close friends with non-Jews," only a minority (44%) of the traditionalists—the most intensely Jewish respondents in our sample—could hold such a view. Of course, not only do the traditionalists have serious doubts about the possibility of these ties. On the whole, those who feel "strongly" optimistic about the possibilities of close friendly ties with non-Jews are relatively rare. While the 22%–24% of the non-traditionalist Jews were optimistic about such ties—clearly more than only 9% of the traditionalists—even these figures are quite low.

In table 4.1 we also present information not only on attitudes but also on the extent to which the four varieties of respondents do in fact maintain friendships with non-Orthodox Jews and Gentiles. The proportions who reported that "all" of their friends were Orthodox rises dramatically from 0% among the non-Orthodox, to 7% among the nominally Orthodox, 13% among the centrists, and fully 46% among the traditionalists. Similarly, the proportions who reported having mostly ("all" or "most") Orthodox friends increases dramatically as we move from the non-Orthodox left to the traditionalist right (i.e., 3%, 36%, 75%, and 96%). In other words, speaking of the extremes, hardly any (3%) of our largely Conservative non-Orthodox control group reported that most of their close friends were Orthodox; they contrast sharply with the traditionalists, almost all of whom had predominantly Orthodox friendship circles.

The results pertaining to friendships with non-Jews follow a similar pattern. Only a quarter of the non-Orthodox and the nominally Orthodox reported having no Gentile

125

friends as opposed to about half the centrists and two-thirds of the traditionalists.

Thus, at least in terms of friendship patterns, Orthodox behavior runs contrary to the rhetoric that speaks of the potential for Jews integrating into the larger society (Jewish and Gentile) while simultaneously maintaining strong commitments to a Jewish way of life. The greater one's observance of traditional rituals, the more one is ensconced in a predominantly Orthodox informal community. This is not to say, however, that the Orthodox community is completely segregated from the outside world, either non-Orthodox or non-Jewish. Even traditionalists are not hermetically sealed off in a ghetto and maintain some ties, even a few close friendships, with outsiders.

Identification with American Orthodoxy

The extent to which people identify with a particular group can be understood partially by the extent to which they feel close to the group and the extent to which they feel close to those outside the group. But not only do we want to know about affect (feelings), we also want to know about cognition (images). To what extent do people believe they are similar to other members of their group, and to what extent do they see themselves as similar to those outside the group?

We asked respondents to tell us how close they felt both toward most Orthodox Jews and most non-Orthodox Jews. We also asked them a second, parallel pair of questions on the extent to which they thought they were similar to most Orthodox and most non-Orthodox Jews. The results are reported in table 4.2.

Louis Wirth once suggested, "The ghetto is not only a physical fact; it is also a state of mind" corresponding to "attitudes of social distance and of . . . group consciousness."[32] As we might well expect, proportions feeling "very close" toward most Orthodox Jews rise dramatically from the non-Orthodox through the three Orthodox groups. Only a small fraction of the non-Orthodox felt "very close" toward most Orthodox Jews as compared to nearly a third of the nominally orthodox, a bit less than half of the centrists, and almost three-quarters of the tradition-alists.

Although the proportions who expressed this most in-

Table 4.2: Self-Perceptions of Closeness and Similarity to Orthodox and non-Orthodox Jews by Orthodoxy

	Orthodoxy			
	Non-Orthodox	Nominal	Centrist	Traditional
How close do you feel toward most Orthodox Jews?				
Very close	9	29	43	73
Somewhat close	43	59	49	26
Total	52	88	92	99
Non-Orthodox American Jews?				
Very close	24	15	12	17
Somewhat close	51	56	47	33
Total	75	71	59	50
How similar do you think you are to most Orthodox Jews?				
Very similar	4	9	27	57
Somewhat similar	29	52	58	32
Total	33	61	85	89
Non-Orthodox American Jews?				
Very similar	25	8	4	4
Somewhat similar	45	40	39	25
Total	70	48	43	29
Orthodox Closeness Index	−19	15	32	51[a]
Orthodox Similarity Index	−29	7	33	57

[a]Orthodox Closeness/Similarity Indices = (% feeling "very close/similar" to Orthodox Jews − % feeling "very close/similar" to non-Orthodox Jews) + ½ (% feeling "somewhat close/similar" to Orthodox Jews − % feeling "somewhat close/similar" to non-Orthodox Jews). Thus strong feelings were given twice as much weight as equivocal feelings.

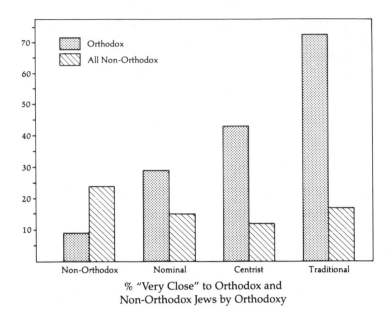

% "Very Close" to Orthodox and
Non-Orthodox Jews by Orthodoxy

tense attachment varied considerably among all four groups, the proportions who felt at least "somewhat close" reveal a large gap between non-Orthodox and Orthodox respondents of *any* variety. Far fewer non-Orthodox felt "somewhat" or "very close" (52%) than did members of the three orthodox groups (88%, 92%, and 99%).

We may infer from these findings that those who hold the most Orthodox beliefs, who are most stringent and punctilious in their observance, also claim to feel closest to other Orthodox Jews (who, as we saw in the previous table, make up the bulk of their friends). To be sure, we cannot say the extent to which the beliefs and practices stimulate the friendships or the extent to which friendships buttress beliefs and practices. What we can say is that in the bundle of behaviors and beliefs we call being Orthodox, friendship with other Orthodox Jews is an undeniable element.

The results from the companion question on feelings of closeness toward non-Orthodox Jews parallel those of the previous question, although in the opposite direction and in a somewhat more muted fashion. Feeling close to the non-Orthodox diminished with traditionalism; the more observant felt less close to (or more removed or even alienated from) the non-Orthodox.

When we looked first at those who claimed to feel "very close" to non-Orthodox American Jews, we discovered that of all of our respondents the non-Orthodox claimed to feel closest to the rest of American Jewry. Nearly one-quarter of them professed such feelings.

Moreover, when we compared the "very close" feelings that the Orthodox felt toward other Orthodox with those feelings they claimed to hold toward non-Orthodox Jewry (29% vs. 15% for the nominally orthodox; 43% vs. 12% for the centrists; and 73% vs. 17% for the traditionalists), it is clear that the intensity of the bond that Orthodox Jews of all denominations share with their fellow Orthodox is significantly greater than that they feel toward the general Jewish population. At least at the affective level, they are indeed a group within a group.

Combining the "very close" with the "somewhat close" feelings, we discovered a threshold "break" lies between the nominally orthodox and the centrists. That is, the nominally Orthodox were closer to the non-Orthodox in their professed feelings of closeness toward "most non-Orthodox American Jews." In both groups about three-quarters felt some sort of closeness to the general Jewish population. In contrast, the centrists and the traditionalists were more like each other in these feelings; only about a half felt in some way close to non-Orthodox Jewry. That is, both of these groups are sufficiently tied up with Orthodoxy and Orthodox Jews to feel a concomitant distance from other kinds of Jews.

Undoubtedly, part of this distance also comes from the experience many Orthodox Jews have had with their non-Orthodox counterparts. One Orthodox informant encapsulated this feeling as follows: "You know the Jews are the worst when it comes to tolerating my Orthodoxy. They always say 'You observe that? You don't really have to; I don't.' Gentiles are often more tolerant. They never claim to know more than me about what Jews can and can't do."

The two other questions on perceived similarity to the Orthodox and to the non-Orthodox largely recapitulate patterns found in the answers to the two "closeness" questions. The more observant more often said they thought themselves similar to other Orthodox Jews. A majority of the Orthodox (89% of the traditionalists, 85% of the centrists, and 61% of the nominally orthodox) thought themselves similar to other Orthodox American Jews. And indeed, looking around at their friends, they were right. Most of those around them were practicing a kind of lifestyle and sharing beliefs like theirs. This is what generated their sense of community and empathy.

Correlatively, the more observant were less likely to say that they felt similar to non-Orthodox Jews. Here too they were right. Relatively more involved in a ritual life that set them apart from other Jews, these Orthodox Jews were not enough like the others to allow for a self-image of being different and for a sense of distance.

It is important here to note as well some of the lines of fracture among the Orthodox. Thus, while huge majorities of the centrists and the traditionalists felt themselves in some way to be similar to other Orthodox Jews, the traditionalist total is made up mostly by those who thought themselves "very similar" to other Orthodox Jews while the centrist figure is made up mostly by those who thought themselves only "somewhat close" to other Orthodox Jews. Clearly, while the centrists experience a sense of cognitive unity with their Orthodox kith and kin, the intensity of that unity is less than that experienced by the more traditionalist Orthodox. This less intense sense of cognitive unity is even more marked among the nominally Orthodox, where only 9% of the total 61% who felt similar to other Orthodox Jews felt "very similar."

Two indices reported at the bottom of table 4-2 summarize the feelings of closeness and similarity to the Orthodox and the non-Orthodox. The indices for both sentiments (closeness and perceived similarity) award "credit" for feeling closeness or for perceiving similarity to the Orthodox, and they subtract credit for parallel feelings toward the non-Orthodox. We gave twice as much credit (or deficit) for the stronger feelings or perceptions ("very . . .") as the weaker responses ("somewhat . . ."). The indices could range from − 100 (signifying total remoteness/dissimilarity from the Orthodox) to + 100 (signifying total closeness/similarity to the Orthodox).

Within each of the four groups, the scores on the two indices are remarkably alike. In both respects the non-Orthodox scores, − 19 (for closeness) and − 29 (for similarity perceptions), clearly leaned away from the Orthodox and inclined toward the non-Orthodox. The nominally Orthodox (scores = 15 and 7) tilted slightly toward the Orthodox. The centrists (32 and 33) were clearly identified with the Orthodox. But of all the groups, the traditionalists (51 and 57) undeniably saw themselves as much closer to and much more similar to most Orthodox Jews than to most non-Orthodox Jews.[33] To be sure, we are not talking about a fragmented community where the divisions are deep and unbridgeable. There were, after all, none who scored anywhere near either a total sense of distance (− 100) or a complete feeling of closeness (100).

What we do see, however, are clear and incontrovertible tendencies of association. Greater ritual observance is closely associated with a sharper and more distinct definition of group boundaries. The more observant more often saw themselves as set apart from the larger world of American Jews, while they more often closely identified with a separate and distinct community of Orthodox Jews.

Charitable Giving as an Illustration of Group Boundaries

In much of what we have written thus far, we have suggested that in many respects American Orthodoxy in general and Orthodox traditionalism in particular is associated with a sectarian orientation which sees Orthodoxy not just as a superior Jewish way of life—"you expect more from Orthodoxy," as Rabbi Reuven Bulka expresses it—but often as the only authentic and legitimate way to live Judaism.[34]

Often, philanthropic issues provide a setting in which to uncover these sectarian sentiments, for at least since bibli-

131

cal times the Jewish people have allowed themselves to be "counted" by what they give to the communal fund.[35] In that regard, we have looked at the extent of Orthodox participation in broad "nonsectarian" Jewish philanthropic life. The relative paucity of Orthodox participation in this giving has long been a concern among some Jewish philanthropic lay and professional officials. Historically, philanthropic leaders, especially those in early twentieth-century New York where some of the earliest and most significant campaigns were mounted, were drawn from what were seen by many as acculturated, if not assimilated, old-line German stock and East European business communities.[36] For this reason and others connected with differences in social class, residence, generation, acculturation, religious orientation, and social networks, the Orthodox came to look upon the collections made by these other Jews as somehow excluding them. Nevertheless, committed to the concept of Jewish charitable giving, the Orthodox constructed and maintained their own infrastructure of philanthropic institutions, distinct from such major community-wide philanthropies as the United Jewish Appeal, Israel Bonds, and the charitable federations. They instead focused most of their attention on the prominent yeshivas—symbols of Orthodox commitment to intensive Jewish life—local day schools or synagogues and other recognizably Orthodox institutions to which the general Jewish philanthropies for many years gave (in the perception of many in the Orthodox community) few if any funds. Thus, among the ways that the Orthodox demonstrated their *otherness* was through their sectarian philanthropy. We wondered whether this was still the case for contemporary Orthodoxy.

Recent analysis of giving among the general Jewish population has revealed that ritual observance is directly related to Jewish philanthropic giving.[37] That is, those who observe little or nothing tend to feel little or no responsibility or pressure to give to Jewish charities. Conversely, those who do maintain some level of ritual observance do give. As a result, some analysts have suggested to the charitable federations that there is a pecuniary payoff for encouraging a higher level of Jewish observance among the population.[38]

Looking only at the federations, UJA and others like it, the principle that "*mitzvas* are worth money," however, seemed to break down when it came to Orthodox Jews. Here were Jews who did maintain a high level of ritual observance but who simply did not give at a proportionately high level to the charities. Indeed, despite the recent heightened philanthropic activities of the more observant (and the greater level of observance among the philanthropically active), UJA/federation professional fundraisers continue to complain, if only anecdotally, that the Orthodox are still underparticipating in the community-wide philanthropic campaign, especially in light of the commitment of Orthodox Jews to the Jewish community.

If this is so, such behavior would be consistent with the theme we have been developing in this chapter. That is, commitment to Orthodoxy entails not merely commitment to Jews as opposed to Gentiles but also a commitment to Orthodox sectarianism as against commitment to the wider Jewish community. As they gave to their own Orthodox in the past, we might expect that they continue to do so in the present. Moreover, we might expect that, as we move away from traditionalism and its relatively high degree of sectarianism, we shall find increased donations (although still limited) to the general Jewish causes.

To examine these matters, we asked our respondents two related questions concerning charitable giving. First, we asked them to allocate a hypothetical $100 among three sorts of charitable causes: "general causes" (such as the Cancer Society), "general Jewish causes" (such as UJA), and "orthodox institutions" (such as yeshivas). We then asked them how much in fact they had contributed to each of these three types of charitable causes over the last year. We found (see table 4.3) that the proportions allocated hypothetically and those reported for actual giving were almost identical. At least in the aggregate, people acted according to the principles they set forth for themselves and according to the logic we have outlined.

Several facts leap out at us when we look at this table.

Table 4.3: Charitable Giving (Hypothetical and Actual) by Orthodoxy

	Orthodoxy			
	Non-Orthodox	Nominal	Centrist	Traditional
Hypothetical giving ("if you had $100 to give, how much would you give to . . .?), e.g.:				
Cancer Society	28	14	12	7
U.J.A.	56	41	31	16
Yeshivas	16	45	57	77
Total	100	100	100	100
Actual giving ("In actuality how much did you give last year to . . . .?), e.g.:				
Cancer Society	285	187	157	92
U.J.A.	575	691	416	188
Yeshivas	201	688	975	1,375
Total	1,061	1,566	1,548	1,655
Percentages:				
General	27	12	10	6
Jewish	54	44	27	11
Orthodox	19	44	63	83
Total	100	100	100	100

First, in absolute terms, on average, the traditionalists gave more money to charity than anyone else. And the other Orthodox Jews gave more than the non-Orthodox ones. Clearly, there is some relationship here worth noting. Moreover, Orthodox Jews are more likely to give to Orthodox charitable institutions, and the more Orthodox are more likely to give more to those institutions. In broad terms, we suggest that as traditionalism increases, so too does charitable support for Orthodox institutions; correlatively, increases in traditionalism are associated with declines in support both for general causes and for general Jewish causes.

Each of the four groups displayed a distinctive pattern of philanthropic attitudes and behavior. The non-Orthodox

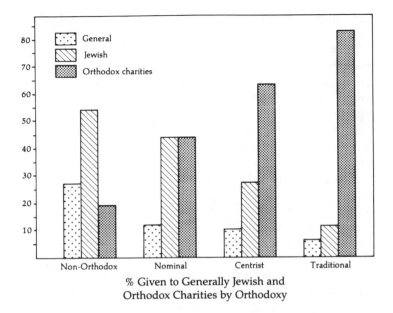

% Given to Generally Jewish and
Orthodox Charities by Orthodoxy

allocated most of their philanthropic dollar to general Jewish causes. Of the remainder, most (more than a quarter of
the total) went for general causes, and the smallest portion
(a sixth of the total) went for Orthodox institutions.

In contrast, the nominally Orthodox were much less devoted to general causes, somewhat less committed to general Jewish causes, and they gave about two-and-a-half
times as much proportionally to Orthodox institutions.
Thus, the nominally Orthodox reported that only one-
eighth of their charitable dollar went for general causes
while the rest was evenly divided (more than two-fifths in
both cases) between general Jewish and specifically Orthodox causes.

The centrist Orthodox displayed yet a third pattern of
giving. They were just as unlikely as were the nominally
Orthodox to support general causes (about a tenth of their
actual giving). But the centrists were much more likely to
support Orthodox institutions and much less likely to give
money to general Jewish causes. In fact, most (about three-
fifths) of their charitable dollar went to Orthodox institu-

tions, and they allocated less than a third to general Jewish causes.

It is as if the centrists were willing themselves to partially leave the orbit of Orthodoxy in their own lives, but all the while they maintained links with the traditionalists even if only by means of their sectarian giving. In light of this finding, an old Jewish custom is worth recalling here. Historically, as certain Jews moved out into the world of commerce and away from the world of Torah study and its associated piety, they often coupled this action with a commitment to financially support those of their brethren who remained in the yeshivas and the sphere of tradition. While some earned, others learned. That custom of those who have moved away from traditional Jewish life without abandoning it completely, continuing to provide maintenance for those who have remained bonded to the tradition, is still part of Orthodox Jewish life. And it is seen most vividly in the centrists (and to an extent in the nominally Orthodox) who, while standing at least partially in the non-Orthodox world, continue to give significant portions of their charitable assets back to the Orthodox.

The traditionalist Orthodox most clearly revealed a sectarian philanthropic pattern. They gave even less than the other groups: only 6% to general causes and a meager 11% to general Jewish causes; almost all their philanthropic dollar (about four-fifths) was donated to specifically orthodox institutions. And, as already noted, they gave on average more money, in absolute terms, than anyone else in our sample. Clearly, when one includes Orthodox Jewish charities in the analysis, the principle that "*mitzvas* are worth money" holds even among the traditionalist Orthodox. They do give more in line with their greater observance. They simply give it to institutions that are part of their traditional Orthodox world.

With utter clarity, these findings demonstrate the extraordinary extent to which ritual traditionalism is associated not only with separation, withdrawal, and distinction from the larger American society; it also implies the drawing of a group boundary around the Orthodox, fencing out not only non-Jews but non-Orthodox Jews as well.

Commitment to Group Perpetuation: Jewish Education of the Children

The commitment to the sustenance of a self-sufficient and self-contained Orthodox community is manifest not only in the charitable domain but in the ways in which the four groups provide their children with formal Jewish education. As we indicated earlier more than a simple pedagogical choice is involved here. People select schools not only for the substance of and values inherent in the education they provide their children but also for the social ties and identity they generate and support. Thus, the choice of a particular kind of school is at once a statement of educational priorities, an expression of social ties, and a symbolic gesture. One might argue, it is a kind of act of communion through which people demonstrate who they are and how they are to be bonded to others. The selection of particular alternatives in Jewish schooling by American Jewish parents is no idle matter, but it reflects their Jewish commitments, worldviews, and aspirations.

To help understand this crucial aspect of Jewish commitment, we asked respondents to report the choices they have made (or are likely to make) for their children's Jewish education. We offered them several alternatives, the most frequently chosen of which were the traditional yeshiva, modern Orthodox day school, Conservative day school, Hebrew school (afternoon school), and Sunday school.

These choices are packed with symbolic, social, and pedagogic meaning to all Jews. They have become particularly important for American Jews. Those earlier in the list generally share several features: they demand more hours of study specifically devoted to Jewish studies, and with that increased emphasis on Jewish curriculum comes a devotion to the world symbolized by those books. In brief, more time spent in sacred literature means greater attachments to the people who choose to guide their lives by these books.[39] Additionally, yeshivas and day schools are sponsored by ideologically more traditional movements than afternoon or Sunday schools; hence enrollment in them is a kind of tacit ideological identification with at least some aspects of these movements.[40]

137

While it is not possible here to review all the nuances of difference that distinguish these schools from one another, some simple distinctions beyond those we set out in Chapter 1 can be made. Perhaps the most basic—as already suggested—is in the matter of the amount of time each institution devotes to Jewish studies. Traditional yeshivas allot the greatest amount of time to sacred learning, and where time is given over to secular (sometimes called "general") studies, this time is as brief as possible. Indeed, in a number of instances the time spent in general studies is only what is considered sufficient to fulfill the requirements set by the civil authorities.[41] Moreover, the staff who teaches Jewish studies in traditional yeshivas often comes from the more contra-acculturative and insular sector of orthodoxy—in part because more often then not many from the more modernist wing have chosen other less parochial careers.

Modern Orthodox day schools offer a range of options between equal time for both Jewish and general studies or increasing the time spent on either one. In principle, however, the schools appear to be generally committed to approximating an even balance. They view both realms as having a legitimate claim upon their students. And if spiritually these institutions are attached to sacred studies, practically they appreciate the logic and importance of a high quality secular education. Unlike traditional yeshivas, the day schools look upon the mixing of the two curricula as desirable. Indeed, many of them, while explaining their *raison d'être* in terms of their commitment to Jewish studies taught in an atmosphere dedicated to Orthodoxy, in practice emphasize the high level of their secular studies. While the traditional yeshivas nominally measure success by the number of their students who continue to study in yeshivas or *kollels,* the day schools pride themselves in the number of admissions their students gain to the prestigious colleges and universities.[42] To be sure, where day schools hire traditionalists to teach their Jewish studies, they often find themselves in a divided struggle for the hearts and minds of their students: Jewish studies with its contra-acculturative, parochial emphasis and secular studies pushing them out into American, contemporary culture.[43]

In many respects the Conservative day school certainly resembles its modern Orthodox counterpart. Both are full-time Jewish schools which teach secular and Jewish subject matter. The major difference between the two, obviously, is in their divergent ideological sponsorship, with all its implications for curriculum, staffing, and ambience. Perhaps a major distinction here concerns the constituency from which the two types of day schools draw their students. While the Orthodox day school, at least nominally, expects a continuity between what the school teaches and the level of Jewish observance in the home, the Conservative day school seems de facto to have fewer such expectations. To be sure, the Conservative day school is a relatively new institution, and accordingly its character has not been fully formed. It owes its existence to the demise of its predecessor institution—the five-day-a-week afternoon Hebrew school—the popularity of the Orthodox day school, the deterioration of public school education in America, and the decline of integrationist anxieties on the part of a generation of Conservative Jewish parents. These parents are secure about "being" American and concerned about the Jewishness of their offspring and, therefore, willing to turn to parochial education with few fears that their children will be ill-equipped to function in and be accepted by the host American society.[44]

The day school has experienced tremendous growth during the decades since World War II (see Chap. 1 for figures of this growth). Every city in the United States with a Jewish population of 7,500 had at least one Jewish day school, as did four out of five of the cities with populations of 5,000–7,500. The overwhelming number of these (which included 425 day schools and 138 Jewish high schools) were under Orthodox auspices.[45] People who in the past might have had to choose between the yeshiva or an afternoon school now have the new option of the day school with its dualistic emphasis on secular and Jewish education. For the modern Orthodox—both those in the center and those slightly left of center—it has, as we shall show below, become the modal institution for the education of their children.

The afternoon Hebrew School—once a five-day-a-week and relatively intensive form of American Jewish education—is today at most a three-day-a-week part-time activity. This school differs markedly from the others thus far mentioned in that it is a part-time institution which supplements public school education. Thus, unlike the yeshiva or day school students, those attending the afternoon (and Sunday) school have the experience of going to a public school with non-Jews and one that excludes religion or any kind of sectarianism from the curriculum. That is, they are products of an educational process that mixes integration (in public school) with sectarian segregation (in the Hebrew school).

In addition, at the afternoon and Sunday schools (which are essentially even more attenuated versions of the afternoon school) not only is the level of Jewish studies quite low but so too is the commitment to Jewish life which is implied by such a limited time investment. While there are numerous options for supplemental school education in the high school years, most Hebrew school students, in contrast with most full-time Jewish school students, complete their formal childhood Jewish education at Bar/Bat Mitzvah age. Although all three movements sponsor afternoon Hebrew schools, the largest number of such schools have been sponsored by the Conservative movement, primarily through their synagogues.

As already intimated, Sunday schools represent the least intensive Jewish educational alternative. Almost universally sponsored by the Reform movement, Sunday schools offer about two or three hours of Jewish education a week for about thirty-five weeks a year. By and large, most of those who attend such schools do so for about five or six school years. No matter how intensive those Sunday school hours are, the curricular possibilities they offer are undeniably limited. Among those receiving Jewish education in America today, those attending Sunday schools tend to come from families with the weakest commitment to conventional Jewish life.[46]

The social and religious distinctions we have described

are familiar to most of those who send their children to these schools or who have themselves attended them. This is particularly true among the Orthodox whose sensitivity to the symbolic significance of Jewish studies decisions is sharpened by their special cultural attachments to this literature.[47] In light of the significance we may ascribe to each choice of Jewish schooling, the distributions of preferred alternatives by level of orthodoxy (table 4.4) are not very surprising.

The proportion preferring yeshiva education for their children rises dramatically from no more than one in ten among the non-Orthodox and the nominally Orthodox, to a third of the centrists, and well over two-thirds of the traditionalists.

Only a small number of non-Orthodox chose the modern Orthodox day school as compared with majorities of the nominally Orthodox and centrists. This is obviously the school of choice among the centrists and a preponderance of the nominally Orthodox. As for the traditionalists, almost all of them who did not opt for the yeshiva preferred the day school. The only group with a sizable proportion choosing the Conservative day school (or other non-Orthodox full-time alternative) was the non-Orthodox where one in five did so. As one would expect, if the Or-

Table 4.4: Jewish Educational Intentions for Children by Orthodoxy

	Orthodoxy			
	Non-Orthodox	Nominal	Centrist	Traditional
Form of Jewish education (do/did/would) give your children?				
Traditional Yeshiva	7	10	32	70
Modern Orthodox day school	12	54	61	29
Conservative day school/other full time	20	5	1	0
Hebrew school	43	19	2	1
Sunday school	6	2	1	0

141

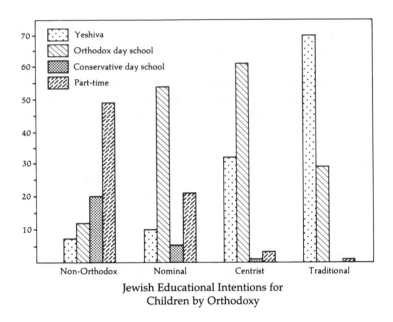

70 — ☐ Yeshiva
☐ Orthodox day school
60 — ☐ Conservative day school
☐ Part-time

Jewish Educational Intentions for
Children by Orthodoxy

thodox choose a full-time option (as, indeed, most did),
they overwhelmingly prefer a school under Orthodox auspices.

While the nominally Orthodox and their non-Orthodox
counterparts may have seemed quite close in their rejection of the yeshiva as a prime educational choice, the difference between these two groups becomes clear when we
look at afternoon Hebrew schools. Almost half of the non-
Orthodox said they prefer the afternoon Hebrew schools,
a proportion over double that among the nominally Orthodox. Hardly any of the centrists or traditionalists chose the
Hebrew school, or any alternative other than an Orthodox
day school or yeshiva. Clearly, an Orthodox Jew who sends
his children to an afternoon school is separating himself
from the dominant currents of Orthodox education.

Finally, very few of our respondents said they preferred
the Sunday school. Of those who did select this option of
marginal Jewish education, the largest proportion (6%) is
found among the non-Orthodox. One might suppose,
therefore, that the great bulk of those attending such

schools come from a population that is far less traditional than those in our sample.[48]

To recapitulate, then, these figures suggest a portrait of dramatically different tendencies in educational preferences among the four groups. A plurality of non-Orthodox preferred the Hebrew school, the rest divided evenly between Conservative and Orthodox full-time education. Most of the nominally Orthodox preferred the modern Orthodox day school, and the remainder chose the Hebrew school. The centrists largely preferred the Orthodox day school, with a healthy minority opting for the yeshiva; among the traditionalists the reverse was true: the majority chose the yeshiva, and a large minority selected the day school.

The patterns of choices of Jewish schooling by the members of each group indicate a devotion to Jewish continuity. Apparently, as parents, our respondents seek to pass on to the next generation the same general approach to Jewish living they are currently enacting in their own lives. And by virtue of the fact that there is a collective consistency in their choices, these selections cannot help but reinforce each group's cultural boundaries. Through the schools (as well as through other institutions they utilize in common), individuals in the Orthodox community who choose the same sort of education as others who share their way of life necessarily intensify their contact with one another. Thus concentrated, they cannot help but perpetuate themselves and harden the social boundaries within which they live.

Moreover, we have here a portrait of intergenerational continuity in particular styles of Orthodoxy (or non-Orthodoxy) which extends not only forward in time but backward to the religious upbringing of our respondents as well.

Jewish Educational Background: Group
Persistence and Fluidity

As earlier noted, the Orthodox community has in recent years established large numbers of yeshivas and day schools to provide formal training for life as an Orthodox Jew in America. Ostensibly, these institutions are there to perpetuate the ways of Orthodox Judaism by providing proper training and a suitable cultural environment for the transmission of a way of life. Some might argue that the schools have taken on gatekeeper as well as socialization functions. That is, not only do they prepare youngsters—and until recently this has meant many more boys than girls—for life in the Orthodox community but, to an unknown extent, the argument might run, those without such training find themselves less than totally comfortable and inadequately socialized into Orthodoxy. The unschooled might, of course, become Orthodox—picking up some practical information (what sociologist Alfred Schutz called "recipe knowledge") in the process of their religious and social development—but in large measure, their lack of schooling would always make them at best neophytes and at worst outsiders.[49] This would be because the experience of becoming Orthodox happens most naturally during the years of schooling and inside Jewish institutions. Indeed, newcomers—those who "return to Judaism"—often find that they must attend a yeshiva of some sort as part of their rite de passage. Thus, while ostensibly a vehicle for training its members, Jewish education and entry into Jewish schools could be said also to serve latently as a barrier to the easy entry of non-Orthodox outsiders.

While no one can doubt the importance of Jewish education in the socialization process, one way to assess its conclusive and definitive importance for entré into Orthodoxy is to compare the respondents' childhood Jewish school attendance patterns with their current level of orthodoxy. In table 4.5 we present the results.

Historically, men, especially the Orthodox, were more likely to have attended full-time Jewish schools as youngsters than women. Accordingly, we consider men and women separately.[50] Among the men we note two sorts of patterns in the data on Jewish school background. While less than one in five of the non-Orthodox attended a full-time (Orthodox) Jewish school in their youth, at least half of the men in each of the other groups did so. Moreover, prior enrollment in a traditional yeshiva is closely asso-

Table 4.5: Jewish Educational Background by Orthodoxy

	Non-Orthodox	Nominal	Centrist	Traditional
	Orthodoxy			
	Predominant form of Jewish educational background			
Men:				
Traditional Yeshiva	8	19	31	49
Modern Orthodox day school	10	33	23	19
Total	19	52	54	68
Women:				
Traditional yeshiva	3	5	14	34
Modern Orthodox day school	6	12	25	30
Total	9	17	39	64
	Years of Jewish educational background			
Men:				
16+ years	2	2	4	19
12–15 years	14	33	46	40
Total	16	35	50	59
Women:				
12+ years	13	23	36	69

ciated with current traditionalism. Each transition from a more lax to a more observant group is marked by a large increase in the proportion of yeshiva alumni (reading from the graphical and ideological left to right, we have: 8%, 19%, 31%, and 49%).

At first glance, when we compare the figures on the educational background of the men and the schools to which they send their children, it appears—at least with regard to the traditional yeshiva—that all groups, except for the traditionalists, have more or less perpetuated the pattern of their education in that of their children. Thus, about 8% of the non-Orthodox went to a traditional yeshiva, and

7% of their children do. For the nominally Orthodox the figures are 19% for the fathers, and 10% for the children. Among the centrists, we find 31% among the fathers and 32% among their children. But among the traditionalists there is a significant jump. Only 49% of the fathers attended yeshivas while fully 70% of the offspring do, did, or are expected to attend such schools. Clearly, this institution is growing in popularity, and its success may presage a move to the right in the next generation of Orthodox in America.

When, however, we look more closely at the table, we can see more of this change in the coming generation over the one that is now fully adult. Among the latter, we found that, among the men, education in a full-time Jewish school is important but in no way is it either a sufficient or necessary precondition for contemporary affiliation with Orthodoxy. If a small majority of currently Orthodox men had a yeshiva or day school education, then it follows that a large minority of them did not; yet they still managed to find their way into the Orthodox community. Moreover, even in the case of the traditionalist Orthodox, while prior study at a traditional yeshiva is perhaps conducive to or at least associated with subsequent adult Orthodoxy—and nearly half the traditionalist Orthodox men reported having that kind of an education—it is obviously not an absolutely indispensable precondition to passage into the traditionalist Orthodox community. Thus, the gatekeeping function of yeshiva or day school Jewish education appears not to have been a precondition for the current adult generation; but for the next—those now in yeshivas and day schools—the story appears to be different.

Looking at the women, we find similar relationships between Jewish education and traditionalism, but at a lower level. Many fewer non-Orthodox and nominally Orthodox women attended a traditional yeshiva in line with the prevailing norm in previous generations which limited yeshiva study to males. Nonetheless, among the traditionalists, almost as many women went to some form of full-time Jewish school as the men, but they were almost evenly divided between yeshiva and day school alumnae (34% and 30%) while the men predominantly attended yeshiva (49%

vs. 19% for day school alumni).[51] Clearly, there are still differences among the Orthodox with regard to the sorts of
Jewish education offered men versus that offered the
women. The latter are still less likely to be provided with
the intensive experience of the yeshiva and as such are
kept out of the elite society of "Torah sages."

Even so, we do find with the women, as we did with the
men, a steady increase in full-time alumnae associated
with increases in ritual observance (i.e., 9%, 17%, 39%,
and 64% for the four groups from left to right). That is,
there is a correspondence between level of observance and
intensity of Jewish education. Similarly, we find a parallel
increase in attendance at traditional yeshivas, although
only traditionalist women displayed a sizable proportion
of yeshiva alumnae (3%, 5%, 14%, and, among the traditionalist women, 34%). There is in all this an echo of sociologist Everett Hughes's assertion that a person "partici-
pates in some fashion in a complement of institutions
corresponding to his peculiar wants and his status in the
community."[52]

Parental Religiosity: More Evidence of
Continuity and Permeability

To obtain a complete picture of intergenerational transmission of Orthodoxy and the permeability of the group
boundaries of the Orthodox community, we need to examine variations in parental religiosity among the four
groups. We asked our respondents to report on four aspects of their parents' religious practice. These include
whether parents maintained two sets of dishes, whether
they refrained from turning on lights on the Sabbath, and
how often they attended synagogue (we asked separate
questions for mothers and fathers). From these four questions we can get a reasonable portrait of variations in parental religiosity by level of Orthodoxy (see table 4.6).

Looking first at one of the most common practices
among Orthodox Jews—having two sets of dishes (i.e.,
keeping something of a kosher kitchen)—we quickly ascertain a small but noticeable minority of currently Orthodox

Table 4.6: Parental Religiosity by Orthodoxy

	Orthodoxy			
	Non-Orthodox	Nominal	Centrist	Traditional
Parents maintained two sets of dishes	67	83	83	90
Parents refrained from turning on/off lights on the Sabbath	27	42	61	83
	Synagogue attendance			
Father:				
Every day	5	4	15	48
Once a week or more (but not every day)	16	30	31	29
Once a month or more (but not every week)	25	33	25	12
High holy days (or a few other occasions too) or less often	55	34	29	11
Mother:				
Every day	4	2	13	10
Once a week or more (but not every day)	16	36	33	41
Once a month or more (but not every week)	26	33	23	32
High holy days (or a few other occasions too) or less often	54	28	31	18

respondents who were reared in homes whose religious practice suggests they were far from Orthodoxy. About one in ten of the traditionalists and one in six of the two other Orthodox groups reported their parents failed to maintain two sets of dishes for meat and dairy. As we would expect, the comparable proportion among the non-Orthodox was even higher: about one-third. Thus, although those who are currently more observant are more likely to have been reared in a home where a minimal prerequisite for kashrut was observed, still a small group of currently Orthodox (about 10% among the traditionalists and 15% among the centrists) have apparently considerably intensified their religious practice in comparison with their upbringing.

Even more striking evidence of this dynamism of increasing Orthodoxy can be found in our data on parental observance of the prohibition on turning lights on and off on the Sabbath. The proportions who reported such parents increase steadily from a quarter of the non-Orthodox, to two-fifths of the nominally orthodox, to three-fifths of the centrists, and to over four-fifths of the traditionalists. Clearly, those who are currently more observant had more observant parents than those who are less observant today. But we find the discrepancies between parental and contemporary respondent ritual behavior at least as interesting as the similarities.

We recall from our data on ritual behavior that all of the traditionalists refrained from turning on lights on the Sabbath as did almost all (92%) of the centrists, very few (18%) of the nominally Orthodox, and hardly any (2%) of the non-Orthodox (see table 2.1). Combined with the parental data, these figures point to considerable change between generations. About a third of the centrists—in this sample—have taken on religious obligations their parents did not observe, as did about half as many traditionalists.

This portrait of both generational correspondence and change also emerges in our data on parental synagogue attendance. The "typical" father of our non-Orthodox respondents attended only on the High Holidays (or a few other occasions); the fathers of the nominally Orthodox attended about once a month or more; the fathers of the centrists went about once a week or slightly more often; finally, the fathers of the traditionalists attended, most generally, every day.[53]

As an aside, for all but the traditionalists, the service attendance patterns of mothers are very comparable to those of the fathers of the same respondents in the same Orthodoxy group. Mothers of traditionalist respondents were much less likely to attend every day, and more likely to attend once a month or once a week than were comparable fathers—but then women's attendance in the synagogue was traditionally a rare occurrence among the most observant Jews of previous generations. For them, a woman's proper place was at home, caring for children.

From these data we can infer that parents indeed have been highly influential in rearing Orthodox youngsters (our respondents). More observant respondents do indeed derive from more observant upbringings. However, the discrepancies between parents and children also displays intergenerational change, as we have already suggested. It is clear, then, that modern Orthodoxy allows for considerable entry and exit intergenerationally if not, possibly, intragenerationally as well.

Conclusion

To be Orthodox inevitably induces a withdrawal from psychic, institutional, and informal participation in the larger society not only of non-Jews but, in many ways, of non-Orthodox Jews as well. Contemporary Orthodox Jews appear to have every intention of perpetuating their way of life in the next generation. Some individual parents may well fail in this attempt, although, if our inferences from our data on parents and respondents are correct, most will not. To be sure, as we have tried to show, the Orthodox community, as coherent and as bounded as it may be, still allows for formerly non-Orthodox Jews to join it and, in true fashion, cannot prevent some of its erstwhile members from departing its confines as well.

But, Orthodoxy is not a monolith. In this chapter, our emphasis has been on affective and cognitive dimensions by which contemporary American Orthodox Jews distinguish themselves from the non-Orthodox and from one another. These matters are undoubtedly interwoven with symbolism and ideology. Nevertheless, the data makes clear that at least at one level of analysis, Jewish orthodoxy is *as much a matter of sociology as of theology.* While what they believe is surely important, people display and express their Orthodoxy through their decisions of social belonging and communal ties. The questions are often not what we believe or which commandments we ought to observe in order to be counted among the Orthodox. Rather, the implicit questions can also be, Who are we like and to whom do we feel close? To whom do we give our charity and with whom do we want our children to spend their school time? What institutions are we ready to belong to and with which will we allow ourselves to be publicly identified? These are of course not decisions unique to Orthodox Jews; they are the stuff of everyday life for all of us. But when these sorts of questions are asked and decisions reached by the Jews we have examined, the Orthodox look to the past, to their own patterns of life, to those of their parents and friends, and align themselves and their children accordingly.

Some questions remain. Among them are those that ask whether or not Orthodoxy changes not only affiliations but also one's worldview and ties to the ethos of the host society in which most Jews find themselves. These issues will be discussed in the next chapter.

5   The Ethos of Orthodoxy: Political,
     Social, and Sexual Attitudes

> Assimilation, it is true, makes progress insofar as
> some Jews come into more intimate contact with
> non-Jews and all Jews more and more adopt the cul-
> tural patterns of their surroundings. But at the same
> time, Jews also create the instruments that continue
> to hold them together and help them maintain a
> separate social identity.
>
> Jacob Katz, *Out of the Ghetto*

The previous chapters have traced lines of cleavage among traditionalist Orthodox, those in the center, and those who are generally little more than Orthodox in name. And we have also compared and contrasted all these Orthodox Jews to those who, albeit not altogether nonobservant or nonbelieving, nevertheless choose not to call themselves Orthodox. We have detailed how the more traditionalist observe ritual practices more frequently, how they express more fervent beliefs in established religious tenets, and how they are more deeply embedded in and committed to the community of fellow Orthodox Jews. Concomitantly, we have demonstrated how those Jews who are further away from traditionalist positions and loyalties tend to be relatively less observant ritually, less fervent in their religious beliefs, and less firmly bonded to other Orthodox Jews (or, as they might prefer to characterize this last quality, more open to creating ties with other communities of people).

In light of all this, one would be surprised if this pattern of variation did not display itself in what might be called the ethos of Orthodoxy, the moral and evaluative elements, the underlying attitude toward themselves and their world that their way of life reflects.[1] In particular, we would expect the more traditionalist Orthodox to display an ethos in which they express somewhat greater detachment from, if not downright skepticism of, certain features of contemporary life and American culture, to espouse more conservative political views, and to conduct a more conservative personal life, as might be exemplified most vividly in their attitudes toward premarital sex. In these—and other

153

cultural, social, and political areas—the most traditional should stand in sharp contrast to the bulk of non-Orthodox American Jews who as a group have a largely deserved reputation for having an ethos that supports liberal world-views, if not a sort of "super-modernism." Moreover, because they are situated between the traditionalists and the non-Orthodox, the centrists and those who, however tenuously, hold onto the Orthodox label might be expected to display some sort of ambivalence. The potentiality for sharp value conflicts and the clash of worldviews within these intermediate groups along with the implied struggle to resolve or at least ameliorate the conflicts between the Orthodox ethos and the one characteristic of the cultural, social, and political domains of the larger society is the subject of this chapter.

Reverence for the Past, Ambivalence about the Present

For many reasons, all Orthodox Jews ought to view the modern world with greater wariness and trepidation than more integration-minded Jews. To the great bulk of Jews, modernity—and particularly the events of the last 150 years—has meant an opening to opportunities, an escape from the ghettoization of their immediate ancestors, and an end to enforced cultural and social isolation. To the Orthodox, modernity has meant these things as well. Yet, while their non-Orthodox counterparts looked upon these consequences of modernity as largely positive, the Orthodox—as we have already intimated—saw them as threatening and not altogether congenial to the Jewish survival. Not only were they concerned about assimilation, which they saw as "the suicidal extinction of the Jewish being," they were also anxious about the possible contamination of the Jewish way of life by perspectives and experiences that came out of a largely Christian culture which informed and shaped the societies that greeted them on the other side of the ghetto's boundary.[2]

Those Orthodox who were ready to get out wanted to "get out as Jews, with our own spiritual treasures."[3] They wanted to hold on to their reverence for the past, even as they moved—or rather as they were nudged—into a world that tried to emphasize progress and the future. And so when at last they ventured out of the "four cubits of Jewish life," the Orthodox, while taking advantage of what the modern world had to offer, did so with caution and less than blazing enthusiasm.

And yet, as we have already seen, Orthodoxy is not monolithic. Almost from the beginning, some Orthodox became more open to what they perceived as the advantages of life outside or at the edges of the Jewish orbit, while others turned away from the outside world as much as possible.[4]

In line with this antecedent pattern of responses, and given the variations in ritual behavior, belief, and communal bonding as we have already discovered among the Orthodox, we should not be surprised to encounter still today a number of significant differences between the more traditionalist Orthodox and the others with regard to their enthusiasm for selected aspects of the modern world, particularly those which offend or endanger their reverence for the past, their religious faith, and their quasi-traditional home and community life.

For example, the more traditional might well view engagement with contemporary affairs as a distraction from what to them are the genuinely significant areas of cognitive engagement, such as the study of sacred texts; or they may view such involvement as diverting good Orthodox Jews from giving their maximal psychic energy in the public sphere to the affairs of the Jewish (and, more particularly, the Orthodox) community. For them, certain aspects of the modern world may not only be seen as competing with Orthodox involvements, they may actually be perceived as endangering them in some ways. Moreover, popular culture—as perhaps epitomized by movies and newspapers—might be seen as something to be eluded or at best tolerated but not followed.

Even the scientific world, perhaps the epitome of modern progress, has always been a two-edged sword for the Orthodox. On one side, it symbolizes the world of technological advancement, the incarnation of universalism and rationality, and antagonist (at least in theory) to bigotry and intolerance, which has afforded many benefits to mankind in general and to Jews in particular. However, to more traditional Jews—like more fundamentalist members of other religious communities—its other side is the challenge and indeed the undermining threat that science and its commitment to unbridled progress and change presents to beliefs in religiously inspired and accepted versions of creation and history. Where the scientific method predominates, an attachment to religious ritual seems arcane and archaic.

Related to these attitudes toward modernity, contemporary culture and affairs, and science are variations among more traditional and more modern Orthodox Jews in their attitudes toward the past and present (or future) generally. The traditionals, more than the moderns, conceive of themselves as struggling against the seduction and invasive modern world—with its celebration of change and novelty—to preserve the truly essential aspects of ancient Jewish life and tradition. They cannot altogether escape from the modern world (although many of those who are even more traditional than the most traditionalist in our sample do even more to fence out contemporary society and its influences). But neither do they—at least in their own conceptualization—admit to its legitimacy or readily honor its authority. The past may be gone or fighting a losing battle against the present and future, but certain aspects of it need to be both preserved and applied in the modern condition. What's "new," traditionalists assert in deeds and words, may not always be "improved." Change is not always for the better. There's much to be said even today for "that old-time religion."

One last point. While we may find variations in attitude and outlook that distinguish among the Orthodox and between them and other Jews, these variations may not always be supported in action. That is, people often claim to believe one thing while they in fact do another. Although one may be tempted to conclude from such contradictions that some people are less than honest with themselves and others, that discovery would not be important for our consideration of Orthodox Jewry, for this apparent hypocrisy is not a quality unique to them by any means. Rather, what *is* important to us here, if such contradictions between stated beliefs and actions are discovered, is the persistence of the claim to be traditional in outlook. Even if the assertion of an Orthodox ethos puts them in contradiction with themselves, some Jews nonetheless still choose to make this assertion. That in itself is noteworthy for it suggests that there are people who *choose* to present themselves as more Orthodox than they really are. In a world where most people choose to present themselves as "up-to-date," flexible, and forward looking, the fact that some people adopt an opposite public face is news.

We may begin with an examination of the extent to which the Orthodox of all types are involved in the contemporary world and popular culture. We look as well at their openness to science and scientific inquiry.

The Contemporary World

As seen in table 5.1, we asked two questions which indicated actual participation in the contemporary culture: "During the work week, how often do you listen to or watch news broadcasts or read the daily newspaper?" and "During the last year, did you go to any R- or X-rated movies?" In both instances, participation was nearly equivalent across all four observance groups. Roughly nine in ten in each of the four groups we have been examining said they viewed, heard, or read about the news "every day."

Between 57% and 72% (with no clear-cut association with traditionalism) of the four groups said they had attended a somewhat risqué movie in the last year. Thus, at least in terms of exposure and involvement, the more traditional respondents in the sample were no less active than their more modern, even non-Orthodox counterparts.[5]

But despite the absence of significant and consistent variation in modern cultural engagement, as exemplified by following the news or going to all kinds of movies, we do find regular patterns of differences in stated attitudes to contemporary life. We asked two questions about perspec-

Table 5.1: Indicators of Contemporary Involvement and Commitment by Orthodoxy

	Orthodoxy			
	Non-Orthodox	Nominal	Centrist	Traditional
During the workweek, how often do you listen to or watch news broadcasts or read the daily newspaper?				
Every day	86	89	86	94
During the last year, did you go to any R- or X-rated movies?				
Yes	69	57	72	64
It is important to learn and know about matters of contemporary life:				
Strongly agree	62	55	54	41
Agree	37	43	42	54
The past is largely irrelevant to the present:				
Strongly disagree	46	54	66	80
In principle, there are no fields of scientific inquiry a good Jew should not pursue:				
Strongly agree and agree	88	84	81	75
My children should learn about the theory of evolution in school:				
Strongly agree	37	33	26	17
Agree	56	56	59	57

tives on the past and present. The first asked for reactions to the statement, "It is important to learn and know about matters of contemporary life." As might be expected, agreement (answering "agree" or "strongly agree") to this near platitude was almost universal among all groups. However, the non-Orthodox were substantially more likely to "strongly agree" than were the traditional Orthodox (62% vs. 41%), with the other two groups scoring in between (55% and 54%). To us, these findings mean that the non-Orthodox were enthusiastic more often (or at least less reserved) about participation in contemporary affairs, while the more traditional groups more readily experienced some doubt or hesitation about expressing such an unqualified commitment to contemporary involvement.

We find even more substantial differences in response to the question, "The past is largely irrelevant to the present." Here only a minority (46%) of the non-Orthodox "strongly disagreed" as contrasted with the vast majority (80%) of the traditionalists. The other two Orthodox groups again scored in between (54% and 66%). In other words, unqualified affirmation of the importance of the past is closely related with the acceptance of traditional Orthodox ritual obligations. The centrist, nominally Orthodox, and non-Orthodox respondents had less trouble adopting the modern, perhaps characteristically American ahistoric view of the world, one that sees the present as largely detached from the past. For traditional Jews, of course, the infusion of meaning and Divine purpose into the course of events, from the past into the present and onward to the future, is a central sustaining tenet of Jewish belief and practice.

Finally, table 5.1 displays responses to two questions on attitudes toward science. The vast majority of respondents from all four groups agreed with the statement: "In principle, there are no fields of scientific inquiry a good Jew should not pursue." That is, they associated themselves with the principle of unbridled research, believing that they could do so without undermining their status as "good Jews." In this, our sample of Orthodox Jews show themselves to have been influenced by their educational backgrounds—which are weighty. Among men in this sample, almost two-thirds of the self-identified Orthodox had a postgraduate degree, and over 80% had a college degree. The differences in education by traditionalism were minor: most of our most traditionalist group reported postgraduate degrees, and over 80% said they had received a college degree. Among women, over 40% had postgraduate degrees (although only a quarter of the traditionalists so claimed), and over two-thirds had a college degree (as did 60% of the most traditional).

Despite their extensive secular educations, however, the traditionalist Orthodox were outscored (albeit slightly) by the non-Orthodox (88% to 75%), with the centrist and nominally Orthodox groups in between (84% and 81%). In contrast, the query on the far more religiously sensitive question of teaching the theory of evolution uncovered much more dramatic differences. As we would expect among such a relatively well-educated sample population, all four groups had vast majorities (ranging from 74% among the traditionalists to 93% among the non-Orthodox) agreeing that their "children should learn about the theory of evolution in school." However, far fewer of the more traditional indicated unqualified or robustly enthusiastic approval of the idea by responding with "strongly agree." Here the proportions systematically decline as traditionalism increases: from 37% among the non-Orthodox, to 33% among the nominally Orthodox, to 26% among the mainstream Orthodox, and only 17% among the most traditional.

Clearly, while this highly educated group of Orthodox Jews values learning about science and other matters of contemporary affairs, the more traditional have reservations about such attitudes or carefully circumscribe them. In particular, as we have seen, the more traditional— though involved in and committed to contemporary life— do not extend such commitments so far as to seriously negate the importance of the past. Though they recognize the worth of learning about science generally, they are not totally comfortable with learning about areas of science that at least in popular attitudes are associated with the subversion of traditional beliefs. The traditionalists, then, more than the others, display an ambivalence toward the modern world in which they are all inescapably a part.

The Orthodox: A Conservative Exception to the Liberal Rule

American Jews, indeed Jews in Western societies, tend overwhelmingly to be politically liberal. To be sure, American Jewish attitudes on public issues, electoral preferences, and political involvements range over the entire political spectrum. Nevertheless, national polls, social research studies, and other less formalized sorts of evidence have demonstrated that the center of the Jewish political distribution is something of the order of fifteen to twenty-five percentage points to the left of the American center, depending on the issue, measure, or election.[6]

The most widely noted evidence of persisting Jewish liberalism, of course, appears almost every year or two in the form of electoral results. For decades, roughly three-quarters of American Jews have voted for Democratic congressional candidates. In several recent big-city mayoral elections between white and black candidates, Jews have led all other white ethnic groups in their electoral support of black candidates. In presidential races—with the exception of 1980—Jewish votes for Democratic candidates have exceeded the national average by fifteen to twenty-five percentage points. In 1984, for example, Jews were the only white ethnic group to give majority support to Walter Mondale.[7]

Jews' liberal tendencies emerge in other ways as well. They are reportedly overrepresented as political activists of all sorts in liberal and social change–oriented causes—be they operatives, contributors, organizers, or intellectual leaders. Moreover, their liberalism extends beyond a narrow partisan definition. Indeed, it is connected to, reflects, and buttresses other allied cultural and social attitudes. For example, surveys of attitudes toward nonconforming groups (such as Communists) or nonconforming behavior (such as premarital sex or abortions) report that Jews express among the most tolerant views of all ethnic or religious groups.[8] The latest survey data on Jewish public attitudes document that their levels of political liberalism and cultural tolerance in a wide variety of areas are higher than the American average.[9] These areas include support for affirmative action for minorities, the Equal Rights Amendment (in its time), civil liberties for homosexuals, government aid for abortions for poor women, and less forcefulness and more diplomacy in American dealings with the Soviets as well as endorsement of the goals and philosophy of welfare programs for the poor. In the same surveys, Jews steadfastly opposed any lowering of the church-state barrier (in the form of aid to private schools or of introducing a moment of silent meditation in the public schools), and they expressed a very dim view of the politically conservative, Christian-oriented Moral Majority. Among all Americans in the early 1980s, self-proclaimed conservatives outnumbered liberals by a three-to-two ratio; among Jews, the proportions were the reverse. In the spring of 1984, four times as many Jews identified as Democrats than as Republicans; at the same time, among all Americans, Democrats held only a three-to-two lead over the GOP.

But why have Jews been overwhelmingly liberal? Perhaps the key feature of their existence that has contributed to the liberalism of the Jews has been their minority status. A society that offered Jews admission only if the Jew became "naturalized," changed from his "unnatural" Jewishness, if he underwent what the Germans called *verbesserung*, did not really open improvement or better conditions. Such emancipation was simply another form of enforced conversion. Whereas traditional societies offered Jews entry if they became Christians, so-called modern societies seemed to offer access if they became secular.[10] Finding themselves afloat in an often hostile sea of Gentiles, Jews have for generations been aware that they would benefit most in a society that promoted tolerance and countenanced pluralism. At the core of the ethos of liberalism is an attitude that "legitimates the ideology of cultural pluralism" and as such accepts the rights of people to be different without having to sacrifice their human or civil rights.[11]

To be sure, while cultural pluralism allows Jews to remain Jews even as they enter the larger society, it also fosters exposure to intimate contact with non-Jews. That contact leads at times to what some have called "cultural relativism," which "weakens and often shatters the protective walls around all the traditionally integrated worlds of meaning; the 'others,' once distant strangers, now become neighbors in a sometimes uncomfortable way."[12] In a pluralistic world, Jews live among Gentiles—but Gentiles can also live among Jews. Liberalism that encourages pluralism thus often leads to reform, reconstruction, and change. It is not for nothing that Reform and other non-Orthodox Jews frequently call themselves "liberal Jews" and their philosophy "progressive Judaism."

But minority status and the support for pluralism that it fosters has not been the only source for Jewish liberalism. Education and professional affiliation have been another. In the process of modernization and acculturation, Jews in the United States—as in other Western societies over the last century or so—have tended to achieve a higher educational level than the general society in which they find themselves. Moreover while Jews, as a group, have the highest level of educational attainment in the United States, it is the Jews with a postgraduate degree who are the most liberal of all. Closely connected with this finding is the relationship between cosmopolitan intellectualism and political liberalism: Jews who read intellectual or culturally upper-middle-brow publications are far more liberal than the rest. In short, higher education and participation in the cosmopolitan intellectual subculture are two complementary channels by which Jews fortify their liberalism. In fact, higher education has such a strong influence on Jewish political attitudes that rich Jews are much more liberal than their wealthy Gentile counterparts, and they are generally no less liberal than less affluent Jews. One important reason for these apparent anomalies is that Jews come by their affluence, perhaps more than other groups, by way of higher education. Thus, among those with the same level of education, wealthier Jews are indeed less liberal than the less affluent, but very few wealthy Jews these days lack a B.A. or even higher degree.[13]

Jews have gravitated to the intelligentsia and allied professions. It happens that members of these professions—academia, law, journalism, media, social service professions, and cultural occupations—tend to espouse some of the most liberal political views. These professionals—Jews and non-Jews alike—are even more liberal than the larger group of generally liberal postgraduate degree holders from whom they are drawn. Thus, there at least two groups of factors that act to make Jews liberal: (1) their minority status, and (2) their high social status consisting of high educational attainment and considerable occupational concentrations in intellectual and cultural professions.

To be sure, many observers have claimed that Jews are liberal because of the historic Jewish value of compassion, charity for the poor, and identification with oppressed minorities. But the case of the Orthodox points up a problem with this explanation. If the argument is correct, one would think that those most familiar with historic Jewish values, the Orthodox, the most traditional, would also be the most liberal. But that is, as we shall see, not the case.

There are some problems as well with using minority status as an explanation for liberalism, as pointed up by the case of the Orthodox. The Orthodox are after all those whose social lives are most enclosed within the minority group—the minority among a minority. Accordingly, they should be among the most liberal. In fact, they are not.

One reason is that historic Jewish values simply are not unambiguously liberal. They offer legitimation for both conservative and liberal stances in several areas. They are particularist as well as universalist; they extol the revered and ancient perhaps even more than the "new and im-proved"; they sanction collective authority as well as individual liberties; and they can validate the aristocratic oli-garchy of the rabbis as much as, or more than, popular democracy. In brief, being "Torah true" does not necessar-ily mean being liberal.[14]

On the contrary, one might argue that the further away one goes from the Torah-true way (the *halacha* is after all "the way," *one* way and not another), the more one must become associated with liberal ideas that legitimate free-dom of choice, that give approval to many ways. That is why most of the non-Orthodox have tended to prefer lib-eral to conservative traditional Jewish values, while tradi-tionalists—who are *halachic*—have tended to make the op-posite choice. According to this principle, we might expect that those Orthodox Jews who have moved away from "the way" through contacts with Gentiles, educational ad-vancement, and professionalization, those who have aligned themselves more closely with the mainstream of American life, will be more liberal than those who have re-mained insular, attached to the relatively more isolated world of Jewish tradition.

But there is a catch here. At what point do education—that is, secular education—and professionalization and the liberal ethos that accompanies them outweigh or at least mitigate the more conservative ethos of Orthodoxy? And what happens when the opposing influences are close to perfectly balanced? To take a simple example, what happens if one's education and political affiliations lead one to believe that in a pluralist society homosexuality is simply one of several legitimate sexual orientations, while one's commitment to the way of *halacha* suggests that it is sinful depravity? What stand does one take? We might hypothesize that those more inclined toward traditionalism will undoubtedly look at homosexuality as wrong, while those who tend in the other direction will, if not altogether be prepared to endorse its legitimacy, either prevaricate or at least weaken their opposition to it.

Or consider the matter of educational policies. Many Orthodox Jews feel they have little to lose and much to gain from the adoption of what are often conservative-sponsored (and church-supported) educational policies. Attempts to introduce prayer or celebrate Christian holidays in the public schools have little effect on Orthodox families nowadays since most send their children to yeshivas and day schools.[15] Moreover, in a certain sense, such attempts confirm rather than offend many Orthodox Jews' view of American society. Stated in its crudest form, this view puts little store in the pluralist conception of American society. Instead, it concedes the society is inherently Christian, and perhaps some Orthodox would go so far as to say Jews should be taught to understand that.

Another conservative educational policy proposal, increasing aid for private and parochial schools, also sits well with many Orthodox Jews. With so many of their children in private religious schools, the prospect of having some of their tax dollars supporting Christian schools is but a small price to pay for government support of Orthodox school budgets and tuitions.

Insofar as the government does make policies affecting the citizenry's moral choices in such areas as abortion, gender equality, and sexuality, Orthodox Jews should be more inclined to support policies encouraging a more traditionalist morality. A more culturally conformist public policy can only help to facilitate the perpetuation of a more traditionalist morality and life-style in their semi-insular communities.

As we noted above, personal relations with those outside one's group do tend to diminish particularism and parochialism by introducing a plurality of worldviews into one's life. Chapter 4 demonstrates that the Orthodox do tend to restrict their intimate associates not merely to Jews but—especially among the more traditionalist—to Orthodox Jews in particular. And the more traditional, the more enclosed one is in an Orthodox community, the less concerned one is with the needs of non-Jews and of non-Orthodox Jews (as the charitable donation findings in Chap. 4 showed). Thus, the interpersonal insularity of Orthodoxy should also strengthen their Jewish and Orthodox group particularism and, thereby, cultural, social, and political conservatism as well.

In sum, more traditional Jews have several reasons for rejecting the liberalism of the non-Orthodox Jewish majority. These reasons include, in some instances, clear *halachic* dictates, unambiguous institutional interests, a preference for more traditional personal life-styles, an interest in public policies that protect traditional mores in private life, and insular personal networks. The findings related to various social attitudes demonstrate the operation of all these factors (see table 5.2).

As already noted, one area where the conflict between traditional religious norm and contemporary latitudinarian attitudes come most to the fore is that of homosexuality. The Torah and Jewish tradition appear unequivocal in their condemnation of homosexuality as an "abomination." In contrast, the last decade or so has witnessed a growing gay rights movement in the United States. The movement's leaders have argued that homosexuality should be freed of the stigma once attached to it and that it represents a perfectly valid, respectable, and legitimate life-style choice. In response, many rabbis and other American religious leaders have criticized the growing acceptance of homosexuality in the larger society, while expressing sympathy for homosexuals as individuals. As might be expected, Orthodox rabbis in general have been in the forefront of the opposition to the gay rights movement. In contrast, the Reform movement has sanctioned homosexual synagogues by including them in their movement, the Union of American Hebrew Congregations.

In recent research, Jews nationwide overwhelmingly en-

Table 5.2: Political and Social Attitudes by Orthodoxy

	Orthodoxy			
	Non-Orthodox	Nominal	Centrist	Traditional
Homosexuality is wrong:				
Strongly agree and agree	40	64	66	92
The government should give aid to nonpublic schools:				
Strongly agree and agree	34	46	65	75
The government should not pay for abortions:				
Strongly disagree and disagree	66	56	55	36
A wife should make her own decisions even if she disagrees with her husband:				
Strongly agree and agree	78	71	65	46
The Equal Rights amendment (ERA) should be passed:				
Strongly disagree and disagree	61	48	47	29
Affirmative action should be used to help disadvantaged groups:				
Strongly agree and agree	48	46	44	37
The death penalty should be abolished:				
Strongly disagree and disagree	62	61	60	59

dorsed the liberal notion that homosexual individuals should have the same rights as other people.[16] A substantial minority, however, felt troubled by the rise in the visibility of homosexuality. These discrepant views can be accounted for by the strong commitment on the part of most Jews to restricting the activities of the government in what they regard as the private sphere. As a minority seeking integration and wary of how the larger society will apply and enforce its moral standards, Jews have an interest in official tolerance of nonconforming groups. It is as if to say that if the society can accept and the government can protect the free exercise of homosexuals' civil rights, then the position of the Jews—a less stigmatized minority—is that much more secure. Commitment to official tolerance of homosexuals, however, may have little connection with one's private opinion of them, the latter being often affected by deeply rooted religiocultural values.

When we asked our respondents in this study whether they thought "homosexuality is wrong," 40% of the non-Orthodox replied in the affirmative, a proportion strikingly similar to the proportion of all sorts of Jews nationwide who are "troubled by the rise of homosexuality" in the recent survey. As one would expect, the proportions agreeing that homosexuality is wrong were significantly higher among the nominally and centrist Orthodox groups (64% and 66%), and almost unanimous (92%) among the most traditional.

There are two ways one can look at these findings. One may focus on the obviously strong correlation of Orthodox traditionalism with moral condemnation of homosexuality—increases in the former certainly were associated with increases in the latter. This said, we can, however, look at another crucial feature of these findings: over a third of the two intermediate Orthodox groups—those who stood between traditionalist Orthodoxy on the one extreme and non-Orthodoxy on the other—refrained from endorsing the straightforward view that "homosexuality is wrong." In effect, they were repudiating an unambiguous, normative view of traditional Judaism in favor of the more latitudinarian modern view. This is a religiously significant lapse. To account for a departure from the point of view mandated by biblical law by such a large number of relatively observant Orthodox Jews, one must assume that the affective influences of modernity are greater than many would have imagined.

We have already seen that these Orthodox Jews have had significant contact with the non-Orthodox world and that they are open to the influences that seep in by virtue of it. We see here that these influences reach quite deeply into the ethos, such that even fundamental attitudes may be effected—or, as some might put it, eroded.

But the tolerance of homosexuality by some of the non-traditionalist Orthodox who are nevertheless substantially more observant than most American Jews is but one of the deviations from the classic ethos of Orthodoxy that we have encountered in our sample population. Generally, we have found them far more open than commonly assumed to the influences of modern America.

To be sure, in this Jews are not necessarily unique. A discrepancy between acceptance of official doctrine and personal attitude among some of our Orthodox Jews is, in some ways, parallel to a similar phenomenon among the coming generation (the young leadership) of American Protestant Evangelicals who, as James Hunter has shown, while still adhering to and supporting prohibitions against premarital, extramarital, and homosexual relations, have "softened" their attitudes towards these prohibitions.[17] Clearly, in modern America, at least some observant individuals have found that they need *not* adopt the moral and doctrinal teachings of their organized faith, and thus may reject those teachings particularly in areas that touch upon what they see as the sphere of private morality.[18]

Earlier, we noted that the Orthodox—especially the more traditionalist Orthodox—tend to send their children to private Jewish schools. As a result, both individually (as tuition-paying parents) and collectively (as members of a community with a stake in religious schooling), the Orthodox have more incentives to support public aid to private schools. Indeed, only a third of the non-Orthodox agreed, "The government should give aid to nonpublic schools." But when we cross over to look at the Orthodox attitude toward this principal, we find three-quarters of our traditionalists, most of the centrists, and nearly half of the nominally Orthodox agreeing in one way or another with the statement.

Sending one's children to day school or yeshiva has an obvious impact on attitudes toward government aid. Among non-Orthodox and nominally Orthodox respondents, only about a quarter of those not sending (or planning to send) their children to full-time Jewish schools supported public assistance to nonpublic schools. Of their counterparts who were day school or yeshiva parents (or planning to be), about half favored government aid.[19]

The homosexuality and the school aid questions touch upon areas where there is an explicit rationale (religious or institutional) for greater conservatism among more traditionally Orthodox elements. In both instances, we have seen that the Orthodox tend toward positions that are markedly more conservative than the general Jewish population, although in the case of the nontraditionalists there are notable minorities that diverge from the majority conservative view.

Among Orthodox Jews, a predominating social conservatism extends to other areas as well. For example, Jews, more than any other identifiable group in the American population, supported passage of the Equal Rights Amendment (ERA) when it was a live issue in the 1970s and early 1980s. About two-thirds to three-quarters of Jews surveyed in public opinion polls at the time were pro-ERA as contrasted with slim majorities in the population. Similarly, two-thirds of the non-Orthodox in our sample agreed, "The Equal Rights Amendment should be passed." But again, as in the earlier cases, as traditional Orthodoxy increased, ERA support fell. It dropped to a slim majority among the nominal and centrist Orthodox and to a paltry 36% among the most traditional Orthodox group. The extent of opposition to the ERA is all the more impressive if we recall that most of our so-called traditional Orthodox Jews are not drawn from the most extreme sections of the entire Orthodox community but rather are simply the most traditionalist edge of an overall mainstream Orthodoxy which was willing to respond to a university-generated social survey.

One might perhaps argue that opposition to the ERA among the Orthodox is not generated by religiocultural conservatism but rather by other factors—perhaps having to do with political strategy or concerns about the preservation of the constitution. Perhaps Orthodox Jews are willing to offer women independence in other domains. To see if this was the case, we asked a question that would test their support for traditional familialism, at the woman's expense. We asked for their reaction to the statement: "A wife should make her own decisions even if she disagrees with her husband."

Unlike the homosexuality question or even the one on aid to private schools, however, this question seemed to have no obvious religious or institutional preordained answer. While one might interpret Jewish law to take one or another position on this question (in principle, after all, the *halacha* covers all aspects of life), most people—who are not among the learned *halachic* virtuosi—would not be expected to know the Torah position on this matter. Accordingly, responses here were largely dependent upon unstated understandings, a feel for what was appropriate and in line with the ethos of the respondent. Thus the response to this question offers an opportunity to examine the persistence of the ethos of Orthodoxy across the various boundaries of observance.

In line with general liberal American attitudes, the vast majority of our non-Orthodox respondents agreed with this statement, as did almost as many of the nominally Orthodox and a slightly smaller number of those we call the centrists. In this case, at least, the latter two groups abandoned the ethos of Orthodoxy in favor of the ethos of liberalism. This was decidedly not the case among the most traditional of our sample, of whom only a minority endorsed this expression of autonomy in decision making for wives. They remained far more embedded in the ethos of Orthodoxy which appeared to spill over into a general tendency to take nonliberal positions on a variety of issues.

The same sorts of patterns are reflected in other responses. Consistent with their reputation for support of government subsidies for the poor and their tolerance of nonconforming life-style decisions, majorities of Jews in national public opinion surveys have endorsed government financial support of abortions for poor women. These views may be contrasted with those of Americans generally who provide only slim pluralities favoring merely the legality of abortions in such cases. When confronted with the question, "The government should not pay for abortions," two-thirds of our non-Orthodox respondents—consistent with Jews in other surveys—supported government aid for abortions (i.e., by disagreeing with the statement). But again, as before, as traditionalism increased, support for the liberal policy option fell; it dropped slightly among the two nontraditional Orthodox groups and more sharply to about a third among the most traditional.

If one wonders over the fact that Orthodox Jews could even acknowledge the legitimacy of abortion, something

171

the Bible would fundamentally prohibit, one needs to realize, first, that Judaism is not as categorically opposed to abortion as, for example, the Catholic Church, and, second, that it is possible that our respondents were thinking about abortion for others, conceivably for poor pregnant Gentile women. Accordingly, an issue such as abortion illustrates the value concerns of traditional Jews where neither *halacha* is unambiguous (such as with homosexuality), nor where there is a clear economic incentive (such as with public aid for private schools). Rather, here we have an issue—like the one on wives' independent decision making—where a generally conservative ethos is extended to the public policy domain, even in an area where we can assume most traditional Orthodox Jews feel they personally will have relatively little direct interest (i.e., the vast majority probably assume that neither they nor most of their close friends and relatives will ever have recourse to an abortion, let alone need government assistance to pay for one).

What about those questions that seem to be irrelevant to the ethos of Orthodoxy, where the implications of established moral teachings are less clear? Here, the association of responses with degrees of Orthodoxy are far less distinct. For example, in response to a question on whether "affirmative action should be used to help disadvantaged groups," only a few percentage points separated the extent of support among the non-Orthodox (at 48%) from the most traditional Orthodox (37%), with the two other Orthodox groups in between. In fact, none of the groups of these Orthodox Jews showed any overwhelming support for affirmative action.

To many Jews, affirmative action programs connote racial quotas,[20] which are particularly odious to those (like the Orthodox) with a strong Jewish group consciousness. Nevertheless, in contrast with the other issues discussed above, affirmative action does not directly touch upon deep-seated and unambiguous moral teachings and the ethos of Orthodoxy. So traditionalist Jews do not markedly differ from the other Orthodox Jews on this.

Apparently, the same can be said for the death penalty.

When we asked whether "the death penalty should be abolished," the proportions disagreeing (whether "strongly" or not) were virtually identical for all four groups (between 59% and 62%). The majority of all these people—including the non-Orthodox—are not opposed to the death penalty (but then neither is the *halacha*).

Once again, what these data point to is evidence of a predisposition among Orthodox Jews to take conservative positions on a variety of public and moral issues. The factors leading to this probably include the specific teachings of rabbinic Judaism, the institutional concerns of the Orthodox community, and its cultural conservatism particularly in matters pertaining to the family and certain aspects of sexuality. Where one or more of these factors can be assumed to be operative, we find more conservative views among the Orthodox than among the non-Orthodox as well as among the traditional Orthodox relative to their more modern counterparts.

However, there are also signs, particularly among the less traditionalist Orthodox, that in certain matters—especially those on which Jewish law and tradition may *seem* ambiguous or even silent, and the Orthodox corporate community relatively neutral—the ethos of Orthodoxy is somewhat offset by the ethos of Jewish liberalism and the effects of modern America. This is, where neither religious doctrine, nor particularistic concerns, nor conservative personal morality directly pertain to a particular question, differences in the responses of the four groups are slight or inconsistent. This suggests limits to the sweep of the Orthodox ethos. Or, put another way, people's Orthodoxy in certain practices, briefs, and affiliations does not necessarily extend to all features of their existence.

Perhaps nowhere are these limitations on the Orthodox ethos seen more dramatically and graphically than with regard to attitudes toward sexual behavior.

Variations in Sexual License

One of the most salient and central changes to accompany the transition from traditional to modern society, whether in eighteenth-century Europe or in developing countries of the contemporary Third World, has been the significant liberalization of sexual behavior and attitudes. The sexual revolution of the 1960s was marked by increases in the legitimation of eroticism, declines in the age of first sexual intercourse, as well as growth in the instances of and permissiveness toward premarital and extramarital sexual relations.

Premarital sexual relations were also strictly limited by Jewish law and tradition. A man was even prohibited from being alone with a woman unless she was his wife. The laws of betrothal are quite specific about what exactly may transpire between an unmarried man and an unmarried woman.[21] And while some might argue that sexual intercourse constitutes a sealing of the bonds of legal marriage, few if any authoritative sources today would accept such a method of coupling as a legitimate means of wedding. Thus, it would be largely accurate to say that from the point of view of the tradition, premarital sex, even with one's betrothed, is prohibited. Although Scripture is prominently marked with instances of the breach of these rules, for the most part the common view among traditional Jews is that their ancestors have more or less devotedly observed the rules.[22]

But as life and the attitudes toward sex have changed so, like everyone else, the Jews have changed. In studies of today's sexual behavior, Jews generally are reported to have the most liberal attitudes of all American religious groups. Orthodox Jews, though, have a reputation for far more conservative sexual attitudes and practices.

Yet we have already shown that while the Orthodox Jews we have studied do in fact display conservative attitudes, they are differences between the most traditionalist in our sample and the others—the centrist and nominally Orthodox. The latter have appeared to hover between the conservative tendencies of the traditionalists and the liberal attitudes of most contemporary American Jews. Accordingly, we would expect this same stance with regard to sexual attitudes. That is, we would expect a highly conservative attitude manifest among the traditionalists while the other Orthodox (the centrists somewhat and the nominals even more) are subject to intense countervailing liberal pressures. To the middle-of-the-road Orthodox, the greater permissiveness of the non-Orthodox toward premarital sexuality, and the opportunities for dating members of the opposite sex with those standards, hold out prospects of both legitimacy and opportunity for violating the far more conservative norms of their traditionalist counterparts.

Many of the young Jews in our sample—recently married or not—no doubt directly experienced these tensions or are keenly aware of them among those close to them. Indeed, the spiritual leader of one of the congregations that make up a large part of our survey was widely reported to have sermonized against the practice of "t'fillin dates," a term that aptly captures the essence of the conflict and the paradoxical solution to the problem of trying to accommodate Orthodox adherence and modern sexual standards. The term refers to the practice of young adult men taking their t'fillin with them on evening dates so that they will be able to fulfill the religious obligation to don the t'fillin during their daily prayers in their date's apartment the following morning.

To assess the accuracy of our images of traditionalists' sexual conservatism and the others' incipient liberalism (with the implicit tension for those Orthodox caught in the middle), we asked, "Would you approve or disapprove of premarital sex in each of the following circumstances?" We then offered alternative scenarios. "If the couple is (1) engaged to be married, (2) dating seriously, (3) just good friends, (4) casual acquaintances." The proportions of each group who disapproved of premarital sex in each of the four circumstances is presented in table 5.3.

Although we have not shown the data here, the differences between men's and women's responses were small, though tending in the direction of women expressing disapproval somewhat more often. However, variations between older (over thirty-five) and younger (thirty-five and under) respondents were substantial and significant. Hence, we present the results separately for older and younger members of each Orthodoxy group, except for the most traditional where there were too few cases to allow us to divide them into separate age groups and still obtain

Table 5.3: Disapproval of Premarital Sex by Orthodoxy and Age

If the couple is . . .	Non-Orthodox	Nominal	Centrist	Traditional
	Orthodoxy			
	Would you approve or disapprove of premarital sex in each of the following circumstances?			
	Engaged			
Disapprove:				
Old (36+)	23	33	60	
Young (18–35)	3	17	46	92
	Dating seriously			
Disapprove:				
Old (36+)	33	57	72	
Young (18–35)	8	23	59	97
	Just good friends			
Disapprove:				
Old (35+)	65	68	85	
Young (18–35)	20	41	79	100
	Casual acquaintances			
Disapprove:				
Old (35+)	77	82	93	
Young (18–35)	58	55	81	100

reasonably stable results. Since most of the traditionalists in our sample who responded to this question were thirty-five years old or younger, we listed the entire group in the "younger" rows of the table.

Several patterns in table 5.3 are particularly noteworthy. First, for all levels of Orthodoxy, we found, as noted, that younger respondents consistently reported more indulgent attitudes toward the practice of premarital sex than their older counterparts. Second, among all but the traditionalists, disapproval rates declined dramatically as the hypothetical relationship between the couple becomes more intimate. For example, among younger Orthodox respondents in the centrist category, while the vast majority disapproved of premarital sex between casual acquaintances, and nearly as many withheld approval for it be-

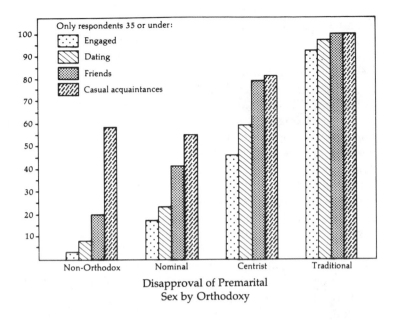

Disapproval of Premarital
Sex by Orthodoxy

tween those who are "just good friends," only slightly
more than half were against premarital sex between those
who are "dating seriously," and less than half disapproved
of an engaged couple engaging in sex. Moreover, the centrists were by no means alone in this pattern of response.
Those under the age of thirty-five who were in our nominally Orthodox category display the same pattern, except
that they are even more permissive. In this group, less
than a quarter opposed premarital sex for those dating seriously, and only 17% disapproved of it between the engaged couple. Indeed, barely half of the young nominally
Orthodox challenged the practice of sex between casual acquaintances—and this from people who choose to call
themselves "Orthodox." In fact, only among the traditionalists in our sample population do we discover uniform attitudes toward premarital sex that we would expect from
those Jews who call themselves "Orthodox" and whose observance, beliefs, and associations seem to qualify them as
such.

While the young appear to be more liberal on matters of
premarital sex than those over thirty-five, the older re-

spondents are by no means paradigms of restrictiveness. To be sure, most centrists seem to draw the line on premarital sex at all levels, yet still nearly a quarter of them would not disapprove of intercourse between those who are "dating seriously," and 40% did not disapprove of it between the engaged. These must be considered significant minorities. The analogous finds are even more dramatic in the nominally Orthodox category. Clearly, while there is evidence of restraint here which sets Orthodox Jews apart from most Jews, liberal attitudes toward premarital sexuality which have become a hallmark of modern American life have made inroads in many precincts of Orthodoxy—in all precincts except those we have identified as traditionalist.

Here, as in other cases, the Jews who make up the centrist category are in many ways the most interesting for they must navigate between the two extremes, neither of which they wholly reject. Relative to their counterparts on the more liberal left, they certainly seem more classically Orthodox in that they are willing to curb sexual freedom in the domain of premarital relations—although not quite as extreme as their counterparts to the traditionalist right. But these curbs, while they reflect the ethos of Orthodoxy, reflect it rather faintly—too faintly, according to many Orthodox rabbinical figures and lay leaders who have expressed increasing concern with what they view as the decline in morality, by which they mean a departure from traditional normative standards in the family and family-building spheres.

Summary and Conclusion

In many ways, non-Orthodox American Jews have deservedly acquired a reputation for adopting social, political, and sexual attitudes more liberal than their non-Jewish contemporaries. Disproportionate numbers are probably enamored of and involved in contemporary affairs and "progressive" intellectual endeavors (such as science) and social movements. Moreover, as earlier noted, American Jews generally have a well-documented tendency to endorse liberal candidates, parties, and positions on major public issues; and in the personal realm, in an area exemplified by their sexual attitudes, they are no less permissive, if not more so, than their social class counterparts.

In contrast, the most traditionalist Orthodox generally espouse the most conservative orientations in these areas. They are far more reverent of the past and suspicious of the present and future; they are typically more nonliberal on public policy questions for reasons having to do with religious law, institutional concerns, and private morality; and they have the most restrictive attitudes toward sexual practice, suggesting a traditionalism in other matters of personal and private morality as well. In short, the ethos of Orthodoxy is clearly expressed and supported in the life of those we have called "traditionalists."

Between these two poles stand the modern Orthodox who express views between the liberalism of the non-Orthodox and the conservatism of the traditionalists. Such evidence suggests, at least implicitly, that most of those who make up contemporary Orthodoxy may well be subject to countervailing pressures. In some cases, they get pulled by contemporary non-Orthodox currents while in others they float toward traditionalism.

6   Whither Orthodoxy?

"All social reality is precarious."
                 Peter L. Berger and Thomas Luckmann

At the end of Chapter 5 and at various points throughout our analysis, we have referred to differences between younger and older Orthodox Jews in our sample. Since, in general, age is certainly an important factor in behavior, belief, communal orientation, and social outlook, we decided to focus more intensively on it in the case of Orthodox Jews. To be sure, youth (even up to thirty-five years of life, our cut-off age) is a turbulent time, a period of changes, and therefore it would be hazardous to suggest that what people do or believe and the way they orient their lives while they are young will necessarily remain the same as they age. Thus, if we have so far seen differences between those over and those under thirty-five years of age, we need to qualify this finding with the caveat that we can only speculate about the future and whether today's young will or will not become like their older counterparts as they too age.

To understand more fully the issues implicit in a comparison of younger and older Orthodox Jews, it is useful to review briefly the evolution of Orthodoxy. That is, we cannot comprehend the distinctions between the generations of American Orthodox Jews without considering the background against which they are expressed.

As we pointed out in Chapter 1, for many years countless observers shared pessimistic assumptions about the future of American Orthodoxy—especially its most traditionalist aspects. During most of this century, as Jews moved into the host societies among whom they found themselves, it was commonly assumed that Orthodoxy faced a precarious if not a bleak future. Either it would be swept up in the swift currents of modern society or it would remain a small, stagnant pool of Jewish existence. Indeed, as demographer Calvin Goldscheider has shown in his analysis of Jewish continuity and change, for a long time in America the flow across generations of American Jews was "clearly away from Orthodoxy."[1]

Then, at the start of the last third of this century, developments occurred that raised questions about the direction of this flow. First, as suggested in the first pages of this book, the reality was that Orthodoxy among Jews did *not* disappear. While previous generational evolution had perhaps displayed a diminution of Orthodoxy among American Jews, by the beginning of the last decade and twenty-five years after the Holocaust the losses among the Orthodox appeared to have leveled off. We have seen in Chapter 4 that, at least these days, Orthodoxy begets Orthodoxy (see tables 4.5 and 4.6). In an America that was moving away from the melting pot ideal of assimilation toward the salad bowl model of ethnic diversity, where "black is beautiful" and people talked of "the rise of the unmeltable ethnics," Orthodoxy was increasingly at home. Looking at the losses that their non-Orthodox counterparts had experienced and their own endurance, Orthodox leaders began to express a greater confidence in their movement's durability and, indeed, its vitality; even non-Orthodox leaders came to accept this upbeat assessment of the Orthodox future. In fact, after the assimilationist trends of the 1950s and even more so of the sixties, the pessimism about survival once directed at Orthodoxy now was projected by many Jewish elites onto other brands of Judaism.[2] Triumphalism, a confidence in their own long-term survival above all other kinds of Jews, became the dominant theme of Orthodoxy.

Second, and perhaps as a consequence of this newly emergent triumphalism, the Orthodoxy that was surviving in America was not private and hidden, it was not the "Jew-in-the-home-man-in-the-street" variety that allowed the Orthodox to remain indistinguishable from other Americans. Rather, many Jews were openly declaring and identifying themselves as Orthodox, often stressing their adherence to precisely those traditions that diverged from American norms. That is, they were often obtrusively ethnic and stringently traditionalist. This trend, sometimes called the "rightward" flow of Orthodoxy, led to some modernist Orthodox Jews feeling (in the words of one such Jew) that "our side is losing control of American Orthodoxy."[3] From this perspective, the more traditional elements within Orthodoxy had increased their influence at the expense of the modernists in a variety of ways.

The nature of this move toward traditionalism can be expressed in the very terms developed in our previous chapters. Traditionalism, in part, suggests that the ritual observance standards for membership in the Orthodox community have risen. Deviations from official norms are less frequent and less accepted. Formerly minor transgressions—once overlooked—are no longer tolerated; or, in other words, the scope of "ritual inattention" has narrowed.[4] A move to the right also means a more fervent belief in what can be called "fundamentalist" tenets, which in Jewish terms means a conviction that God, through Scripture and rabbinic elucidation, clearly and fundamentally expresses how Jews ought to behave and what they ought to believe.[5] On a communal level, the rightward flow implies greater insularity, more involvement within Orthodox networks, less openness to the non-Orthodox, and less official cooperation with their rabbis, leaders, and institutions. It also means increased enrollment as well as more years of attendance in day schools and yeshivas. Finally, a shift toward Orthodox traditionalism also may encompass a move to the political and cultural right.

Whether such shifts toward traditionalism have occurred in American Orthodoxy can be empirically tested, and we shall try to do so in this chapter. In other words, we wish to establish whether the impressions and sentiments of many observers of Orthodoxy who have asserted this move to the traditionalist right are based on fact. Are the Orthodox Jews of today, the coming generation, more or less traditionalist then those of the older generation?

The Traditionalist Shift and the Larger Context

Since Jews and Jewish life—even in the case of Orthodoxy—do not exist in a vacuum, part of the reason for the change in the image of Orthodoxy and its public expression lies in concurrent changes in the thinking about religion, ethnicity, and Jewish survival in the United States. While admittedly speculative, we propose that it is no accident that changes in the way many observers understood these three issues took place just around the same time as did changes in the way Jews—whether Orthodox or not—understood Orthodoxy. Alternatively, we can make a more modest statement: prevalent conceptions of American religion, ethnicity, and Judaism through the first two-thirds of this century at least comported with the pessimism and modernist leanings of Orthodoxy; and prevalent conceptions in these spheres in the last twenty years conformed with the significantly greater optimism and seeming traditionalist tendencies in American Orthodoxy.

To elaborate, it would be fair to say that most scholars and journalists writing about American religious life before the early 1970s embraced what may be called the "secularization paradigm." Max Weber first defined this as the process of "disenchantment,"[6] by which he meant that the spiritual and the metaphysical were being replaced by the rational and the calculable. According to this paradigm, the great march of Western history is in a direction away from strongly held traditional religious beliefs and practices and toward the weaker and more circumscribed influence of religious leaders and institutions. Moreover, insofar as religion had any future, it was with those theological liberals who deemphasized formal theological content and played up religion's relevance and appropriateness for modern living. Traditional religion might at best give way to the more secular civil religion in which corporate, social entities might take the place of the gods.[7]

In the last twenty years, however, several developments have stimulated many to seriously question the secular paradigm. To quote Martin E. Marty: "First, contrary to expectations, religion is very much in evidence. . . . Second, . . . religion has diffused throughout the culture, and has assumed highly particular forms in the private lives of citizens. Third, traditional religion has not fallen away, as expected, but has survived and staged an impressive comeback."[8] In the last number of years, America has witnessed the emergence of passionate, nonconventional religious movements and communities, a rise in the popularity of evangelicalism (20% of the American population, according to James Davison Hunter);[9] and the continuity of Christian fundamentalism, embracing tens of millions of Americans, including some very prominent public figures. "Through the two generations when secularism reigned, one large subculture resisted its sway. It included hasidic and other mystical or orthodox movements in Judaism; numbers of American-born 'sects' like the Latter-Day Saints, Jehovah's Witnesses, and Adventists; pentecostal and charismatic movements in conventional Christianity; traditionalist Catholicism, to a lesser extent; and to a greater one, evangelical and fundamentalist Protestantism. That subculture is now resurgent, and in 1980, it could claim the loyalty of all three major presidential candidates, along with entertainers and entrepreneurs, athletes and beauty queens."[10] Anthropologist Mary Douglas suggests that "modernization turns out to be quite compatible with . . . doctrines that sacralize life in external ritual forms of celebration, compatible even with all the narrowness of spirit and intellectual closure thought to be maladaptive in modern life."[11]

In 1963, Seymour Martin Lipset used the observations of both foreign visitors and American chroniclers to show that all-pervasive religion had for a long time characterized American culture.[12] And Gallup polls in the 1970s found Americans more ready than ever to identify themselves as "born again."[13] In 1978, David Hay and Ann Morisy could assert that at least a third of the American population reported having a religious experience.[14] To quote Marty again: ". . . theorists not only found more evidence of religion than they had forseen, but had to account for it as well, [and] they began to waver in their support for the secular paradigm."[15] In light of these and other tendencies, the projection of continued decline in traditional religion seemed less plausible; and, we argue, the projection of an inevitable decline in Jewish Orthodoxy seemed less compelling.

Not only was religion—even in its most traditionalist forms—resurgent, ethnicity was too. This likewise affected

Jewry. Jews are, after all, distinctive in that they are one of the few groups in the United States that appear both on the roster of American religious movements as well as on the list of American ethnic groups.[16] Hence, thinking about America's ethnic future ought also to effect thinking about the American Jewish future. Here too—as noted earlier—we find intellectual trends that may serve to reinforce both Orthodoxy's confidence and its traditionalist tendencies.

Through the 1960s, most social scientists and others assumed that ethnic attachments were a relic of America's not-so-distant immigrant past. For years, as we have said, the melting pot model was dominant in thinking about American ethnicity. That model contended that serious ethnic involvement and differences evaporate by the third or fourth generation, that is, among the grandchildren or great-grandchildren of immigrants. Will Herberg's influential essay *Protestant—Catholic—Jew,* first published in 1955, reflected this thinking in that it both perceived and predicted the complete amalgamation of various nationality groups within three religious rubrics.

Then, starting perhaps in 1963 with the publication of Beyond the Melting Pot by Nathan Glazer and Daniel Patrick Moynihan, the intellectual climate began to turn. Increasingly, observers proclaimed the vitality of American ethnic groups and argued for the persistence of ethnic loyalties—the so-called salad bowl model which unlike the melting pot allowed for ethnic diversity within an overall sociocultural unity.[17] Several developments fostered this shift in thinking about the prospects for ethnic continuity. These included the emergence of the Black Power movement in the mid-1960s, the political assertiveness of Southern and Eastern European ethnic groups in the early 1970s, and, to no small extent, the extraordinary rise of Jewish consciousness stimulated by the 1967 Six Day War in Israel and agitation of American Jews in support of Soviet Jewry.[18] Finally, and by far not the least important factor was the immigration of millions of newcomers—both legal and illegal—to the United States, particularly from Asia and Latin America. This migration fueled a resurgence in a public consciousness of ethnicity and of ethnic conflict as well as of the likelihood for ethnic persistence.

If ethnicity and religion have become more comfortably a part of American life (albeit some would argue that the nature of these ethnic and religious expressions is more symbolic rather than real),[19] then, one might suppose, there has been less to inhibit the Orthodox from becoming more overt, sometimes even brazen, in displaying and acting upon their particular group peculiarities.[20] The sprouting of *yarmulkes* on the heads of Orthodox Jews from the campus to the boardroom, the ubiquitous availability of kosher food as well as the political assertiveness of Orthodoxy in local and national contexts are but a few of the indications of these more confident, uninhibited tendencies. In brief, what may be called a new ethnic permissiveness and tolerance for religious expression probably may have helped foster changes in the image and reality of American Orthodoxy.

Tied to these changes was a third element: a deep-seated change in American Jewry which may also have fostered a rightward shift—real or apparent—in American Orthodoxy. As we have implied earlier in our remarks about Jewish communal life, sometime between the mid-1960s and the mid-1970s, the chief communal concerns of organized American Jewry switched from what may be called "integrationist" or "acculturative" to "survivalist" or "contra-acculturative" agendas.[21] No longer were Jews as concerned with their acceptance as Americans—they took that for granted; instead, they became far more attentive to, even anxious over, their survival as Jews.

This shift reverberated throughout the Jewish world on many levels. Survival issues—such as the continued existence of Israel, freedom for Soviet, Syrian, Ethiopian, and other endangered Jewries, and a growing concern with the Holocaust—came to occupy center stage in the consciousness of individual Jews and became the agenda of major Jewish organizations. These matters were of particular concern to young Jews, especially those who had received the best that Jewish education and communal life could offer in the late fifties and early sixties and who had become, in the spirit of the times, activists. Under the stimulus of the young and for a variety of other reasons, politically active Jews diminished (but by no means ceased) their once enthusiastic involvement in non-Jewish causes and adopted a more group-centered agenda.

Jewish education became more important to many. An estimated 41% of Jewish children between the ages of three and seventeen are now receiving some kind of Jewish education. While 72% of them are in supplementary schools, enrollment of Orthodox, Conservative, and even Reform Jews in all-day Jewish schools has surged dramatically over the last twenty years.

In addition, federations—the local centralized Jewish charitable campaign organizations—became more parochially Jewish in several dimensions. They saw to it that their charitable dollars served increasingly Jewish clientele and sharply increased funds for Jewish day schools and bureaus of Jewish education. Moreover, the Americanized, integrationist-oriented lay leadership of the past either adopted the ethos of the new Jewish survivalism or was replaced by a more Jewishly assertive leadership.[22] Finally, federations encouraged their professionals to possess greater knowledge of Jewish cultural matters. This they accomplished either by selecting staff with a strong Jewish background (a surprising number of key federation professionals were, for the first time in memory, identifiably Orthodox) or by seeing to it that the undereducated staff received on-the-job Jewish education.[23]

Against this background, Orthodoxy specifically and Jewish traditionalism generally grew in stature in the eyes of survivalist-oriented Jews, Orthodox or otherwise. By any measure, the Orthodox seemed more able to assure Jewish continuity. Compared to the non-Orthodox, they seemed to be characterized by lower divorce rates, less frequent intermarriage, more ritual involvement, and a deeper attachment to Israel.[24] And as we have seen, they were having more children, the ultimate instruments of Jewish survival.[25] Orthodoxy was no longer viewed as the stagnant pool.

This view of the triumph of Orthodoxy affected the Orthodox community itself. So-called modern Orthodoxy and its integrationist trends, so popular in the days when particularism and ethnicity were out of vogue and religion was subordinate to secularity, found itself under ideological attack from the traditionalist right wing. In this atmosphere, accommodating to modernity, cooperating with the non-Orthodox, responding positively to larger social trends (such as feminism), and displaying doctrinal flexibility, all increasingly took on something of an unsavory connotation. More than before, these tendencies came to signify surrender (even if unwitting) to a Jewish (or an American) world plagued by many of the ills Orthodoxy was committed to countering.

A fourth and final reason to explain the image of triumphalism and of a rightward shift in American Orthodoxy entails the coming of age of Orthodoxy, its institutions, and its ideology. At one time, to be Orthodox in America meant being foreign-born and working class. Moreover, the popular ideology of the Orthodox—such as it was—was in many respects closer to a "cargo cult" from Eastern Europe than a well-developed and articulated belief system appropriate to modern America. In the age of the Second Generation Jews, a time that encouraged Americanization, Orthodoxy enjoyed low status. Many of those who stayed Orthodox—the grandmothers and grandfathers (or, more accurately, *bobbehs* and *zaydehs*)—seemed to do so more out of inertia than volition. The ideological vitality Orthodoxy had in its nineteenth-century dawn seemed to have been sapped on the trans-Atlantic journey. The earliest of the first-generation American Orthodox Jews were quiet defenders of their way of life—staying true to the tradition themselves but often failing to pass on that tradition fully to their children. And Orthodoxy suffered severe intergenerational defections. Their institutions were filled with the old and the poor.[26]

In time, though, two complementary processes well may have strengthened Orthodoxy. First, over the years Orthodoxy has shed many less ideologically committed inertial members (losing their children as well). Second, Orthodoxy built and solidified its institutional base, particularly after the Second World War. At that point, as explained in Chapter 4, their institutions were filled with new life while their ideological champions arrived—and all this happened just at a time when America was about to become receptive to Orthodoxies and ethnicities of all types.

We think that all these factors promoted at the very least a resurgence in Orthodox confidence, if not an accompanying, and, we argue, a related shift to the ideological right as we have defined it above. And we think the young— those who were coming of Jewish age in this period—and many of the strongest voices of Orthodoxy were infected with this confidence and swept up in the traditionalist flow. There has been anecdotal evidence of this flow: Orthodox parents speak of their children's greater devotion to stringent observance of the more traditional ritual practices; informed observers claim that rabbinic responsa over the last several decades have tended to go in a more conservative direction; stories abound of *baaley t'shuva*, those who have returned to traditional Orthodoxy, turning up in the most assimilated of families.[27] And, clearly, Orthodox institutions have proliferated, giving Orthodoxy at least the appearance of greater affluence, visibility, and potency.

Clearly, we cannot assign specific weights to the various influences. America's conservative religious revival, the legitimation of ethnicity, the Jewish turn from integrationism to survivalism, and the institutionalization of Orthodoxy have all contributed to the expectation of a rightward flow in Orthodoxy. Until now, no systematic quantitative confirmation has been available to substantiate the anecdotal evidence of the rightward turn. We have no idea of the scope and extent of the rightward trend. We do not really know whether or not the young are more traditionalist in their Orthodoxy than their elders? We do not know if, indeed, there is a rightward flow whether it is a limited or broad-based trend. Does it affect only one or another aspect of Orthodox Jewish identity (whether ritual practice or religious belief or schooling), or is it all-encompassing? To answer these questions, evidence from survey questionnaires is quite appropriate and valuable.

The ideal sort of quantitative evidence to address these issues would consist of surveys of Orthodox Jews conducted at different points in time, perhaps once every decade for the last thirty years or so. Unfortunately, such data are unavailable. Instead, this analysis is limited to two one-shot surveys conducted about the same time in different populations, in particular: the data set we have been analyzing heretofore, and another survey data set (about which more presently). With survey evidence collected at one point in time, we are forced to turn to age-related differences as an indirect way of assessing over-time trends.

The rationale for this method is based on the idea that one way in which populations change is that ultimately youngsters replace their elders. If younger adults are noticeably different from their elders, we can infer that some broad-based social change is or has been underway. To be sure, looking at the differences between younger and older people does not unequivocally establish trends since we may be looking at phenomena that reflect life-cycle effects more than generational change. Maybe young people simply rebel against the way of life of their elders: so when the old are traditionalist the young are modernist and vice versa. Or maybe if we had surveyed the older generation thirty years ago, they might have been more like today's young people; or perhaps in thirty years today's young people might reply in ways similar to their elders. We do not believe this is so, as our analysis of the evolution of Orthodoxy implies—but in all honesty we cannot be sure, and thus our findings must be considered as suggestive but not conclusive.

All of this is to caution that the appearance of age-related differences alone ought not be taken automatically as evidence of broad-based social change in Orthodoxy, either as evidence of prior change or as a portent of developments in the near future. Too many confounding influences make such an immediate inference unwarranted if not dangerous. Rather, such differences ought to be seen as raising the possibility of population-wide trends, provided such interpretations are consistent with the available qualitative evidence and relevant social theory.

To some extent, age is a proxy for generation. The bulk of American Jewish migration was concentrated in the decades around the turn of the century; in addition, a good number of Jewish refugees from the Holocaust—including a large (some would argue a *decisive*) number of Orthodox—immigrated in the late 1940s.[28] As a result, older Jews tend to represent the earlier generation; more of them were born in Europe (first generation) or are the children of the foreign-born. In contrast, by far, more of the younger Orthodox are third generation (grandchildren of foreign-born). We did not measure generation of nativity directly in this sample, but we can reasonably postulate that the overlap of age and generation found elsewhere is found in our sample as well.[29]

Generation is widely associated with declines in traditional Jewish practice, at least through the third generation.[30] Indeed, the three-generation hypothesis of acculturation that proposed that as Jews established themselves in America they would become uniformly more like all Americans and less definitively Jewish became a standard feature of the sociology of American Jewish life.[31] Following that hypothesis, we might expect younger Orthodox Jews to score lower than their elders on most of our dimensions of traditionalism. In fact, the comparatively high levels of traditionalism we find among the younger Orthodox in the results reported below point to a fascinating distinction between Orthodox and non-Orthodox Jews, one we certainly try to explain.

To examine whether in fact Orthodoxy has been moving right and what that trend may mean, we supplement the data set we have been analyzing with data from the 1981 Greater New York Jewish Population Study.[32] That study interviewed a random sample of 4,505 Jews in the New York metropolitan area, a region that contains almost a third of the American Jewish population and probably about half the American Orthodox population. The virtue of the data set for our purposes lies in its superior sampling design and in its coverage of all Jews, not just the Orthodox. As such, it allows us to examine trends within Orthodoxy with a great measure of confidence in the representativeness of the sample which will in turn provide the context within which to understand our nonrandom sample of Orthodox Jews drawn from several synagogues and mailing lists.

While the New York data are superior from a sampling point of view, they cannot offer much insight into the detailed aspects of Orthodox identity we have been exploring—which is why we have used our own survey results for the bulk of our discussion of Orthodoxy in America. Since the New York survey obviously was not conducted with a specific interest in Orthodoxy, the interviewers asked only a few questions immediately relevant (i.e., those on a few traditional ritual practices, on Jewish schooling, on denominational affiliation, and on parental religiosity). From these questions we can sketch only a few age-related and parent-child differences, but we cannot draw upon much detail in several dimensions of Orthodox Jewish identity. For that purpose we shall return to our own survey, the results of which we have used throughout this study.

Rising Standards of Ritual Practice and Yeshiva Schooling

The rise in what may be regarded as the expected standards of membership in Orthodoxy can be seen in a number of ways. We may begin by looking at the two panels of table 6.1 which summarize some differences among young (under thirty-five), middle-aged (thirty-five to fifty-four), and older (over fifty-five) Orthodox Jews. The upper panel represents the results found among those New York Jews who identified themselves as "Orthodox." Contrary to the image of a fully observant community, only two-thirds of this group reported they refrained from handling money on the Sabbath—a prohibition mandated by Jewish religious law—and less than half reported fasting on the fast of Esther. Clearly, a large minority of Orthodox Jews in the New York area would qualify at best as "nominally Orthodox" by our definition.

The lower panel represents the results found among those who reported that their parents were highly observant (the measure of that observance being their refusal to handle money on the Sabbath). We put these two panels together because they enable us to compare today's Orthodox with yesterday's.

Interestingly, as we have been suggesting, younger Or-

Table 6.1: Scoring High on Measures of Orthodox Identity by Age for Orthodox Respondents (%)

	Less than 35	35–54	55 or over
Handles no money on the Sabbath	79	77	58
Fasts on the Fast of Esther	63	52	34
Attends services weekly:			
Men	82	66	56
Women	27	48	35
Ever attended yeshiva or day school:			
Men	89	71	43
Women	67	46	19

Respondents whose parents were highly observant
(parents refrained from handling money on the Sabbath)

	Less than 35	35–54	55 or over
Handles no money on the Sabbath	62	44	28
Fasts on the Fast of Esther	54	31	17
Attends services weekly:			
Men	59	35	29
Women	26	25	17
Ever attended yeshiva or day school:			
Men	74	41	38
Women	48	31	11
Identifies as Orthodox	61	36	33

Source: 1981 Greater New York Jewish Population Study

thodox Jews are indeed more observant than their older counterparts. Whereas just over half of those fifty-five and over reported handling no money on the Sabbath, well over three-quarters of those under thirty-five so claimed. Similarly, only one-third of the older Orthodox observed the Fast of Esther as compared with almost twice as many younger adults. In terms of the categories of Orthodoxy about which we have been thinking throughout this study, we might guess that while a good many of the older Jews in this sample are nominally Orthodox, as we move toward the younger ages on the spectrum more traditionalists can be counted and hence ritual observance increases (i.e., money is not handled on Sabbath and the Fast of Esther is observed).

We can see parallel changes in the service attendance

patterns of the Orthodox. The number of men who attend services at least weekly was greater among younger men. Two-thirds of the older Orthodox men attended services weekly or more as compared with over 80% of those under thirty-five. The opposite result for women is perplexing, but we speculate that it may likewise be a sign of increased traditionalism. As we pointed out in Chapter 4, in the traditional Orthodox community women did not attend the synagogue except once or twice a year. Hence, as women become more traditionalist, we might expect a drop in their weekly attendance in the synagogue.[33]

Part of the reason for the greater seriousness with which younger Orthodox Jews observe the formal norms of Orthodoxy can be found in the changing patterns of attendance at yeshiva or day school. While men's childhood attendance at such schools significantly exceeds that of comparably aged women, among both sexes, yeshiva or day school, attendance has climbed dramatically. (Our data appear below on table 6.2.)

Among the men, only a minority of those over fifty-four reported having attended a full-time Jewish school; in contrast, almost nine of ten men under thirty-five had been to a yeshiva or day school as a child. The women report a parallel trend. Of the older women, less than one in five went to full-time Jewish schools; of those under thirty-five, the figure reached two-thirds. (To be sure, as seen in table 4.5 of Chapter 4, among traditionalist Orthodox overall about two-thirds of both men and women had a yeshiva or day school education, and among centrists overall nearly half did so.)

Certainly for the men, and to a lesser extent for the women, yeshiva or day school attendance has become something of a prerequisite for membership in the Orthodox community—a fact established in table 4.4 of Chapter 4. We now add to that fact these age-related figures from table 6.1 which can be understood as a reflection of a historical record. Looking at these, we must say that the change in the proportions attending full-time schools over the last twenty or thirty years has been truly startling. The difference in yeshiva or day school attendance between those fifty-five and over and those less than thirty-five among men is more than two to one and among women more than three to one.

The findings cited above speak to the question of whether those who call themselves Orthodox are becoming increasingly observant and learned. Their ritual observance is likely to be more punctilious—if the rituals of handling money on Sabbath and fasting on the Fast of Esther are any indicators. And if the yeshivas and day schools they attend teach them anything, they are likely to be more learned or at least more exposed to Orthodox Jewish life and values.

If we are satisfied that, of those who call themselves Orthodox, the younger among them may well tend to be more strongly Orthodox, we now wish to determine if the intergenerational outflow from Orthodoxy that was once overwhelming has indeed been thwarted. That is, if Orthodoxy has been in some way getting stronger, if there is some genuine basis underlying its leaders' confidence, then we should discover evidence of increases in what may be called "the Orthodox intergenerational retention rate." If there is such an increase, the extent to which the children of Orthodox parents act Orthodox as adults—either by identification or by way of observance—should increase as age declines.

The Greater New York Survey failed to ascertain whether respondents' parents were Orthodox per se. But it did ask about parents' observance patterns. Here as before we can use one ritual—refraining from handling money on the Sabbath—as a reasonable indicator of parental Orthodoxy. To ascertain the reality of intergenerational retention, we can examine the observance and schooling patterns of those respondents whose parents were reported to have refrained from handling money on the Sabbath.

Indeed, the New York area data on those whose parents handled no money on the Sabbath do lead us to believe that Orthodox Jews are doing better in holding on to their own. Of those fifty-five and over, less than a third were observing the same restriction themselves as contrasted with more than twice as many young adults (under thirty-five) with the same sort of parents. Similarly, while most of these young adults fasted on the Fast of Esther, less than a fifth of their older counterparts made the same claim. Among children of the Sabbath observant, yeshiva or day school education also rises with youth. Among men, the proportion who had some full-time schooling was twice as large among those under thirty-five as it was among those fifty-five and over (74% vs. 38%); among women, the ratio between the younger and older groups exceeds four to one (48% vs. 11%). Last, the proportion who simply call themselves Orthodox is far greater (almost two to one) among younger children of the traditionally Sabbath observant as among their older counterparts.

In short, insofar as these data can be taken as a sign of the success with which Orthodox parents manage to raise Orthodox children, the findings point in the same direction. Increasingly, the adult children of Orthodox parents claim to be Orthodox themselves, practice a higher level of observance, and report having attended a yeshiva or day school.

The New York area findings, based as they are on a random sample of the region's Jewish population, certainly provide evidence of the two trends we have been discussing. On the basis of the patterns of observance and educational background, Orthodoxy does seem to be moving toward the religious right. On the basis of data on the children of observant parents, Orthodoxy does seem to be improving its ability to hold on to its own.

Our own specialized survey allows us to further elaborate on the shift to the right (see table 6.2). Insofar as we can explicitly compare the age-related trends in the New York study with those in our particular sample, the trends are substantively similar. In our sample, the proportions who fasted at least part of the day on the Fast of Esther increased from about half of those fifty-five and over to over 80% of those under thirty-five. This pattern parallels the New York area trends, albeit at a higher level. For each age group, the proportion fasting in these data exceeded those in the New York data.

One reason for this discrepancy may be the difference between the two surveys in question wording. The New York questionnaire provided a simple "yes" or "no" choice

Table 6.2: Percent Scoring High on Measures of Orthodox Identity by Age

	Less than 35	35–54	55 or over
Fasts part or all day on Fast of Esther	82	70	51
Attends services weekly:			
Men	91	92	83
Women	68	48	54
Yeshiva or day school was main form of Jewish education:			
Men	68	56	39
Women	58	25	9
Yeshiva or day school main form of Jewish education "you do/did/ would give your children"	99	90	66
Indices:			
Ritual observance	59	44	35
Faithfulness	51	48	33
Torah-true	40	39	34
Personal God	38	31	25
Orthodox closeness and similarity	41	47	62
Parochialism	31	28	26
Conservatism	28	25	44
No non-Jewish close friends	49	44	44
Most close friends are Orthodox Jews	80	69	63
Mean % of charity devoted to Orthodox causes	58	60	54

to the question, "Do you fast on the Fast of Esther?" Our Orthodoxy questionnaire offered three choices: full-day, part-day, or not at all. The number of full-day fasters in the latter survey is very close to the numbers in the New York area sample who answered "yes" to the Fast of Esther question. Certainly those in the New York sample who answered affirmatively included not only full-day but part-day fasters as well. If so, then the proportion fasting in the Orthodox survey certainly exceeds the proportion in the New York sample. This, in turn, implies that the Orthodox sample is to some extent more ritually observant than the random sample of New York area Orthodox Jews. Nevertheless, the import of the age-related patterns in the two samples is the same: younger Orthodox Jews are more observant than their elders, indicating that the ritual standards for identification with Orthodoxy have indeed been rising.

The service attendance patterns reinforce the notion that our Orthodoxy sample is more observant than the random sample of New York area Orthodox. For both men and women, for every age group, more of the Orthodoxy survey respondents attended services weekly than did their New York area counterparts. Younger respondents attended more than their elders of the same sex (in the Orthodoxy sample), but here the age differences were less pronounced and less consistent than they were in the New York data.[34]

The educational patterns in the Orthodoxy sample also parallel those found in the New York data. Here again, we have discrepant questions but substantively similar age trends. The New York data referred to *any* attendance at a full-time Jewish school; the Orthodoxy questionnaire asked about "the *predominant* form of Jewish education." All other things being equal, we would expect higher percentages in the New York questionnaire.

With this said, it is significant to note that in the Orthodoxy sample, the proportion with a predominantly full-time Jewish education rises dramatically with declines in age. Among men, the proportion of young people with such schooling is almost double the proportion among those 55 and over (68% vs. 39%). Among women, hardly any of the older group reported a full-time education (9%), as contrasted with a quarter of the middle-aged, and a clear majority of those under thirty-five.

In other words, in both populations, far more younger Orthodox men showed evidence of a yeshiva or day school education, on the order of twice the magnitude among older men. Moreover, while women's attendance trailed that of the men, the growth in women's full-time schooling substantially exceeded that of the men. In fact, the gap between men and women in full-time schooling was narrower among younger than among older groups. And among the younger, more intensive Jewish education was predominant.

We also asked, "What sort of Jewish education do/did/ would you give your children?" About two-thirds of those fifty-five and over gave one of the full-time answers. It is interesting that this figure comes close to the number of young Orthodox adults who said they actually had such an education. It is as if the reports of the parents (fifty-five and over) were confirmed by the educational experiences of their putative children (the respondents under thirty-five). Among those slightly younger, the number who provided a full-time Jewish education for their children climbed to 90%; and the commitment to such an education among the youngest adults is almost total. We might propose that, for today's young Orthodox, intensive Jewish education is no longer simply an alternative; it is a requirement. Piecing together the actual schooling of the different age groups with their reports and intentions for their children's education, we can adduce a clear trend over three generations from infrequent toward universal full-time Jewish schooling.

Contrasting Trends in Aspects of Orthodoxy

Having established the rough correspondence between the random sample of the New York area data and our selective sample of Orthodox Jews drawn from several sources, we can now proceed to examine age-related differences in other dimensions of Orthodox Jewish identity. To do so, we will rely on several indices constructed so as to summarize the most significant items appearing in our earlier chapters. For convenience, the indices and the items they draw upon can be outlined as follows (see questionnaire in Appendix for complete question wording):

1. Ritual observance: As noted in Chapter 2, this index incorporates fasting on Tisha B'Av and the tenth of Tevet; refraining from eating cold salads at a nonkosher friend's house; refraining from eating warm "kosher" foods at a nonkosher friend's house; not working at a job on the Sab-

bath; refraining from turning on and off lights on the Sabbath; having meat and dairy dishes.

2. Faithfulness: Belief that God definitely exists; that the Torah was given to Moses at Mount Sinai; that the Messiah will come; and denial that "God plays a negligible role in everyday life."

3. Torah-true: Disagreement with several potentially heretical ideas: that "one should not follow the . . . Torah in blind faith;" that I am not "a 'sinner' even if I transgress . . . Jewish law"; that "*halacha* must sometimes be ignored"; that "the modern world has become too complex to be ruled by Torah; as well as agreement that ancient Jewish practice is appropriate for the present day, and that the dictates of the Torah alone rather than kindness alone is a good reason to "give alms to the poor."

4. Personal God: Belief in the efficacy of prayer in causing the recovery of one's gravely ill child; trust in God's favor as an explanation for personal success; a conviction of the importance of prayer as an answer to one's problem or worry; confidence in the idea that winning a million dollars in the lottery is brought about with God's help; and assurance that "God will punish those who transgress his commandments."

5. Orthodox closeness and similarity: Feeling close "toward most Orthodox Jews"; and thinking oneself similar "to most Orthodox Jews," what we might also call, "Orthodox cohesiveness and bonding."

6. Parochialism: Disagreement that "An Orthodox Jew can be close friends with" non-Orthodox Jews and with non-Jews; and that "it is important to learn and know about matters of contemporary life."

7. Conservatism: Opposition toward the Equal Rights Amendment, homosexuality, affirmative action, government aid for abortions, and abolition of the death penalty; support for government "aid to nonpublic schools."

The indices correspond with the issues investigated in the previous chapters. Chapter 2 explored ritual observance; Chapter 3 analyzed the items under the rubrics of Faithfulness and Personal God; Chapter 4 explored feeling close to the Orthodox community and openness to friends and interests outside Orthodoxy; and Chapter 5 analyzed the social and political attitudes. These chapters showed that the more ritually observant (as measured by our first index based on ritual behavior) reported higher scores on most of the individual items in each of the six other dimensions of Orthodox identity. In other words, those more observant of *mitzvas* also more often expressed greater faithfulness, more explicitly "Torah-true" attitudes, stronger belief in a personal God, increased closeness to Orthodox Jews, resistance to cosmopolitanism, and conservative social attitudes.

To simplify the analysis in this chapter, for each index, we defined a "high" scoring group. Thus, we decided to focus on the more traditional segment, a collection that ranged in size from over a quarter to half the total sample. That is, we distinguished the groups that were most faithful, most "torah-true," most believing in God, most bonded to the Orthodox, and most socially conservative. Table 6.2 reports the extent to which the proportion of these more traditional segments varied over the three age groups.

The age-related patterns outlined thus far in this chapter suggest that we should find similar patterns with respect to these other dimensions. That is, the young should be "more Orthodox" than their elders (and, presumably, their forebears). But the results are far from uniform.

In a majority of the items, younger Orthodox Jews (those under thirty-five) were, indeed, substantially more conservative or traditional than their elders. The greatest differences and where younger adults scored higher than their elders are with regard to ritual observance and belief in a personal God (on faithfulness, they score higher too— but just slightly). That is, they do more *mitzvas,* and believe in God and His omniscience and activity more than those older than they.

In the other areas of Orthodox identity, while the young score higher, the differences are not nearly as pronounced. The "Torah-true" index measures commitment to obeying the dictates of the Torah, to living the halachic life, no matter what complications modernity may generate. Here, the young—despite their higher levels of ritual performance, profession of belief in fundamentalist tenets of the faith and in an active and personal God—score just slightly higher than older Orthodox Jews. In like fashion, we find small yet measurable differences between old and young with respect to "parochialism," the index that measures openness to friendship with the non-Orthodox (Jewish or not) and to involvement in the affairs of contemporary life.

One may speculate on the reasons for these differences. Certainly the enthusiasm and fervor of youth must play some role in the process. It is likely as well that their having come of age at a time when Orthodoxy was vital and no longer on the cultural defense led to a stronger attachment to its way of life and values.

But if this has been a time when being an Orthodox Jew in America was acceptable and legitimate, then it also has been a time when to be Orthodox meant that one did not have to remain tied to the parochial community of other Orthodox Jews. One could be uncompromisingly Orthodox and still be out in and part of the world. One could be cosmopolitan. And this was something the young, those coming of age in this time, understood. Table 6.2 reflects that reality.

As the figures make clear, more of the older respondents claimed to feel especially close and similar to other Orthodox Jews; in addition, they were readier to express the conservative social and political attitudes. These are measures of insularity, of holding back. Moreover, we recall from the previous chapter that those under thirty-five were also far more sexually permissive than their elders. The relative social liberalism of younger Orthodox Jews, then, is fairly consistent and broad-based. In these respects, the young—in spite of their religious fervor and increased ritual observance—seem relatively more cosmopolitan and liberal and the old more parochial and traditionalist. Do these age-related patterns extend to other aspects of social integration or insularity?

To further explore questions related to parochialism and insularity, the bottom of table 6.2 reports age variations in three items: charitable commitment to Orthodoxy, friend-

ship with non-Jews, friendship with Orthodox Jews. Charitable commitment refers to the average percentage of their
charitable dollar respondents said they would donate to
specifically Orthodox causes rather than other Jewish or
nonsectarian charities.

We found that the young and old were about as likely to
report having no non-Jewish friends; and they reported
giving equal proportions of their ideal charitable dollar to
Orthodox causes (in all cases more than half). However, to
a measurable extent, more younger respondents reported
that most of their friends were Orthodox.

Insofar as these age-related findings can be taken as evidence of either past developments or future trends, they
appear to suggest somewhat contradictory inclinations
among Orthodox Jews, or at least those represented by this
sample. On the one hand, we have clear evidence of a
move to what may be called the theological traditionalism.
The trends suggested include more yeshiva/day school
training, greater punctiliousness in ritual observance,
more fervent endorsement of the principles of the faith,
and a more unswerving belief in the Divine omniscience
and immanence. At the same time, the younger respondents provided some evidence of a greater openness to the
non-Orthodox world, that is, a decline in insularity, a kind
of cosmopolitanism. They expressed less rhetorical attachment to the Orthodox community, and they were decidedly more liberal in political and social attitudes. In addition, the youngsters were no more likely than their elders
to focus their charitable giving on Orthodox causes or to
report non-Jewish friends.

That they did have more close friends within Orthodoxy
does not invalidate our inference of less insularity. Close
friends emerge from the warp and woof of everyday life—
and in that everyday existence, as we have seen, the
younger Orthodox come into a great deal of contact with
other Orthodox Jews. Moreover, having most of one's close
friends be Orthodox Jews may be distinguished from attitudes toward politics, contemporary affairs, and the *idea* or
principle of having non-Orthodox friends. We suggest that
even as the most intimate aspects of younger Orthodox
Jews lives are more bound up within the Orthodox com-

munity, their worldviews are decidedly more tolerant and open than those of their elders. In more technical terms, the more educated (Jewishly and otherwise) younger adults are more apt to more fully compartmentalize their lives into a traditionalist private sphere and a modern public sphere.

Interesting parallels with these findings can be found in the study of American Jewry generally. On the one hand, the extent to which Jews have non-Jewish spouses, friends, and neighbors appears to be rising—that is, they continue in the direction of cosmopolitanization. At the same time, levels of ritual observance, communal affiliation, and commitment to Jewish peoplehood appear to be holding steady—that is, Jewish parochialism still exists.[35]

It seems—and this inference is admittedly speculative—that Orthodox Jews (perhaps like American Jews) are more thoroughly integrating without in any way abandoning the essential aspects of their religious identity. They are in effect becoming a part of America *as Orthodox Jews*. That the ABC network can on its "Nightline" program devote a full half-hour to an Orthodox, Hassidic wedding, a wedding that takes place in the New York City Jacob Javits Convention Center; that an Orthodox Jew, Ari Weiss, donning a *yarmulke*, can become the top legislative aid of the Speaker of the United States House of Representatives; that Orthodox Jewish Talmud study circles can take place daily at lunch hour in the conference rooms and boardrooms of major corporations, law firms, and university faculty clubs are all signs that Orthodoxy is part of American life—and not only on its margins.

To be sure, not all Orthodox Jews are cosmopolitan and parochial, modern and Orthodox, American and Jewish. In fact, the segregation and insularity of some Orthodox may be instrumental in supporting the distinctive Orthodox subculture. The Orthodox still need their talmudists, ritual specialists, and religious virtuosi. Indeed, one of the impending crises of the modern wing of Orthodoxy may possibly be that having sent their young into the cosmopolitan professions, they have left few behind to be rabbis, yeshiva teachers, and keepers of the Orthodox institutions;

and accordingly—as Orthodox Jews—they are increasingly dependent upon those of their coreligionists who have *not* left the parochial confines of the tradition and who remain the rabbis, teachers, and keepers of the institutions. And these parochials may not fully share in an understanding of and sympathy with the modern condition; they may indeed resist and reject it, trying to turn the young against it.

The modernization of younger Jews, their education and affluence, may bring about two seemingly contradictory effects: clearer articulation and compliance with an Orthodox credo and system of behavior, coupled with greater involvement in the larger society. In a sense, the formal training, the strengthened commitment, the greater behavioral conformity make it possible for younger Orthodox Jews to, in a sense, venture forth more confidently into the non-Orthodox world. Who precisely will remain behind in the totally Orthodox world to which they return to study, to pray, and to live with, is a harder question to answer.

7 Conclusion

"At any age, to be an Orthodox Jew in modern society means to live with questions and conflicts."

Chaim I. Waxman,
"Orthodox Judaism and Modern Society"

We have tried in the foregoing pages to define and articulate the character of Orthodox Jewry in contemporary America, and particularly of those who have made some attempts at culture contact. In so doing, we have attempted to address the general question of how those who are attracted to Jewish tradition, religious ritual, ancient beliefs, and a parochial community which shares these attachments do so while simultaneously finding themselves in the more cosmopolitan situation of modernity. That they *have* found ways of coming to grips with their multifaceted lives, of adapting their acculturation, seems beyond question. But, as we have discovered, Orthodox Jews are not all alike, and accordingly their responses to the confrontation between the parochial and the cosmopolitan differ.

Looking at these varying responses, we found ourselves able to distinguish among three broad categories of modern Orthodoxy: those who on the one extreme remain strongly attached to the traditions of Judaism; those on the other extreme who choose to call themselves "Orthodox" but while measurably more observant, faithful, and parochial than the general Jewish population are on the liberal fringe of those who identify themselves as "Orthodox"; and, finally, we found a category of Jews who fill the space between these extremes and display a bivalence, sometimes exhibiting traditionalist tendencies and other times moving toward the relative laxity and liberality of the nominally Orthodox. To be sure, the distinctions between "traditionalists," the "nominally Orthodox," and those we have called "centrists" are not ones that Jewish law recognizes. From the perspective of the Torah, all Jews by and large share equal responsibilities and a common religious heritage. These are, however, distinctions that we as sociologists recognize and believe to be undeniable. They are based on empirical reality in which, as we demonstrated, there are differing levels of ritual observance, variations in belief, and distinctions in ethos and communal ties.

Each of the groupings helps us to comprehend the character of contemporary Orthodoxy. The traditionalist minority reveal the possibilities of punctiliousness in observance and fervency of ancient religious belief, even in the atmosphere of a contemporary world where most people are less observant and far less articulate in their religious beliefs. These Jews continue to seek insulation from America and modernity and tend toward the splendid isolation of totally Orthodox society. Here they observe their rituals, keep their faith, find their friends; and here they give their charity. Moreover, they show us that insularity and parochialism can survive quite well even in a world that seems to be shrinking and where cosmopolitanism and mobility are facts of modern life. And they show us that, at least these days, they have had some success in attracting the young to share somewhat in their point of view and way of life. Finally, they show us that an ethos largely at odds with the dominant trends can be held on to with striking tenacity even by those who find themselves in the situation of modernity.[1]

In a sense, the nominally Orthodox exemplify this as well for they continue to call themselves Orthodox, with—as we have shown—some justification, even as they display behaviors, beliefs, loyalties, and ties that associate them quite closely with the contemporary American scene and society. They can be cosmopolitan *and* parochial. But, if their situation of modernity is restrained by their Orthodoxy, so too their Orthodoxy is limited by their association with ways of life outside of it—and they are a minority of a minority.

It is left to the centrists, who (compared with the nominally Orthodox) are more firmly attached to the parochialities of Orthodoxy without being very remote from or untouched by more cosmopolitan connections, to most dramatically display the character of modern Jewish orthodoxy. Their dualism, an ambivalence coupled with compartmentalization, is what makes them most fascinating. These are the Jews, sitting at the epicenter of the crossroads of the traditional and contemporary worlds, who try to remain open to the outside world and close to their Judaism, who as a group cannot decide whether they are "strictly" or only "fairly" Orthodox because, in fact, they are both. These are the Jews who in some respects merge with the traditionalists and in other ways share in the liberality of the nominally Orthodox. These are "Torah-true" Jews who remain loyal to the formal doctrines and patterns of behavior associated with Orthodoxy but who reflect a practical and informal ideology that is something less than completely formed by the demands and expectations of the Torah. These are people who are both cosmopolitan and parochial.

What these Orthodox Jews (and, by contrast, their traditionalist counterparts) have shown us is that—as a group—Orthodox Jews have passed into the modern world, but they have done so with ambivalence. To handle their ambivalence and swim in these crosscurrents, most American Orthodox Jews have had to live with contradiction. They have done this, as we have said, by compartmentalizing their lives. Thus, as we have shown, they can have an attitude that reflects openness to all sorts of people and a variety of life-styles while in practice they have only Orthodox friends and live a relatively parochial existence. They are modern even as they live a life very much embedded in ancient rituals, customs, beliefs, and traditions. And to mute the contradictions implicit in this dualism, they frame the separate worlds by brackets of inattention. That is, unless forced to, most Orthodox Jews (but particularly the nontraditionalist ones) choose not to focus on the strains. Sometimes this has led to a diminished inner commitment to things Jewish and a concomitant openness to things American (even when the latter appear to contradict Jewish values, loyalties, and affiliations). At other times, it has led to less than an enthusiastic embrace of contemporary America as Orthodox Jews have pulled away from the pressures of assimilation, rejecting cosmopolitan orientations in favor of parochial attractions and intimacies.

Often, however, it has led to a feeling of being at home in each world, even though these worlds are not always at home with each other.

In many ways, modern Orthodox Jews (and particularly the nontraditionalist ones) may be seen as the quintessential American Jews for they strive to be both authentically American and Jewish—even when this seems oxymoronic. They live lives of cultural dualism, with all the pain and privilege this kind of existence affords.

This dualism has affected the fervency and certainty of beliefs just as it has diminished or at least adjusted certain religious practices—from keeping kosher to going to the synagogue or fasting. This is not to say that modern Orthodox Jews are not recognizably more observant and faithful than most American Jews. They are—indeed, among the young even more so than among those over the age of fifty-five. Orthodox Jews are still devoted to God, His Torah, and its commandments as well as the central tenets of rabbinic Judaism. But it does mean that many—if not most—Orthodox Jews today are somewhat less punctilious about their observance of those commandments and a bit less certain about their Jewish beliefs and less fervent in their expression of them.

Centrists, even when they are a majority, do not always capture the imagination of observers nor do they make the most noise. They are far less noticeable than the more exotic and often picturesque traditionalists. Indeed, strictly speaking, we cannot even call them a group for they are by nature a conglomeration of people in the middle facing both directions and pulling toward opposite extremes. Among themselves the centrist tending toward traditionalism and the one closer to nominal Orthodoxy look upon each other as far apart. Thus, centrists are rather an aggregate of the ambivalent, a mass of people not completely aligned with traditionalism nor wholly in favor of settling for an Orthodoxy in name alone.

America, a society that encourages and fosters individualism and that in the last number of years has become more tolerant of pluralism, is precisely the environment in which such a centrist Orthodoxy, a cosmopolitan parochialism, could flourish. This society, while not antagonistic to religious sensibility and increasingly comfortable with ethnic diversity, has created an atmosphere in which even ritually observant individuals feel freer to articulate their own versions of Judaism and Jewish life, where they can deviate rather easily from the formal moral and doctrinal teachings of organized faith. This is a country where people can each be "religious in his or her own way." And modern Orthodox Jews have taken advantage of this. Indeed, for the nontraditionalist (the centrists and the nominally) Orthodox, wherever Jewish law appears to be neutral, individual choice seems to fill the vacuum. While many modern Orthodox Jews lament the dearth of religious leadership, few beyond the most traditionalist wait for the rabbis—the formal voices of Jewish law and religion—to blaze new trails through the thicket of contemporary American life. The lay people act first and only later look for religious legitimation and support, which more often than not is slow to arrive.

As America has allowed for greater expression of ethnicity and religiosity, these Jews have found their cultural dualism easier to bear, and they have bared themselves accordingly; they have displayed more of their Jewishness and emphasized the religiosity more. Turning toward their traditionalist side, they have sent their children in greater numbers into full-time and intensive Jewish education (places increasingly staffed by the traditionalists). Thus, the young—those maturing in this ethnic and religious America and influenced by this parochial Jewish education—are more observant then their parents, more manifestly tied to the Orthodox community (among whom they count all or most of their close friends). They are restrained in their enthusiasm for some of the cardinal values of modernity, including science, and more politically conservative than most Jews.

But, even now, most contemporary Orthodox Jews have not become traditionalists. They still have a liberal side. They still believe they can have ties with non-Orthodox and even with non-Jews. Although conservative, they are still more politically and religiously liberal than their traditionalist Orthodox counterparts, and more aligned with and open to the influences of modern America (including its popular culture). In short, they are (as to an extent the nominally Orthodox are also) cosmopolitan parochials. Indeed, when we look at nontraditionalist Jews, particularly where the effects of their religion are muffled or neutralized (as we did in Chapter 5), we find that they act very much like other American Jews.

Yet all this is not to say that the Orthodoxy reflected by those we have called "traditionalists" is waning or insignificant. On the contrary, we have seen that traditionalist tendencies are growing more pronounced in many areas. This is a time in America that is hospitable if not conducive to these tendencies. A disenchantment with secularity, a rise of ethnicity and religion, the growth of triumphalism and the enhanced pride that Orthodoxy has in its capacity to survive, the growing number of Jewish educational institutions—particularly day schools and yeshivas—and their popularity as a means of Jewish socialization and their staffing by those who have not been de-ghettoized, the visibility of the newly Orthodox *(baaley t'shuvah)*, the increase of the political and moral influence of Orthodoxy in Israel along with Israel's enhanced importance for Jewish identity, and finally a growing concern with Jewish survival have all served to make Orthodoxy in general and traditionalist Orthodoxy (perceived by many both inside and outside its ranks as the most "authentic" Judaism) in particular the "Jewish success story" of the times. To be sure, after all the gloomy predictions of its demise in the middle years of the century, almost any evidence of its capacity to survive would have been news; but that it has flourished is even bigger news.

As we have shown, the more persistent and bolder Orthodoxy of the young is perhaps the biggest news of all, for it suggests that Orthodoxy is not about to disappear. And if nothing else the existence of the young Orthodox offers evidence of the Orthodoxy's capacity to reproduce itself— no small accomplishment when we look at the transformation and evaporation of so much of American Jewry. The story is even more striking when we realize that among the young there has been an increase in the numbers receiving an intensive Jewish education: the tendency to provide full-time Jewish primary and secondary education is practically universal—nearly 100% among all but the nominally Orthodox and almost 70% among the latter. Moreover, the young are more ritually observant, faithful, and attached to a belief in a personal God. They are more bonded to the Orthodox community, the locus of most of their friendships and the source of many of their values. They are, at least at present, more firmly Orthodox than the older generation.

This is not to suggest that the young are exclusively traditionalist in their Orthodoxy. They just lean that way. Nevertheless, these are people who are also young American Jews. As such, they are liberal in their attitudes toward sexuality, open in many of their general political orientations, and clearly ready to share in American popular culture. Thus, while they display traditionalist tendencies, they would still seem to qualify as centrists—Orthodox Jews who have not altogether turned away from the contemporary American way of life and values.

And what of the future? Predictions are always dangerous, particularly in an age when time seems to collapse more readily into the future and changes occur more rapidly than ever before. Still, certain assumptions about the future seem fairly safe. First, the nearly universal intensive Jewish education that has become de rigueur in Orthodox circles will undoubtedly result in an Orthodoxy more knowledgeable about its obligations and life possibilities. The deviations that have stemmed from ignorance may accordingly lessen and a stricter Orthodoxy may be expected, at least at the level of ritual observance where much of the education is focused.

Second, the fact that most Orthodox young people will attend such schools will even further foster network relations among them. People will share friendships from their youth as well as have a common personal history and pattern of socialization. The likelihood that Orthodox Jews will continue to have most of their friends from among the Orthodox is therefore fairly high. In adulthood, such a common educational and social heritage facilitates a sense of intimacy and abets the feelings of quasi-kinship that are

213

so much a part of the Orthodox *kehilla*. And Orthodox Jews are likely to continue to be highly endogamous, finding their spouses from within the world of Orthodoxy. We may, therefore, expect that communal bonding among Orthodox Jews will be a continuing feature of American Orthodox life.

Insofar as the educational institutions that Orthodox Jews attend continue to provide a liberal secular education and encourage university training, and do not encourage a total turning away from American life, their graduates will still feel an attachment to the non-Orthodox world and share in some of its values. And thus, at least in America, we may expect a persistence of the bivalence of American life. To be sure, valences may vary from time to time, depending on who the teachers in the schools are and their success in transmitting either traditionalist Jewish or modern American ways of life and values. Or, to put it differently, much of American Orthodoxy is likely to remain a marginal culture, one in which its members share in two cultures without being central to either one.[2]

As a marginal culture, American Orthodoxy will necessarily remain significantly affected by the changes in the character of American life. So long as America remains receptive to ethnic diversity and religious expression, Orthodoxy here will allow itself to more openly and fully express the Jewish (i.e., non-American) side of its character, for it thus can mitigate the pressures of ambivalence and the strains of cultural dualism. In a pluralist America rather than a monocultural one, in the salad bowl rather than the melting pot, Orthodoxy is likely to be more traditionalist in its public face, although never totally antimodern.

Moreover, should American society swing back toward an attitude encouraging cultural homogeneity, Orthodox Jews may find themselves forced to make a choice between being more manifestly American or more obviously Jewish. Given their network of relations, it is hard to imagine a sudden and complete abandonment of the Orthodox way of life. A melting pot ideal in America, however, could significantly enlarge the number of nominally Orthodox or at least those sorts of trends among centrists. Bivalence after all suggests the possibility of movement into either of two orbits.

That women will play an increased role in Orthodox life also seems certain. Not only are they receiving more education—Jewish and secular—then ever before, but many have come of age in an era of feminism when women have stressed their parity with men. This does not mean that they will overcome the ambivalence of much of modern Orthodoxy, but it does mean that they will become a part of the equation, forcing modern Orthodox Jews to come to terms with yet another element of the situation of modernity that is sometimes at odds with Jewish tradition. And if the yeshivas find a place for women in them, they too will lean to the right as have their male counterparts.

In the years to come, it is likely that ritual observance will continue to play a major role in defining the character of Orthodoxy and that faith will remain embedded in Orthodox life. But while the number of rituals observed and the fervency of faith may rise (or fall), the existence of variations along a continuum of Orthodoxy seems likely to continue to be part of Orthodox life. That is, Orthodox Jews will continue to differ among themselves because, more than simply an expression of ideology or dogma, Orthodoxy in America is the result of social forces. It is the product of communal ties and common behavioral background as well as shared ethos and worldview.

Orthodoxy has reason to feel optimistic about its future. Not only are its mature adults embraced by its way of life, but its youth are so as well. Moreover, the divisions within the fabric of its population, the variations among those who identify themselves as Orthodox, are in fact a strength rather than a weakness for they provide these Jews with a range of models of behavior, belief, and way of life. That Orthodoxy is not a monolith is healthy for it. It means that Orthodoxy can flex and mold itself to the vagaries of fortune. This may be troubling to those who perceive it from any particular internal viewpoint for they necessarily see others (or even themselves) as falling short of the ideal.

But, evaluated from the outside, the multifaceted character of the community must be seen as a sign of organic vitality.

To be sure, there are real challenges ahead for Orthodoxy. There are issues we have merely touched upon briefly but that constitute real concerns for insiders. One is the lack of a dedicated and talented cadre of Jewish educators to provide training for future generations who would be both modern *and* Orthodox. Another problem is an increasingly insular rabbinate, particularly one trained in the yeshivas and *kollels* which have remained as separate as possible from mainstream America and lay Judaism, and one that often cannot speak to the concerns of most Orthodox Jews in America. If more and more rabbinic leaders take the position that, in the words of one such rabbi, "the opinion of the *balebatim* [lay people] is the reverse of the opinion of the Torah," the middle may well find itself even more dependent on its own devices than it now is.

The dependence on America must also be a cause for concern for it means that the future of Orthodoxy is not always within the control of only its members. There is no complete insularity, no total retreat to the ghetto, no escape from the situation of modernity. It means that for all the internal communal planning, Orthodox Jews must be prepared for the possibility that forces beyond their control will affect them. And that is true even for the traditionalists who will continue to have to contend with a changing situation of America and the outside world—even if only to find new ways of rejecting and escaping them.

Yet with all of that, there *is* a future for Orthodoxy in America. It is one of bivalence, adapted acculturation, of contention and cooperation, reinterpretation and compartmentalization, the cosmopolitan coupled with the parochial, the past meeting with the present. Moreover, it is a future in which the people in question are always having to fine-tune their lives so that they manage to handle its various valences. And thus it is a future that will bear watching in the days and years ahead.

Notes

Chapter One

1. See Rosenthal 1960, pp. 275–288; see also Katz 1987, pp. 257–269.

2. Mayer 1973, pp. 151–165.

3. Sklare [1955] 1972, p. 43.

4. Mayer and Waxman 1977, p. 101.

5. See Sklare [1955] 1972, characterizing comments made by Rabbi David Gordis, p. 264.

6. Massarik (1974, p. 2) places the number at round 11% based upon a National Jewish Population Survey. This figure is cited and supported by a number of others, including Mayer and Waxman 1977.

The local Jewish population studies, sponsored by the federations (central philanthropic agencies), report wide variations in the proportion Orthodox, ranging from 20% in Baltimore to perhaps only 2%–3% in Western and Pacific communities. The 1981 Greater New York Jewish Population Study reported a 13% frequency. Weighting the several studies by population size, it seems that 10% is a reasonable estimate for a national proportion (see also Tobin and Chenkin 1985, pp. 154–178).

7. Goldscheider 1986, p. 104.

8. Sklare [1955] 1972, p. 264.

9. Liebman 1987, p. 11.

10. Gurock 1987, p. 64.

11. Schiff 1966, p. 48. Most day schools are Orthodox in sponsorship.

12. Gurock 1987, p. 64.

13. Some, particularly those who escaped America by way of Shanghai, did indeed pledge to one another that they would create Orthodox institutions as an act of thanksgiving to God for their having been saved from destruction.

14. Mayer and Waxman 1977, p. 100.

15. Schiff 1981.

16. Gastwirth 1974; Raphael 1985, p. 139.

17. Cited in Raphael 1985, pp. 138–139.

18. Raphael 1985, p. 140.

19. Ibid., pp. 140, 151.

20. Ibid., p. 154.

21. Sklare [1955] 1972, p. 264.

22. Neusner 1972, p. vii.

23. *Halacha*, the Hebrew word for Jewish law, means literally "the way."

24. See, e.g., Bernstein 1979; Gurock 1983, 1988, and 1987, pp. 37–84; Heilman 1982b, 1982c; Hoenig 1932; Raphael 1985; Rosenblatt 1951; Rothkoff 1972; Schwab 1950.

25. Works on this process of Jewish modernization include Endelman 1979; Etkes 1987; Katz 1973; Mahler 1971; Meyer 1987; Roth 1959; Silber 1987.

26. Durkheim 1954, p. 475.

27. Maine 1885, pp. 164–165.

28. This is what Max Weber called *Zweckrationalitat*.

29. Katz 1987.

30. Katz 1973.

31. Katz 1987, p. 1.

32. Ibid., p. 2.

33. Ibid., p. 11.

34. Cited in Kallen 1958, p. 9.

35. Katz 1975, p. 1.

36. When the nineteenth-century enlightened Jew Moses Mendelssohn was requesting permission from the Prussian sovereign to be granted the authorization for residence in Berlin, a privilege not commonly allowed Jews, a letter was written on his behalf by a Catholic friend who began his request as follows:

> A bad Catholic who is an intellectual asks a bad Protestant who is an intellectual to grant the right of residence in Berlin to a bad Jew who is an intellectual.

Commenting on this letter, Milton Himmelfarb points out, that while Mendelssohn was not all that bad a Jew, he had to be presented as one in order to gain the right of residence in Berlin. Catholics and Protestant could be good or bad as they pleased and still retain the right to live in Berlin (see Himmelfarb 1973, p. 369).

37. Katz 1973, p. 209.

38. See the essays by Israel Bartal, Emanuel Etkes, Michael Silber, Michael Graetz, Joseph Michman, Hillel J. Kieval, Lois Dubin, Todd Endelman, and Michael A. Meyer in Katz 1987.

39. On assimilation, see Doob 1960, p. 265; Sommerlad and Berry 1970.

40. Deutscher 1968, p. 26.

41. Quoted in Howe 1976.

42. Randall 1940, p. 377.

43. Herskovits 1949, p. ix.

44. Blau 1966, p. 27.

45. Gordon, however, deservedly famous for this phrase, was not simply advocating acculturation with it, the message most frequently assumed to be the primary one embedded in the aphorism. He was also reminding people to remain Jewish in spite of their acculturation. As Aharon Zeev Ben-Yishai suggests, Gordon "was also disappointed in the Jewish maskilim, particularly the young, who were carried away by the assimilationist trend, rejecting indiscriminately and forsaking Jewish values and the Hebrew language which Gordon loved without reservation" (*Encyclopedia Judaica*, vol. 7, pp. 801–802).

46. Of Mendelssohn's children, "two turned Catholic, two Protestant. Two remained Jews—but last generation Jews" (Karp 1976, p. 312).

47. E. W. Burgess (*International Encyclopedia of the Social Sciences* 1930, vol. 1) defines accommodation as this kind of social adjustment, while G. E. Simpson calls it a "process of compromise."

48. *Encyclopedia Judaica* 1972, vol. 6, p. 80; vol. 5, p. 901.

49. Herskovits 1949, p. 531.

50. For a fuller discussion of these issues, see Heilman 1982b and 1982c.

51. Although there are reports of the use of the term "Orthodox" with respect to Judaism as early as 1795, within the Jewish community the designation "Orthodox Jew" is generally agreed to have been first employed in 1807 by Abraham Furtado, a communal leader in Bordeaux and secretary of the Paris Sanhedrin, the assembly of Jewish notables convened by Napoleon for the purpose of clarifying the relations between the civil state and the Jews. He called those Jews "Orthodox" who refused to join civil society, who continued to cling to ancient practices and dogmas.

It is worthwhile noting that, while championing the past and tradition, Orthodoxy is in this sense a modern movement in that it sets itself up as voluntary community, a group of people who individually choose to turn their backs on acculturation and modernity. For an extended discussion of this thesis, see Friedman 1987.

52. Berger 1979, p. xi. For an illustration of the differences, see Emanuel Etkes penetrating analysis, "Immanent Factors and Ex-

ternal Influences in the Development of the Haskalah Movement in Russia" (1987).

53. Berger 1979, p. 3.

54. Katz 1986, p. 4.

55. Himmelfarb 1973, p. 283.

56. Waxman 1983.

57. These Jews are "quasi-tolerators," people who unenthusiastically tolerate or endure modern, non-Jewish culture either because they wish thereby to deny its inherent value or because they consider themselves hostages to it (see Heilman 1982b, p. 27).

58. Jung 1968, p. 115.

59. Redfield, Linton, and Herskovitz 1936, p. 152.

60. Breuer 1958, p. 277.

61. Lamm 1986, p. 2.

62. Katz 1987, p. 7.

63. There were, of course, precursors to Hirsch, among them Naftali Herz Wessely.

64. Grunfeld 1956, p. xviii. We do not mean to suggest that what the rabbis did was always in perfect harmony with the laity. Certainly there were discrepancies, but the rabbis in this respect largely mirrored the general attitudes of their congregants. Had they not, they would have lost their leadership positions.

65. Hirsch 1971, p. 236.

66. Ellenson 1980.

67. Grunblatt 1982.

68. This is perhaps most dramatically true in the case of the community that emerged out of the offspring and followers of Samson R. Hirsch and his sons-in-law the Breuers. Here, in what is today a stronghold of Agudas Yisroel Orthodoxy, modernity is viewed as something to which one makes concessions but does not wholeheartedly embrace.

69. See Sharot 1973.

70. As Jacob R. Marcus notes, "Most of the Jews whom we know by name in the eighteenth century were observant to some degree" (1953, p. 459).

71. For the concept of a "worked-through Orthodoxy," see Heilman 1982b, pp. 25, 36 (see also Gurock 1987, p. 64).

72. Gurock 1988.

73. To be sure, three of the men who were primarily instrumental in the creation of the Young Israel—Israel Friedlaender, Mordecai Kaplan, and Judah Magnes—were not dominant influences in American Orthodoxy and went on to achieve reputations for other achievements.

74. Gurock 1987, p. 64.

75. "We now call ourselves 'Centrist Orthodoxy.' There was a time, not too long ago, when we referred to ourselves as 'Modern Orthodox'" (Lamm 1986, p. 11). The choice of the term "centrist" comes from the decision of some Orthodox Jews to identify themselves as having chosen to avoid either extremes of the liberal left or the conservative right. Although we shall use the term "centrist" as well in our subsequent analysis, we use it in a very specific way—as shall be made clear when we introduce the term in our text—to indicate an aggregate that lies between two other alternatives on a continuum. Of course, right and left wing, precisely because they are short and ambiguous terms, probably remain the most popular.

76. Much has been written about the yeshivas and their role in shaping Orthodox Jewish consciousness (see, e.g., Weingarten 1976; Helmreich 1982). The idea of separating yeshiva students from their communities—while firmly established in many residential yeshivas in America—has its origins in the Lithuanian yeshiva established about 200 years ago in Volozhin (Shaul Stampfer, personal communication).

77. Berkovits 1971, p. 7.

78. Helmreich 1982, p. 31.

79. Raphael 1985, p. 156.

80. Berkovits 1971, p. 16.

81. Quoted in ibid., p. 156. Similar sentiments were expressed by Rabbi Aharon Lichtenstein, a Harvard Ph.D. in English literature and head of the yeshiva in Etzion, Israel ("Torah U Madda" lecture, Yeshiva University, 1988).

82. Hochbaum 1971, p. 91; see also Schiff 1981.

83. Mayer and Waxman 1977, p. 102.

84. Undoubtedly, many of the administrators—including Bernard Dov Revel, the president of Yeshiva College—were at best grudgingly pulled by their student body toward an integrationist approach. Nevertheless, their willingness to be pulled in that direction differentiated them from the more insular and rejectionist Orthodox (see Klaperman 1969; Rothkoff 1972).

85. To be sure, much care is taken to qualify the acculturative stance of modern Orthodoxy. "For those of us in the Centrist camp, Torah U Madda does not imply coequality of the two poles. Torah remains the preeminent center of our lives, our community, our value system. But centrality is not the same as exclusivity. It does not imply the rejection of all other forms or sources of knowledge" (Lamm 1986, p. 5; Lamm is president of Yeshiva University).

86. Gurock 1983, p. 109.

87. That this organization is more widely known by its Hebraic name offers tacit but no less symbolic evidence of its contra-acculturation.

88. Raphael 1985, p. 147.

89. Rosensweig 1986, p. 2.

90. Schiff 1981, p. 277.

91. Although the Lubavitch organization does concern itself with non-Orthodox Jews, it does so mainly to reach out and convert these Jews to a way of life more in line with contra-acculturative Orthodoxy.

92. See Raphael 1985, pp. 150–153.

93. Ibid., p. 151.

94. Rosensweig 1986, p. 2.

95. Some analysts, e.g., speak of a rightward turn of the Young Israel movement, long thought of as a bastion of acculturative, modern Orthodoxy. Shubert Spero marks it from 1963 when the Young Israel national director—a graduate of a transplanted European-style yeshiva—"urged a united Orthodox front which would turn to the 'Gedoley Torah' (leading Orthodox sages in America) . . . and be bound not only by their decisions on purely halachic matters, but also by their point of view on non-legal matters." To Spero this meant that the Young Israels were now turning for advice and direction to the same type of rabbis against whom their predecessors had tacitly rebelled (Spero 1978, p. 88).

96. See Lamm 1986, p. 6. As a motto of this group, Lamm quotes Rabbi Abraham I. Kook: "If you are firmly anchored up above, you will not slip here below."

97. Ritterband and Cohen 1984; Cohen 1988.

98. The local Jewish population studies sponsored by the federations (central philanthropic agencies) report wide variations in the proportion of Orthodox, ranging from 20% in Baltimore to perhaps only 2%–3% in Western and Pacific communities. The 1981 Greater New York Jewish Population Study reported a 13% frequency. Weighting by population size, it seems that 10% is a reasonable estimate for a national proportion. This figure conforms with the 11% figure given by Massarik (1973, p. 2; see also Tobin and Chenkin 1985, p. 171).

Chapter Two

1. Blau 1968, p. 308.

2. Wolpin 1974.

3. Deciding precisely where in that stream one or another region begins may be compared to defining the precise boundaries of the Midwest region of the United States about which there has been some dispute among social scientists, market researchers, and politicians. We may not be certain where it begins, but no one doubts the existence of such a region.

4. Borhek and Curtis 1975, p. 6.

5. Fackenheim 1968, p. 204.

6. There is a certain irony here in that the word "Orthodox" refers to matters of theology, belief, or opinion rather than to practice. Nevertheless, since at least 1803 when Abraham Furtado referred to those Jews who, in contrast to more "enlightened" Jews, were most scrupulous in the observance of their religion as "Orthodox," the term has stuck. In fact, "Orthoprax" would probably have been a more precise term—but it, according to the Oxford English dictionary, did not appear in usage until 1872 ("To be orthoprax, reader, is to do aright according to the commandment of the everlasting God, as to be orthodox is to think aright").

7. This is stated perhaps most succinctly by Rav Yehuda in tractate Pesakhim (50b) of the Babylonian Talmud.

8. Wurzberger 1962.

9. *Moment* 1978, p. 42.

10. Heilman 1976.

11. There is another good reason not to use all the observances. While tradition has it that there are 613 *mitzvas*, by no means do all authorities agree on what all these observances are. Moreover, customs and folkways—some of which have achieved, at least in the tradition, some of the character of observances—would also have to be counted. And folkways and customs vary across ethnic and community lines.

12. See, e.g., Lazerwitz and Harrison 1979; Cohen 1987a.

13. The idea of counting mitzvas as points has a precedent in the way that many Jews tend to think about observance. Not only do many of the traditions surrounding Yom Kippur, the Day of Atonement, present one's good deeds and sins that the Heavenly Court totals up once a year in a *din v'cheshbom* (judgment and account), but contemporary Orthodox Jews have themselves taken to referring to "*mitzva* points" when talking about their religious observance.

14. References to fasting appear in the Bible (Lev. 16; Num. 30; 2 Sam. 1, 12; 2 Kings 21; and elsewhere).

15. See *Encyclopedia Judaica*, vol. 6, pp. 26–46.

16. Berger and Luckmann 1966, p. 65.

17. Evans-Pritchard 1937, p. 70.

18. Guyau 1962.

19. Heschel 1952, p. 89.

20. This folk wisdom does not flow directly from biblical and rabbinical law. Indeed, there are many other laws and practices that are identified in the sacred literature as fundamental to a definition of ritual and religious state of being. But while these may be considered when one Jew closely evaluates the behavior of another, they all seem to pale in the light of Sabbath observance.

21. In our pilot studies we questioned people as to whether they turned lights on and off both with and without a timer. It was clear from the responses and also from our in-depth interviews that most people understood a question that asks them whether or not they turn lights on and off on the Sabbath to mean that this action is taken without the (permissible) assistance of a timer.

22. And we note, the non-Orthodox in our sample are, in turn, more observant than surveys indicate most American Jews to be.

23. See Cohen 1983; Ritterband and Cohen 1984, p. 63m.; Tobin and Chenkin 1985.

24. Our scale of Orthodox traditionalism may be compared with our fastidious dresser. Just as there are many choices of behavior that mark a person as punctilious in his dress, there is a wide selection of questions that can be used to test our respondents' degree of Jewish Orthodoxy.

25. See, e.g., Goldstein and Goldscheider 1985; Cohen 1983, p. 129; Ritterband and Cohen 1984; Tobin and Chenkin 1985.

26. Num. 15.

27. Num. 5:18; Isa. 3:17; B. T. Nedarim 30b.

28. One is tempted to suggest that there is in our findings a sociological analogue to the Talmudic assertion by Rabbi Eliezer ben Jacob who proclaimed: "Whosoever has phylacteries on his head, phylacteries on his arm, fringes on his garment, and a mezuzah on his doorpost is certain not to sin" (Menuhot 43b).

29. Heilman 1976, p. 19.

30. Ritterband and Cohen 1984, p. 151.

31. Halpern 1956, p. 35.

32. Herskovits 1949, p. 553.

33. Sklare and Greenblum 1979, p. 57.

34. This notion of "broadening of the limits of acceptability" comes from Hunter 1987, p. 163. While Hunter was speaking about "the broadening of the meaning of proper Christian living," meaning among young Christian Evangelicals when he used this phrase, much of what he says about them has its parallels in modern Orthodoxy and in particular in its centrist stream.

35. On those occasions that centrists do go to daily morning services in the synagogue, they will likely carry out their prayers there in a hurried fashion—quite unlike the more leisurely pace that characterizes the Sabbath morning services when immersion in the Jewish world is more fervently celebrated. This rushing is a symbolic way of saying that while they are ready to display attachment to the Jewish domain, this attachment is attenuated by another attachment to the world outside. However moving prayer may be, the modern centrist seems to be saying, "I must get moving to make my train to get to work (in the outside modern world) on time." This approach is also in contrast to the longer, more impassioned prayers of the traditionalists, and in particular the yeshiva students or hasidim.

36. Among the most insular of Orthodox women, those who live in the Mea Shearim quarter of Jerusalem and who eschew all contact with the world outside their ghetto, the norm is a shaved head covered by a black kerchief (see Heilman 1986b, esp. pp. 137–154 and 201–214).

37. See Heilman 1976, esp. pp. 95–103.

38. See ibid., pp. 53–56.

39. See Chapter Six for evidence of more traditional observance generally among younger Orthodox Jews.

40. Num. 15:37–39.

41. In his pamphlet "A Hedge of Roses," a sort of modern guide to the meaning and laws of "family purity" which has been distributed through a variety of institutions to young Orthodox women, Rabbi Norman Lamm, currently president of Yeshiva University, writes:

> It is difficult to convey adequately the overriding importance Judaism places upon these laws [of *mikveh*]. . . . Perhaps the best measure of their significance lies in the punishment that the Torah prescribes for their violation—*karet* (excision, being cut off from the people of Israel), the same as that for transgressing the Yom Kippur fast! Moreover, the Talmud assigns priority to Family Purity over public prayer services and the reading of the Torah itself; hence if a community cannot afford to erect all three communal structures, the building of the *mikveh* takes precedence over the building of the Synagogue and the writing of the Scroll of the Torah. The purity of the Jewish family, more than worship by the community or the pursuit of scholarship, is responsible for the perpetuation of the House of Israel. (p. 46)

42. See, e.g., Debra Kaufman (1987, p. 61), who reports that

many of the newly Orthodox women she spoke to about the *mikveh* "felt these laws increased their sexual satisfaction within marriage." And she adds: "Others referred to the 'autonomy' and
'control' they experienced when practicing the rituals of sexual
separation [i.e., *mikveh*]."

43. Heilman 1983b, p. 1 (see also Goldberg 1987; Zborowski
1965.

44. Interestingly, there seems to be an awareness among the
Orthodox as to the religious and cultural importance of lernen.
Much in the way the young among them have begun wearing a
yarmulke as an emblem of their Orthodoxy, many have begun
forming study circles in public places to demonstrate their attachment and commitment to a Jewish way of life (see Chapter 7 for
comparisons of young and old). Perhaps the most dramatic exhi-
bition of this occurred in 1982 when well over 10,000 Orthodox
Jewish men gathered in New York's Madison Square Garden to
celebrate a *siyum haShas,* the completion of a cycle of study of the
entire Babylonian Talmud. The 1982 *siyum,* the largest in history,
was marked by over 50,000 participants the world over, and it
indicated success in the Orthodox effort to get laymen involved in
regular lernen.

45. Cohen and Ritterband 1981.

46. Goldscheider 1983.

47. Henry 1961.

48. For a discussion of American Jewish fertility, see Heilman
1986a.

Chapter Three

1. Marty 1966, p. 168.
2. Heilman 1982a, pp. 1–17.
3. Doob 1960, p. 114.
4. Hirsch 1963, Commentary on Exodus.
5. Cohen 1953, p. 188.
6. It is interesting to note here that when in our pilot questionnaire we asked a different version of this question, the results
were even less encouraging for those who expected to find a
strong belief in God. Our earlier questions asked, "If you found
ten dollars on the street, would you say you did this by the help
of God or by luck?" For ten dollars, even the most observant traditionalists did not believe God got involved. Only when we
raised the ante to the million-dollar lottery did some significant
number of believers find the hand of God at work.

7. Berger 1979, p. 96.

8. Liebman 1983, p. 110.

9. For a discussion of "plausibility structures," see Berger 1979, pp. 17–20.

10. Berger 1979, p. 17.

11. Weber 1958, p. 139.

12. Hunter 1987, p. 32.

13. Cited in Otto 1958, p. 25.

14. Soloveitchik 1965, p. 35; Wurzberger 1962, p. 239.

15. See e.g., B. T. Pesachim 50b.

16. This is the model suggested by the traditional Jewish interpretation of the experience of Sinai wherein the people are reported to have said first "na-aseh" (we shall do) and only later adding "ve-nishma" (we shall comprehend).

17. Jakobovits 1974, p. 22.

18. The word that the Orthodox often use for this "integration" is "assimilation." In the Orthodox world "assimilation" is the contemporary analogue to "heresy" and carries the same pejorative implications.

19. Berger 1979, p. 101.

20. Berkovits 1962, p. 6.

21. Berger 1979, p. 24.

22. Kaplan 1976, p. 45.

23. Durkheim 1954, p. 478.

24. Guyau 1962, p. 141.

25. Katz 1973, p. 147.

26. Douglas 1970, p. 142.

Chapter Four

1. Katz 1972, p. ix.

2. To be sure, this entry into the life of Europe and the West was achieved more as a result of a general public sentiment in the countries of the West in favor of equality for all people than by the victory of those who championed the case of the Jews. It was simply the case that where a "transformation from a semi-feudal to a constitutional state was achieved, there Jewish emancipation, too, became a legally secured fact" (Katz 1973, p. 199, see also pp. 162–163).

3. Blau 1968, p. 303.

4. Jung 1968, p. 129.

5. Rotenstreich 1973, p. 56; Kallen 1958, p. 34.

6. Blau 1966, quoting Eliezer Berkovits, p. 159.

7. Meiselman 1975, p. 53.

8. Sometimes, their Yiddish became "Yinglish," a particular mix of Yiddish and English that yielded the peculiar language that is the common vernacular among many Orthodox—particularly when they are talking among themselves. For a fuller discussion of this Yinglish, see Heilman 1981, pp. 227–253.

9. Liebman 1973, p. 78.

10. Ibid.

11. Wolpin 1974, p. 24.

12. Heilman 1982b, 1982c.

13. Auerbach 1968, p. 307.

14. Lamm 1986, pp. 3 and 6.

15. Sturm, n.d., p. 9.

16. Lamm 1967, p. 30; Kaufman 1966, p. 11.

17. "We define ourselves as a Centrist Orthodox body," writes Bernard Rosensweig describing the Rabbinical Council of America, "some of us a little to its left, some of us to its right" (1986, p. 6.)

18. Riskin 1976, p. 42.

19. Jakobovits 1974.

20. Jakobovits letter in *Commentary.*

21. Pelcovitz 1976, p. 13.

22. Singer 1974, p. 54.

23. Helmreich, 1982. See also Friedman (1987, pp. 241–244) in which he argues that the yeshiva fostered an attitude of increasingly stringent and uncompromising interpretations of the demands Judaism made upon its practitioners.

24. Cohen 1986.

25. E.g., Jeffrey S. Gurock, describing the shifts toward traditionalism in the Young Israel synagogues that as we noted in our Introduction, had been for a long time identified totally with modern, acculturative Orthodoxy, says:

> The rightward shift of Young Israel and other like-minded OU [Union of Orthodox Jewish Congregations] synagogues has been spurred on by . . . : the growth of Jewish day schools and the limited acculturation of the refugee's children and grandchildren. During the interwar period, even the most traditionally observant members of YI [Young Israel] or strictly Orthodox OU congregations attended American public schools and after-school Talmud Torah programs. Immigrant parents, with few exceptions, sent their children to the public schools and expressed their residual Jewish commitment by directing these pupils to afternoon

congregational and communal schools. Those second-generation Jews, positively influenced by supplementary Jewish education, filled the rows of American Orthodox synagogues between 1920 and 1945.

The proliferation of day schools after 1945, a result of the disenchantment of middle-class parents with the educational program offered at public schools coupled with increased confidence in their dual identities as Americans and Jews, has changed Orthodox synagogue life. Third- and fourth-generation children generally know more of Jewish traditional teachings and practices than do their elders. (1987, p. 66)

26. Sklare 1972,

27. Aviad 1983; Willis 1981.

28. Heilman 1976, p. 14.

29. Katz 1980.

30. See, e.g., Cohen 1984, 1988.

31. Cohen 1987.

32. Wirth [1928] 1956, p. 8.

33. To be sure, we do not know if they felt closer and more similar to "traditionalist" Orthodox Jews than to Orthodox Jews in general.

34. Bulka 1983, p. 25.

35. See Exod. 30:11–14.

36. Woocher 1986.

37. Cohen 1980.

38. Ritterband and Cohen 1979.

39. Heilman 1983b.

40. The naive newcomers who do not know this and—although not Orthodox themselves—send their children to a yeshiva, perhaps because the local public schools are not up to par or because they wish to keep their children in a classroom with other Jews, are often startled and chagrined when they discover they have tacitly aligned themselves with a whole world of beliefs, behavior, and affiliations. Some parents become changed Jews as a result, while others withdraw their children from the schools and continue their educational search somewhat wiser about the consequences of Jewish schooling.

Some day schools use the word "yeshiva" in their title, but they are not, strictly speaking, identified with the yeshiva world. Nevertheless, this ambiguity of identity indicates the tendencies for overlap at the edges within Orthodoxy.

41. See Helmreich 1982.

42. As such, outsiders to Orthodoxy can and often do feel less

out of place in modern Orthodox day schools than they do in yeshivas.

43. For a fuller discussion of this, see Heilman 1983a.

44. Charles Liebman makes some instructive comments on this point:

> A crucial difference between the Conservative home and Orthodox home is the Jewish community into which each is related. The Orthodox home is related to a kashrut-observing community of time and place. The Orthodox Jew lives with the sense of an omnipresent community which mediates relationships to other Jews, to Jewish history, and to major Jewish symbols. At the simplest level this means that relationships to the local Jewish community, the national Jewish community and even to Israel takes place through a network of institutions (the synagogue, the day school, American counterparts of Israeli political parties, hospitals and other philanthropic societies, etc.) which share an Orthodox orientation. On the other hand, relationships at the most intimate level, family and peers, are, at least to some extent, governed by a sense of obligation toward the rules and customs of that community. The same sense of community governs relationships to the Jewish past. Now this has a double reinforcing effect. Precisely because of the omnipresent sense of community, the notion of ritual and the efficacy of ritual . . . is natural rather than artificial. Gripped in the web of community bonds, both in a metaphysical as well as a material sense, the Orthodox Jew believes because he experiences. Moreover, the specific injunctions of the community such as kashrut observance are backed by sanctions of community favor or disfavor, approval or disapproval.
>
> Even the best Conservative homes often lack this type of linkage to a Jewish community. Their Jewish community is, on the one hand, far more ephemeral and permeable, less omnipresent than that of the Orthodox Jew. Hence not only are its rules less compelling but rules are not natural. Secondly, the Jewish community to which the Conservative home is linked is not a kashrut-observing community. . . . [but] is linked to a broader Jewish community . . . to whom kashrut is irrelevant. (1981, pp. 27–28)

45. Schiff 1981, pp. 275–289.

46. Heilman 1983a; Himmelfarb 1974.

47. Heilman 1983b.

48. It should be recalled that our non-Orthodox population is largely composed of Conservative Jews. Sunday schools, particularly among the Jewish communities of the Eastern seaboard where most of our respondents reside, are generally patronized by Reform Jews.

49. Schutz 1962.

50. Although the movement for a full Jewish education for Orthodox Jewish women is at least as old as the Beth Jacob Schools founded by Sara Schnierer in Krakow, Poland, in 1917, it was only in the post-World War II era and especially in the last several decades that this education has become nearly as intensive as that of the men's.

51. Some might wonder that even today women claim to have attended a "yeshiva" since such institutions are still predominantly male enclaves. The answer probably lies in the fact that a number of Jewish educational institutions have loosely come to be called "yeshiva" even where, strictly speaking, they are probably closer in character to what we have here called a "day school." In general, "yeshiva" is a term that in the popular parlance of Orthodox life refers to an institution of learning that emphasizes the ethos of Orthodoxy. And while most people who inhabit the precincts of Orthodoxy understand the differences between a "real" yeshiva and those modern institutions that have come to be inaccurately called "yeshiva," they all may not always have responded to our questions with the greatest degree of accuracy.

52. Hughes 1971, p. 8.

53. By "typical" we mean what statisticians call either the "median" or "mode," which in this table turn out to be the same. The median is the halfway point. Thus, for any group, half the fathers went to services as or more often than the "typical" father, and the other half went as or less often. Mode is simply the most popular single answer for any one group.

Chapter Five

1. Geertz 1973, pp. 126–127.

2. Kallen 1958, p. 34.

3. Peretz 1947, p. 245.

4. The differences between those who in Germany were willing to be part of the organized community which included Reform Jewry and those who wanted to secede from it and maintain

their Orthodox exclusivity, or the varying points of view between Mizrachi and Aguda supporters in later years, are but two examples of this kind of division.

5. Since an X or R rating may in theory also be appended to a film because of excessive violence (and not only because of the portrayal of explicit sex or use of obscene language), one might argue that the moral significance of viewing such movies is blurred. Nonetheless, we, like James Hunter who also uses such film ratings for conclusions about worldview and morals, believe that in general the measure works (see Hunter 1987, pp. 174–175).

6. See Cohen 1983, p. 236; Cohen 1984; Singer 1987.

7. The Mondale landslide among the Jews (roughly 68%–32%) was even larger than the Reagan landslide across the country (59%–41%).

8. *Public Opinion* (1984): 28–29.

9. Cohen 1984.

10. Katz 1973.

11. Medding 1977, pp. 127–128.

12. Rupp 1973, p. 208; Berger 1977, p. 61.

13. Cohen 1984.

14. Rabbi Meir Kahane is an Orthodox Jew; the longtime Jewish head of the American Civil Liberties Union is not.

15. See Kranzler 1976, pp. 61–72.

16. Cohen 1984.

17. Hunter 1987, p. 63.

18. A similar case can be found among some American Catholics. While many churchgoing Catholics reject the teachings of their religious officialdom regarding premarital sex, they still maintain a fairly high level of Catholic observance.

19. Similar comparisons among centrists and traditionalists were impossible since hardly any said they would or had not sent their children to day schools or yeshivas.

20. While it is conceivable that one could associate "affirmative action" with benefits for women and other minorities—including Orthodox Jews—it seems unlikely that most of our respondents did so.

21. See B. T. Kiddushin 4 and also Sotah; see Maimonides Mishna Torah 4:1–4.

22. As an aside, in a study of premarital sexuality in nineteenth-century Alsatian villages, social historian Paula Hyman reports that roughly 30% of Gentile brides gave birth within eight months of marriage; among contemporary Jews, the rate was "only" 15%.

Chapter Six

1. Goldscheider 1986, p. 160.

2. For a discussion of assimilation, see Gordon 1964 and Cohen 1987b and 1988.

3. See Liebman 1979. Such views were prominently expressed at a recent gathering (May 15–16, 1987, Long Beach, N.Y.) of American Orthodox Jews meeting under the sponsorship of the Israeli Minister of Religious Affairs.

4. For a discussion of the concept of "ritual inattention," see Heilman 1982a.

5. We are indebted to Charles Liebman and an address on Orthodoxy which he delivered at Queens College on March 25, 1987, for this conception of Jewish fundamentalism.

6. See Weber 1958, p. 139.

7. See Bellah 1968; and in the Jewish case, Liebman and Don-Yehiaya 1983.

8. Marty 1982, p. 149; see also Glock and Bellah 1976.

9. See Hunter 1987.

10. Marty 1982, p. 157; Hunter 1983.

11. Douglas 1982, p. 6; Fitzgerald 1981; Dupre 1982.

12. Lipset 1963.

13. Gallup Opinion Index 1977–1978, p. 43.

14. Hay and Morisy 1978, pp. 255–268.

15. Marty 1982, p. 152.

16. Goren 1980.

17. Yancey et al. 1976.

18. Carmichael and Hamilton 1967; Novak 1972.

19. See Gans 1979 on "symbolic ethnicity"; Glock 1965, esp. pp. 68 and 84–85.

20. This argument can be extended to American Jews generally; see Cohen and Fein 1985; Cohen 1987b.

21. Cohen and Fein 1985.

22. Woocher 1986.

23. Such organizations as Rabbi Irving Greenberg's Center for Learning and Leadership became important instruments for this kind of Jewish training of federation professionals.

24. Brodbar-Nemzer 1986; Goldstein and Goldscheider 1968, p. 130; Cohen 1983, 1987a, 1988.

25. See also Goldscheider 1986, p. 104.

26. Sharot 1973.

27. Aviad 1983.

28. Waxman 1985–1986, p. 30.

29. See, e.g., Cohen 1988, p. 47.

30. Cohen 1983, 1988.

31. See, e.g., Redfield, Linton, and Herskovits 1936; Rinder 1958.

32. Ritterband and Cohen 1984; Cohen 1988.

33. That there is a rise for the middle-aged women may reflect the modernist influences and synagogue emphases that have become a part of this generation's Orthodoxy (see Chapter Four).

34. The differences in our findings cannot be easily explained for it clearly is involved in the whole issue of sampling. We shall simply say, as we have at the outset, that the Orthodox Jews in our sample appear to be more robust in their Orthodoxy than the general population—perhaps as an effect of their relative education and youth as well as finding themselves in the heartland of American Orthodox life, the urban Northeast.

35. Cohen 1988; Goldscheider and Zuckerman 1984, Goldscheider 1986.

Chapter Seven

1. Of course, the contra-acculturative Orthodox are even more insular—but then they may not have to contend with the outside world quite as much as the traditionalists in our sample population. So they may have an easier time of it.

2. See Goldberg 1947, pp. 52–58.

Bibliography

Auerbach, M. "Survey of Jewish History." In *The Jewish Library 2: The Folk*, ed. L. Jung. London and New York: Soncino, 1968.

Aviad, Janet. *Return to Judaism*. Chicago: University of Chicago Press, 1983.

Bellah, Robert N. "Meaning and Modernization." *Religious Studies* 4, no. 1 (1968): 37–45.

Bellah, Robert N., and Glock, Charles Y., eds. *The New Religious Consciousness*. Berkeley: University of California Press, 1976.

Berger, Peter L. "Are Human Rights Universal?" *Commentary* 64, no. 3 (September 1977): 60–63.

———. *The Heretical Imperative*. New York: Anchor/Doubleday, 1979.

Berger, Peter, and Luckman, Thomas. *The Social Construction of Reality*. Garden City, N.Y.: Doubleday, 1966.

Berkovits, Eliezer. "Jewish Education in a World Adrift." *Tradition* (Fall 1962): 3–13.

———. "A Contemporary Rabbinical School for Orthodox Jewry." *Tradition* 12, no. 2 (Fall 1971): 7–17.

Bernstein, Louis, "Generational Conflict in American Orthodoxy: The Early Years of the Rabbinical Council of America." *American Jewish History* 69, no. 2 (December 1979): 226–232.

Blau, Jacob L. *Modern Varieties of Judaism*. New York: Columbia University Press, 1966.

———. "Alternatives within Contemporary American Judaism." *Daedalus* 12 (1968): 300–318.

Borhek, J. T., and Curtis, R. F. *A Sociology of Belief*. New York: Wiley, 1975.

Breuer, M. "Samson Raphael Hirsch." In *Guardians of Our Faith*, ed. L. Jung. New York: Bloch, 1958.

Brodbar-Nemzer, Jay. "Divorce and Group Commitment: The Case of the Jews." *Journal of Marriage and the Family* 48 (1986): 89–98.

Bulka, Reuven, ed. *Diversions of Orthodox Judaism*. New York: Ktov, 1983.

235

Carmichael, Stokely, and Hamilton, Charles. *Black Power*. New York: Random House, 1967.

Cohen, Elliot. *Commentary on the American Scene*. New York: Knopf, 1953.

Cohen, Steven M. "Trends in Jewish Philanthrophy." *American Jewish Year Book*. 1980: 29–51.

———. *American Modernity and Jewish Identity*. London and New York: Methuen/Tavistock, 1983.

———. "The 1984 National Survey of American Jews: Political and Social Outlooks." Pamphlet. 64 pp. New York: American Jewish Committee, 1984.

———. "Jewish Travel to Israel: Incentives and Inhibitions among U.S. and Canadian Teenagers and Young Adults." Pamphlet. 107 pp. Jerusalem: Jewish Education Committee of the Jewish Agency, 1986.

———. "Ties and Tensions: The 1986 Survey of American Jewish Attitudes toward Israel and Israelis." Pamphlet. 115 pp. N.Y.: American Jewish Committee, 1987a.

———. "Reason for Optimism." In *The Quality of American Jewish Life: Two Views*, by Steven M. Cohen and Charles S. Liebman. New York: American Jewish Committee, 1987b.

———. *American Assimilation or Jewish Revival?* Bloomington, Ind.: Indiana University Press, 1988.

Cohen, Steven M. and Fein, Leonard J. "From Integration to Survival: American Jewish Anxieties in Transition." *Annals of the American Academy of Political and Social Science* (July 1985): 75–88.

Cohen, Steven M., and Ritterband, Paul. "Why Contemporary American Jews Want Small Families." Pp. 209–231 in *Modern Jewish Fertility*, ed. P. Ritterband. Leiden: Brill, 1981.

Deutscher, Isaac. *The Non-Jewish Jew and Other Essays*. New York: Oxford, 1968.

Doob, Leonard W. *Becoming More Civilized*. New Haven: University Press, 1960.

Douglas, Mary. *Natural Symbols*. New York: Pantheon, 1970.

———. "The Effects of Modernization on Religious Change." *Daedalus* (Winter 1982).

Dupré, Louis. "Spiritual Life in a Secular Age." *Daedalus* (Winter 1982): 21–31.

Durkheim, Emile. *The Elementary Forms of the Religious Life*. Trans. J. W. Swain. New York: Free Press, 1954.

Ellenson, David. "A Response by Modern Orthodoxy to Jewish Religious Reform: The Case of Esriel Hildesheimer." *American Jewish History* (1980).

Endelman, Todd. *The Jews of Georgian England, 1714–1830: Tradi-*

tion and Change in a Liberal Society. Philadelphia: Jewish Publication Society, 1979.

Etkes, Emanuel. "Immanent Factors and External Influences in the Development of the Haskalah Movement in Russia." Pp. 13–32 in *Toward Modernity: The European Jewish Model,* ed. Jacob Katz. New York: Transaction Books, 1987.

Evans-Pritchard, E. E. *Witchcraft, Oracles and Magic among the Azande.* New York: Oxford University Press, 1937.

Fackenheim, E. L. "On the Self Exposure of Faith to the Modern-Secular World: Philosophical Reflections in the Light of Jewish Experience." *Daedalus* 12 (1968): 200–210.

Fitzgerald, Frances. "A Disciplined Charging Army." *New Yorker,* May 18, 1981, pp. 53–141.

Friedman, Menachem. "Life and Book Tradition in Ultraorthodox Judaism." Pp. 235–255 in *Judaism: Viewed from Within and from Without,* ed. Harvey Goldberg. Albany: SUNY Press, 1987.

Gallup Opinion Index. *Religion in America.* Report no. 145. Princeton: American Institute of Public Opinion, 1977–1978.

Gans, Herbert. "Symbolic Ethnicity: The Future of Ethnic Groups and Culture in America." *Ethnic and Racial Studies* 2 (January 1979): 1–20.

Gastwirth, Harold. *Fraud Corruption and Holiness.* Port Washington, N.Y.: Kennikat Press, 1974.

Geertz, Clifford. *The Interpretation of Cultures.* New York: Basic Books 1973.

Glazer, Nathan, and Moynihan, Daniel P. *Beyond the Melting Pot.* 2d ed. Cambridge, Mass.: M.I.T. Press, 1970.

Glock, Charles Y. "The Religious Revival in America." In *Religion and Society in Tension,* by C. Y. Glock and R. Stark. Chicago: Rand McNally, 1965.

Glock, Charles Y., and Bellah, Robert N. *The New Religious Consciousness.* Berkeley: University of California Press, 1976.

Goldberg, Harvey. "Test in Jewish Society and the Challenge of Comparison." In *Judaism: Viewed from Within and from Without,* ed. Harvey Goldberg. Albany: SUNY Press, 1987.

Goldberg, Milton. "A Qualification of the Marginal Man Theory." *American Sociological Review* 6, no. 7 (1947): 52–58.

Goldscheider, Calvin. "Contraceptive Usage among American Jewish Families." *Papers in Jewish Demography 1981.* Jerusalem: Hebrew University and Institute of Contemporary Jewry, 1983.

———. *Jewish Continuity and Change.* Bloomington: Indiana University Press, 1986.

Goldscheider, Calvin, and Zuckerman, Alan. *The Transformation of American Jews.* Chicago: University of Chicago Press, 1984.

Goldstein, Sidney, and Goldscheider, Calvin. *Jewish Americans: Three Generations in a Jewish Community.* [1968.] Lanham, Md.: University Press of America, 1985.

Gordon, Milton. *Assimilation in American Life.* New York: Oxford 1964.

Goren, Arthur. *The American Jews: Dimension of Ethnicity.* Cambridge, Mass.: Belknap/Harvard, 1980.

Grunblatt, Joseph. "The State of Orthodoxy Symposium." *Tradition* 20, no. 1 (Spring 1982): 3.

Grunfeld, I. *Judaism Eternal.* New York: Bloch, 1956.

Gurock, Jeffrey S. "Resisters and Accommodators: Varieties of Orthodox Rabbis in America, 1886–1983." *American Jewish Archives* (November 1983): 100–187.

———. "The Orthodox Synagogue." In *The American Synagogue: A Sanctuary Transformed,* ed. Jack Wertheimer. New Rochelle, N.Y.: Cambridge University Press, 1987.

———. *The Men and Women of Yeshiva.* New York: Columbia University Press, 1988.

Guyau, J. M. *The Non-Religion of the Future.* [1897.] New York: Schocken, 1962.

Halpern, Ben. *The American Jew: A Zionist Analysis.* New York: Herzl Press, 1956.

Hay, David, and Morisy, Ann. "Reports of Ecstatic, Paranormal or Religious Experience in Great Britain and the United States." *Journal for the Scientific Study of Religion* 17 (September 1978): 255–268.

Heilman, Samuel C. *Synagogue Life: A Study in Symbolic Interaction.* Chicago: University of Chicago Press, 1976.

———. "Sounds of Modern Orthodoxy: The Language of Talmud Study." Pp. 227–253 in *Never Say Die: An Introduction of the Sociology of Yiddish,* ed. J. Fishman. The Hague: Mouton, 1981.

———. "Prayer and the Orthodox Synagogue: An Analysis of Ritual Display." *Contemporary Jewry* 6, no. 1 (Spring/Summer 1982a): 1–17.

———. "The Many Faces of Orthodoxy, Part I." *Modern Judaism* 2 (February 1982b): 23–51.

———. "The Many Faces of Orthodoxy, Part II." *Modern Judaism* 2 May 1982c): 171–198.

———. "Inside the Jewish School: A Study of the Cultural Setting for Jewish Education." Research report. New York: American Jewish Committee, 1983a.

———. *The People of the Book: Drama, Fellowship and Religion.* Chicago: University of Chicago Press, 1983b.

———. "The Jewish Family Today: An Overview." In *Tradition and*

Transition, ed. Jonathan Sacks. London: Jews College Publications, 1986a.

―――. *A Walker in Jerusalem.* New York: Summit Books/Simon and Schuster, 1986b.

Helmreich, William. *The World of the Yeshiva.* New York: Free Press, 1982.

Henry, Louis. "Some Data on Natural Fertility." *Eugenics Quarterly* 8 (June 1961).

Herberg, Will. *Protestant―Catholic―Jew.* New York: Anchor Books, 1956.

Herskovits, Melville. *Man and His Works.* New York: Knopf, 1949.

Heschel, A. J. *The Sabbath.* New York: Harper, 1952.

Himmelfarb, Harold. "The Impact of Religious Schooling: The Effects of Jewish Education upon Adult Religious Involvement." Ph.d. diss., University of Chicago, 1974.

Himmelfarb, Milton. *The Jews of Modernity.* New York: Basic Books, 1973.

Hirsch, S. R. *The Pentateuch.* 2d ed. Trans. I. Levy. New York: Block, 1963.

―――. *Igrot Tzafon.* Trans. I. Levy. New York: 1971.

Hochbaum, Jerry. "Community Action for Orthodoxy: Priorities and Perspectives." *Tradition* 11, no. 4 (Spring 1971): 91–99.

Hoenig, Moses. "In Retrospect: Twenty Years of Young Israel." In *Council of Young Israel Convention Annual 5692* (1932).

Howe, Irving. *World of Our Fathers.* New York: Harcourt, Brace, Jovanovich, 1976.

Hughes, Everett C. *The Sociological Eye.* Chicago: Aldine-Atherton, 1971.

Hunter, James D. *American Evangelicalism: Conservative Religion and the Quandary of Modernity.* New Brunswick, N.J.: Rutgers University Press. 1983.

―――. *Evangelicalism: The Coming Generation.* Chicago: University of Chicago Press, 1987.

Jakobovits, Immanuel. "Letter to the Editor." *Commentary* 58, no. 5 (November 1974): 22.

Jung, Leo. "What is Judaism?" in *The Jewish Library I: Faith,* ed. L. Jung. London and New York: Soncino, 1968.

Kallen, Horace. "The Bearing of Emancipation on Jewish Survival." *YIVO Annual* 12 (1958).

Kaplan, Lawrence. "The Dilemma of Conservative Judaism." *Commentary* 62, no. 5 (November 1976): 44–47.

Karp, Abraham J. "Ideology and Identity in Jewish Group Survival in America." *American Jewish Historical Quarterly* 65 (June 1976): 300–318.

Katz, Jacob. *Emancipation and Assimilation*. Westmead, England: Gregg International, 1972.

———. *Out of the Ghetto: The Social Background of Jewish Emancipation 1770–1870*. Cambridge, Mass.: Harvard University Press, 1973.

———. "Religion as a Uniting and Dividing Force in Modern Jewish History." In *The Role of Religion in Modern Jewish History*, ed. Jacob Katz. Cambridge, Mass.: Association for Jewish Studies 1975.

———. *From Prejudice to Destruction: Anti-Semitism, 1700–1933*. Cambridge, Mass.: Harvard, 1980.

———. "Orthodoxy in Historical Perspective." Pp. 3–17 in *Studies in Contemporary Jewry*, ed. Peter Medding. Vol. 2. Bloomington: Indiana University Press, 1986.

———, ed. *Toward Modernity*. New Brunswick, N.J.: Transaction Books, 1987.

Kaufman, Debra. "Coming Home to Jewish Orthodoxy: Reactionary or Radical Women?" *Tikkun* 2, no. 3 (1987).

Kaufman, M. "The Orthodox Renaissance: Crisis and Challenge." *Jewish Life* (September/October 1966): 6–26.

Klaperman, Gilbert. *The Story of Yeshiva University*. New York: Macmillan, 1969.

Kranzler, G. G. "The Changing Orthodox Jewish Community." *Tradition* 16, no. 2 (Fall 1976): 61–72.

Lamm, Norman. "The Voice of Torah in the Battle of Ideas." *Jewish Life* (March/April 1967): 23–31.

———. "Some Comments on Centrist Orthodoxy." *Tradition* 22, no. 3 (Fall 1986): 1–11.

Lazerwitz, Bernard, and Harrison, Michael. "American Jewish Denominations: A Social and Religious Profile." *American Sociological Review* 44 (August 1979): 656–666.

Liebman, Charles. *The Ambivalent American Jew*. Philadelphia: Jewish Publication Society, 1973.

———. "Orthodox Judaism Today." *Midstream* 25, no. 7 (1979): 19–26.

———. "The Sociology of Religion and the Study of American Jews." *Conservative Judaism* (May/June 1981): 16–33.

———. "Orthodox Judaism Today." Pp. 106–120 in *Dimensions of Orthodox Judaism*, ed. R. Bulka. New York: Ktav, 1983.

———. "Orthodoxy Faces Modernity." *Orim* 2, no. 2 (Spring 1987): 7–21.

Liebman, Charles, and Don-Yehiya, E. *Civil Religion in Israel*. Berkeley: University of California Press, 1983.

Lipset, Seymour M. *The First New Nation: The United States in Historical and Comparative Perspective.* New York: Basic Books, 1963.

Mahler, R. A. *History of Modern Jewry, 1780–1815.* London: Valentine, 1971.

Maine, Henry Sumner. *Ancient Law.* New York: Henry Holt & Co., 1885.

Marcus, Jacob R. *Early American Jewry.* Philadelphia: Jewish Publication Society, 1953.

Marty, Martin. "The Spirit's Holy Errand: The Search for a Spiritual Style in Secular America." *Daedalus* 12 (1966): 160–171.

———. "Religion in America since Mid-Century." *Daedalus* 111: 149–163.

Massarik, Fred. "Jewish Identity: Facts for Planning." Research report. New York: Council of Jewish Federations, 1974.

Mayer, Egon. "Jewish Orthodoxy in America: Towards the Sociology of a Residual Category." *Jewish Journal of Sociology* 15, no. 2 (December 1973): 151–165.

Mayer, Egon, and Waxman, Chaim I. "Modern Jewish Orthodoxy in America: Toward the Year 2000." *Tradition* 16, no. 3 (Spring 1977): 98–112.

Medding, Peter Y. "Equality and the Shrinkage of Jewish Identity." Pp. 119–134 in *World Jewry and the State of Israel*, ed. M. Davis. New York: Arno Press, 1977.

———, ed. *Studies in Contemporary Jewry.* Vol. 2. Bloomington, Indiana: Indiana University Press, 1986.

Meiselman, Moshe. "Women and Judaism." *Tradition* 15, no. 3 (Fall 1975): 40–53.

Meyer, Michael A. "German-Jewish Identity in Nineteenth-Century America," Pp. 247–267 in *Toward Modernity: The European Jewish Model*, ed. Jacob Katz. New York: Transaction Books, 1987.

Moment. "Doing and Believing: A Round-Table Discussion." *Moment* (September 1978): 40–44.

Neusner, Jacob. *American Judaism: Adventure in Modernity.* Englewood Cliffs: N.J.: Prentice-Hall, 1972.

Novak, Michael. *The Rise of the Unmeltable Ethnics.* New York: MacMillan: 1972.

Otto, Rudolf. *The Idea of the Holy.* Trans. J. W. Harvey. New York: Oxford, 1958.

Pelcovitz, Ralph. "America's Bicentennial: A Torah Perspective." *Jewish Life* (Fall 1976): 9–16.

Peretz, Y. L. *Stories from Peretz.* Ed. and trans. Sol Liptzin. New York: Hebrew Publishing Co., 1947.

Randall, J. H., Jr. *The Making of the Modern Mind.* Boston: Houghton Miflin, 1940.

Raphael, Marc L. *Profiles in American Judaism.* New York: Harper and Row, 1985.

Redfield, Robert; Linton, Ralph; and Herskovits, Melville. "Memorandum for the Study of Acculturation." *American Anthropologist* 38 (1936): 149–152.

Reisman, Bernard. "Managers, Jews, or Social Workers? Conflicting Expectations for Communal Workers." *Response* (Autumn 1982): 41–49.

Rinder, Irwin. "Polarities in Jewish Identity." In *The Jews: Social Patterns of an American Group,* ed. M. Sklare. New York: Free Press, 1958.

Riskin, S. "Orthodoxy and Her Alleged Heretics." *Tradition* 15 (Spring 1976): 34–44.

Ritterband, Paul, and Cohen, Steven M. "Will the Well Run Dry? The Future of Jewish Giving in America." Pamphlet. 16 pp. New York: Center for Learning and Leadership, January 1979.

———. "The Social Characteristics of the New York Area Jewish Community, 1981." *American Jewish Yearbook* 84 (1984): 128–161.

Rosenblatt, Samuel. *The History of the Mizrachi Movement.* New York: Mizrachi Organization of America, 1951.

Rosensweig, Bernard. "The Rabbinical Council of America: Retrospect and Prospect." *Tradition* 22, no. 2 (Summer 1986): 2–7.

Rosenthal, Erich. "Acculturation without Assimilation?" *American Journal of Sociology* 66, no. 3 (1960: 275–288.

Rotenstreich, N. "Emancipation and Its Aftermath," In *The Future of the Jewish Community in America,* ed. D. Sidorsky. New York: Basic Books, 1973.

Roth, Cecil. *The Jews in the Renaissance.* Philadelphia: Jewish Publication Society, 1959.

Rothkoff, Aaron. *Bernard Revel: Builder of American Jewish Orthodoxy.* Philadelphia: Jewish Publication Society, 1972.

Rupp, G. "Religious Pluralism in the Context of an Emerging World Culture." *Harvard Theological Review* 66 (April 1973): 207–18.

Schiff, Alvin I. *The Jewish Day School in America.* New York: Jewish Educational Committee Press, 1966.

———. "The Centrist Torah Educator Faces Critical Ideological and Communal Challenges." *Tradition* 19, no. 4 (Winter 1981): 275–289.

Schutz, Alfred. *Collected Papers.* Vol. 1. Trans. Maurice Natanson. The Hague: Nijhoff, 1962.

Schwab, Hermann. *The History of Orthodox Jewry in Germany.* Trans. Irene Birnbaum. London: Mitre Press, 1950.

Sharot, Stephen. "The Three-Generations Thesis and American Jews." *British Journal of Sociology* 24 (1973): 151–164.

Silber, Michael. "The Historical Experience of German Jewry and Its Impact on Haskalah and Reform in Hungary." Pp. 107–157 in *Toward Modernity: The European Jewish Model,* ed. Jacob Katz. New York: Transaction Books, 1987.

Singer, David. "Voices of Orthodoxy." *Commentary* (July 1974): 54–60.

———. "American Jews as Voters: The 1986 Elections." Research report. New York: American Jewish Committee, 1987.

Sklare, Marshall. *Conservative Judaism: An American Religious Movement.* [1955.] New York: Schocken, 1972.

———. "Jewish Acculturation and American Jewish Identity." Pp. 167–188 in *Jewish Life in American Society,* ed. G. Rosen. New York: Ktav, 1978.

Sklare, Marshall, and Greenblum, Joseph. *Jewish Identity on the Suburban Frontier.* 2d ed. Chicago: University of Chicago Press, 1979.

Soloveitchik, Jospeh B. "The Lonely Man of Faith." *Tradition* 7 (1965): 1–50.

Sommerlad, E. A., and Berry, J. W. "The Role of the Ethnic Identification in Distinguishing between Attitudes towards Assimilation and Integration of a Minority Racial Group." *Human Relations* 23, no. 1 (1970): 20–34.

Spero, Shubert. "Orthodox Judaism." In *Movements and Issues in American Judaism: An Analysis and Source Book of Developments since 1945,* ed. Bernard Martin. Westport, Conn.: Greenwood, 1978.

Sturm, Ephraim. "Social and Religious Philosophies of the Early 1900's Which Influenced the Formation of the Young Israel Movement." N.p., n.d.

Tobin, Gary, and Chenkin, Alvin. "Recent Jewish Community Population Studies: A Roundup." *American Jewish Year Book* 85 (1985): 154–178.

Waxman, Chaim I. *America's Jews in Transition.* Philadelphia: Temple University Press, 1983.

———. *American Alyia: Portrait of an Innovative Migration Movement.* Detroit: Wayne State University Press, 1989.

Weber, Max. "Science as a Vocation." In *From Max Weber,* ed. H. Gerth and C. W. Mills. New York: Oxford, 1958.

Weingarten, Shmuel. *The Yeshivot in Hungary: Their History and Problems.* [Hebrew.] Jerusalem: Kiryat Sefer, 1976.

Willis, Carol. *Beginning to See the Light: Pieces of a Decade.* New York: Knopf, 1981.

Wirth, Louis. *The Ghetto.* [1928.] Chicago: University of Chicago Press, 1956.

Wolphin, Nissan. "Letter to the Editor." *Commentary* 58, no. 5 (November 1974): 24.

Woocher, Jonathan. *Civil Judaism.* Bloomington: Indiana University Press, 1986.

Wurzburger, Walter. "Pluralism and the Halakhah." *Tradition* (Spring 1962): 234–235.

Yancey, William L.; Erikesen, E. P.; and Juliani, R. N. "Emergent Ethnicity: A Review and Reformulation." *American Sociological Review* 41 (June 1976): 391–402.

———. "Orthodox Judaism and Modern Society." *Yearbook of Religious Zionism* (1985–1986): 29–44.

Zborowski, M. "The Place of Book-Learning in Traditional Jewish Culture." Pp. 118–141 in *Childhood in Contemporary Cultures,* ed. M. Mead and M. Wolfenstein. Chicago: University of Chicago Press, 1965.

Index

Abortions, 171

Acculturation, 11, 12; adaptation process in, 17, 29; shift to contra-acculturative agenda, 187

Affirmative Action, 172

Age, and degree of Orthodoxy, 190–92, 195, 197, 202–4, 213

Agudas Ha-admorim, 27

Agudath HaRabbonim, 4, 27, 28

Agudath Israel, 27

American Orthodoxy, varieties of, 21–29

Amit Women, 28

Anti-Semitism, 124

Aramah, Isaac (Rabbi), 96

Arba Kanfos, 61

Ashkenazic Jews, 8

Assimilation, 11, 113–15

Av, Ninth of, fasting on, 46

Baal t'shuva movement, 5, 212

BeHaB fasts, 47

Berger, David, 26

Berger, Peter, 16, 93, 95, 97, 98

Berkovits, Eliezer (Rabbi), 25, 98

Bernays, Isaac (Rabbi), 20

Beth Midrash Govoha Yeshiva, 25, 115

Beyond the Melting Pot (Glazer and Moynihan), 186

Black Power movement, 186

Blau, Joseph, 113

Bulka, Reuven (Rabbi), 131

Catholicism, 185

Centrist Orthodoxy: belief in revelation, 88–89; and charitable giving, 135; defined, 23; dietary laws, 54, 60, 63; dualism of, 93–94, 208; and education, 141; fasting practices, 54, 60; parochialities of, 208, 210; ritual observance by, 60, 61 (table), 62–64; Sabbath observance, 54, 60, 61 (table), 63

Chaim Berlin Yeshiva, 24

Charismatic Christianity, 185

Charitable giving, 131–36, 204

Childbearing practices, 77–79

Chok, 102

Christianity: charismatic, 185; pentecostal, 185

Conservative Judaism, 14; and Day Schools, 139

Conservative Judaism (Sklare), 2

Contra-acculturative traditionalists, 11, 18

Contraception, 79

Cosmopolitanism, 122

Cultural pluralism, 117, 210

Day of Atonement, 46, 47, 66

Day Schools, 26; curriculum of, 138–39; growth of, 4, 139; and Orthodoxy, 26

Death penalty, 172, 173

Deutscher, Isaac, 11

Dietary laws, 10, 48–51, 68, 102

Douglas, Mary, 106, 185

Education (*see also* Day Schools; Hebrew Schools; Sunday Schools; Yeshivas): future trends in, 214; importance of, 188; in-

Education (*continued*)
crease in traditional, 120; influence of Protestantism on, 13; public aid to private schools, 169; secular, 26, 214; and the socialization process, 144; trends in, 199–200; variations by type of Orthodoxy, 137–50
Emancipation, 8–9
Emunah, 83–87; central tenets of, 87–95; hierarchy of, 103–4
Equal Rights Amendment, 170
Esther, Fast of, 47, 59, 73
Ethnicity, increase of, 185–86
Ettlinger, Jacob (Rabbi), 20
Evolution, teaching of, 159–60

Fackenheim, E. L., 41
Faith. See *Emunah*
Fast days, 46–48, 59, 60, 62–63, 66, 72–73; and women, 47–48
Frankel, Zacharias, 14
Friendships, intergroup, 122–26, 204
Fringes. See *Tzitzis*

Ghettoes, 8
Glazer, Nathan, 186
God, personal: existence of, 88–89; importance of, 90–95
Gordon, Yehuda L., 12
Greater New York Jewish Population Study, 31, 192, 196
Greenblum, Joseph, 69
Guilt, and Orthodoxy, 105
Gurock, Jeffrey, 26
Guyau, Jean Marie, 104

Halacha, 5, 72, 165; as basic element of Orthodoxy, 42; belief in, 98–103; conflicts with American way of life, 39; and liberal issues, 172; and the modern world, 95–104; trends in observance, 201; variations in, 67–81
Halpern, Ben, 68
Haskalah, 13; acculturative trends of, 15

Hay, David, 185
Head coverings. See *Yarmulkes*
Hebrew language, 10; and Jewish prayer, 14
Hebrew literature, 13
Hebrew Schools, 140, 142
Hebrew Theological College of Chicago, 22
Hedonism, and modern Orthodoxy, 21
Heschel, Abraham Joshua, 51
Hildesheimer, Esriel (Rabbi), 20
Hirsch, Samson Raphael (Rabbi), 20, 90
Hitachdut Harabbonim Haredim, 27
Homosexuality, attitudes of Orthodoxy towards, 166–69
Hughes, Everett, 147
Hunter, James Davison, 185

Intellectualism, and liberalism, 163
Intergroup friendships, 122–26
Israel Bonds, 132

Jakobovits, Immanuel (Rabbi), 118
Jehovah's Witnesses, 185
Jewish Day School, growth of, 3, 4
Jewish liturgy, influence of Protestanism on, 13
Jewish Observer, 115
Jewish prayer, in Hebrew language, 14

Kashrut, 27, 60, 102
Katz, Jacob, 16, 105
Khvolson, Daniel, 11
Kollels, 120
Kook, Abraham Isaac (Rabbi), 69
Kosher, 48–51, 60, 66

Lamm, Norman, 18, 116
Latter-Day Saints, 185
Lazarsfeld, Paul, 55
Lernen, 76–77, 120
Liberalism, political, 160–68, 211
Liebman, Charles, 2
Lipset, Seymour Martin, 185

Maimonides, 87–88, 90
Maine, Henry Sumner, 7
Marriage, sexual conduct in, 76
Marty, Martin E., 85, 184
Maskilim, 11, 12, 13, 17
"Melting pot" model, 182, 186
Mendelssohn, Moses, 12
Mesivta Tiffereth Jerusalem, 24
Mesivta Torah Vodaath, 24
Mikveh, 27, 59, 64, 65, 66, 75, 76
Mitzvas, 14, 60, 61 (table), 96; emphasis on practice of, 42; frequency of observance of, 70–77; future role of, 215; hierarchical structure of, 58; as measure of Orthodoxy, 40–56; as method of identification, 86; relationship to belief, 85–86; relationship to charitable giving, 132–33; rising standards of, 193; trends in observance, 200–201
Mizrachi, 28
Modernization, effects on Orthodoxy, 68–69
Moral Majority, 161
Morisy, Ann, 185
Moynihan, Daniel Patrick, 186

National Conference of Synagogue Youth, 4
National Council of Young Israel, 4
Ner Israel Yeshiva, 24
Niddah, 76
Ninth of Av, fasting on, 46
Nominal Orthodoxy: belief in revelation, 88–89; and charitable giving, 135; and education, 141; ritual observance by, 60, 61 (table), 64–66; Sabbath observance, 60, 61 (table), 65; and use of *mikveh*, 65
Non-Orthodox: and fast days, 55, 60; ritual observance, 60, 61 (table), 66–67; and Sabbath observance, 55, 60, 61 (table)
N'Shai Chabad, 28

Orthodox: awareness of contemporary world, 157–58; charitable giving by, 131–36; childbearing among, 77–79; differences from non-Orthodox in rituals, 55; education among, 22, 143–47; ad *Eumanah*, 83–95; frequency of ritual observance by, 70–77, 196; German, 20; parental religiosity among, 147–50; percentage of population, 2; political liberalism of, 160–68; social conservatism among, 165–71, 173; synagogue attendance by, 194, 199
Orthodoxy (*see also* American Orthodoxy; Centrist Orthodoxy; Nominal Orthodoxy; Traditionalist Orthodoxy): affluence of, 119–20; age level effects on degree of, 190–92, 195, 197, 202–4, 213; emergence of, 7–15; future role of women in, 215; future trends of, 213–16; index of, 53 (table); institutional maturation of, 119; left-wing, 23; modern, 16–17, 23; progenitors of, 16; right-wing, 23; and Science, 155–56, 159; and yeshivas, 25
"Orthodoxy Faces Modernity" (Liebman), 2
Orthoprax Judaism, 86

Parents, religiosity of, 147–50
Parochialism, 122, 205
Past, importance of, 154–57
Pentecostal Christianity, 185
Pluralism, repudiation of, 15
Politics, Jewish attitudes towards, 160–61
Poskim, 49
Premarital sex, 174–78
Protestantism: and education, 13; and liturgy, 13; and synagogue architecture, 13

Rabbi Isaac Elchanan Theological Seminary of Yeshiva University, 28
Rabbinical Alliance of America, 27

Rabbinical associations, 22
Rabbinical Council of America, 4,
28
Racial quotas, 172
Reform Judaism, 14; attitudes to-
wards homosexuality, 166; and
Sunday Schools, 140
Religious tradition, primacy over
secular morality, 103
Revelation, belief in, 88–89
Ritual practices. See *Mitzvas*

Sabbath, observation of, 59, 60,
63, 73; economic consequences
of, 68
"Salad bowl" model, 182, 186
Schools, public aid to private, 169
Science, and the Orthodox, 155–
56, 159
Secular education, 26, 214
Secularization paradigm, 184
Sefer Ha-Chinuch, 90
Seventeenth of Tammuz, fasting
on, 46, 59
Seventh-Day Adventists, 185
Sex, premarital, 174–78
Sexual conduct, 76, 166, 173–78,
203
Shaytl, 62
Shomer Shabbos, 51
Sklare, Marshall, 2, 69
Sofer, Moses (Rabbi), 19
Sturm, Ephraim, 116
Sunday Schools, 140, 142
Synagogue architecture, influence
of Protestantism on, 13
Synagogue attendance, 61 (table),
71, 72, 194, 199
Synagogue Council of America,
117

Tammuz, Seventeenth of, fasting
on, 46, 59
Telshe Yeshiva, 24
Tenth of Tevet, fasting on, 46, 59
"*T-fillin* dates," 175
Third of Tishrei, fasting on, 47, 59
Tikhl, 62
Tisha B'Av, fasting on, 46, 48

Tishrei, Third of, fasting on, 47, 59
Torah: and blind faith, 101–2; divine revelation of, 87, 89
Torah-imderecheretz, 20
Torah Umesorah, 2
Traditionalism, shift towards, 183–
93
Traditionalist Orthodoxy: belief in
revelation, 88–89; and charitable
giving, 134–36; defined, 23; distinguished from Modernist, 19
(table); and education, 138; ritual observance by, 58–62, 60, 61
(table)
Tsom Gedalia, 47, 59
Tzitzis, 61, 74, 75

Union of American Hebrew Congregations, 166
Union of Orthodox Jewish Congregations of America, 4, 22,
120
Union of Orthodox Rabbis, 4, 27
United Jewish Appeal, 132

Weber, Max, 184
Weiss, Ari, 205
Wirth, Louis, 126
Wolpin, Nisson (Rabbi), 115
Women: attending Sabbath ser-
vices, 59, 63, 65; future role in
Orthodoxy, 215; independence
of, 170; married, covering of
hair by, 62, 71; *mikveh*, 59, 64,
65, 66, 75, 76
Wurzberger, Walter (Rabbi), 42

Yarmulkes, 61, 74–75
Yeshiva Orthodoxy, 25
Yeshivas: attendance, as prerequi-
site for Orthodoxy, 195; chari-
table giving to, 132; curriculum,
138; development of, 24; rising
standards of, 193
Yeshivat Etz Chaim, 22
Yeshiva University, 22, 26
Yiddish language, 10
Yiddish literature, 13
Yom Kippur, 46, 47, 66
Young Israel, 22, 28